The Praxis of
Social Inequality in Media

Communication, Globalization, and Cultural Identity

Series Editor: Jan Servaes, Ph.D.

The *Communication, Globalization, and Cultural Identity* series explores and complicates the interlinked notions of "local" and "global" by integrating global dependency thinking; world-system theory; local, grassroots, interpretative, and participatory theory; and research on social change.

In the current world state, globalization and localization are seen as interlinked processes, and this marks a radical change in thinking about change and development. It also marks the arising of a new range of problems. One of the central problems is that the link between the global and the local is not always made clear.

The debates in the field of international and intercultural communication have shifted and broadened. They have shifted in the sense that they are now focusing on issues related to "global culture," "local culture," "(post) modernity," and "multiculturalism," instead of their previous concern with "modernization," "synchronization," and "cultural imperialism." With these new discussions, the debates have also shifted from an emphasis on homogeneity towards an emphasis on differences. With this shift towards differences and localities, there is also an increased interest in the link between the global and the local and in how the global is perceived in the local.

Titles in series are:

The Praxis of
Social Inequality in Media

A Global Perspective

Edited by
Jan Servaes and Toks Oyedemi

LEXINGTON BOOKS
Lanham • Boulder • New York • London

Published by Lexington Books
An imprint of The Rowman & Littlefield Publishing Group, Inc.
4501 Forbes Boulevard, Suite 200, Lanham, Maryland 20706
www.rowman.com

Unit A, Whitacre Mews, 26-34 Stannary Street, London SE11 4AB

British Library Cataloguing in Publication Information Available

Library of Congress Cataloging-in-Publication Data Available

ISBN 978-1-4985-2346-2 (cloth : alk. paper)
ISBN 978-1-4985-2347-9 (electronic)

♾™ The paper used in this publication meets the minimum requirements of
American National Standard for Information Sciences—Permanence of Paper
for Printed Library Materials, ANSI/NISO Z39.48-1992.

Printed in the United States of America

To Bryce, Fiona, Lisa, Myra, Patchanee, Tayo,
and the millions of people who strive for a sustainable future that is just
and equitable, while living within the limits of supporting ecosystems.

Contents

Acknowledgments

We wish to acknowledge and thank Julia E. Kirsch, Vice President/Publisher; Brian Hill, Associate Editor; and Eric Kuntzman, Assistant Editor, at Lexington Books, a division of the Rowman & Littlefield Publishing Group, for their support and assistance.

This project could not have been possible without the interest and commitment of all the authors who contributed—even those whose work didn't make it through the final stages of peer review. We are also grateful to Myra and Patchanee for taking care of our share in the household, hence allowing us to "hide" behind our books and computer screens.

Abbreviations

A2I	Access to Information
ADL	Aspects of Daily Life
AFL	Australian Football League
AHRC	Australian Human Rights Commission
AIR	All India Radio
AKP	Turkey's Adalet ve Kalkınma Partisi (Justice and Development Party)
APC	Australian Press Council
CBO	Community Based Organization
CIC	Citizen and Immigration Canada
CIESPAL	Centro Internacional de Estudios Superiores de Comunicación para América Latina
CONAPO	Mexican Consejo Nacional de Población
CONEVAL	Mexican Consejo Nacional de Evaluación de la Política de Desarrollo Social
DAE	Digital Agenda for Europe
DI	Diffusion Index
EOWA	Australian Equal Opportunity for Women in the Workplace Agency

HCR	Indian Henvalvani Community Radio
HDI	Human Development Index
HITW	Hole in the Wall
HUD	U.S. Department of Housing and Urban Development
ICTs	Information and Communication Technologies
IFJ	International Federation of Journalists
IFRC	International Federation of Red Cross and Red Crescent Societies
IMF	International Monetary Fund
INEGI	Mexican Instituto Nacional de Estadística y Geografía
ISTAT	Italian Istituto Nazionale di Statistica -- National Institute of Statistics
IVRS	Interactive Voice Response Systems
IWC	Immigration Watch Canada
LGBT	Lesbian, Gay, Bisexual, Transgender
MCA	Multiple Correspondence Analysis
MCP	Multicultural Policies
MEAA	Australian Media, Entertainment and Arts Alliance
MIE	Minimally Invasive Education
MSC	Most Significant Change
NGO	Non-Governmental Organization
OECD	Organization for Economic Co-operation and Development
OHRC	Ontario Human Rights Commission
PLA	Participatory Learning and Action
PR	Participatory Research
SC	Significant Change
SSHRC	Social Sciences and Humanities Research Council
UISC	Union Information Service Centers
UNDP	United Nations Development Programme
UNFPA	United Nations Population Fund
WB	World Bank
WGEA	Australian Workplace Gender Equality Agency

Introduction

From Theory to Praxis:
Social Inequality and Its Consequences

Toks Oyedemi and Jan Servaes

In the collection of chapters in *Social Inequalities, Media, and Communication: Theory and Roots* we engage some of the theoretical discourses and historical narratives that help to shape contemporary understanding of social inequality in relation to media and communication. These discourses are particularly poignant for their global perspectives in sharpening knowledge about how social inequality intersects with media and communication. In this current volume, we shift the focus to case studies and empirical analyses of how social inequality shapes media and communication experiences of individuals, groups, and communities.

The essence of praxis of social inequality in media is derived from an essential academic approach to move from theory to praxis. It is derived from scholarship that does not reside solely in abstraction but also aims to engage the real-life consequences and applications of theoretical assumptions. In the scholarship of social inequality, empowerment, powerlessness, social change, and development, issues of *participation*, *agency* and *voice* are often centered (see, for instance, Servaes 2013). This centering arises from the critical study of how individuals, groups, and communities are confronted with experiences of inequality, domination, and alienation, and how they strive, at times, collectively to challenge these experiences.

The focus on the empirical consequences of social inequality and instances of the lived experiences of certain groups and communities helps to address the question, as posed by Jencks (2002), "Does inequality matter?" Jencks (2002) engages a debate between the moral and empirical claims over inequality. While empirical claims relate to the demonstrated evidences of direct effects of inequality, the moral claims tend toward addressing inequality based on the ground of greatest good of society. However, both moral and empirical claims about why inequality is bad are based on its consequences, and, as Jencks notes, merely treating inequality as a moral issue does not make the empirical questions go away. The empirical effects of social inequality are not only based on direct firsthand consequences, the experiences of social inequality are also indirect, largely because they are historical, generational and often shaped by individual and group experiences that are influenced by aspects such as *demographic criteria, unequal power structures,* and *institutionalized policy actions* with consequences on the well-being of many people in society. Especially the latter form the start of Thomas Piketty's observations. Though limiting his assessment to *the economics of inequality,* he contends that the question of inequality and redistribution is essentially a political or policy discussion between a right-wing free-market position and a traditional left-wing position: "Hence only a detailed analysis of the socioeconomic mechanisms that generate inequality can sort out the competing truth claims of these two extreme versions of redistribution and perhaps contribute to the elaboration of a more just and effective set of policies" (Piketty 2015: 2).

Terreblanche's (2002) study of the over 300 years of history of inequality in South Africa attests to the influences of the three Ps (*population, power, and policy*) on the consequences of inequality. Terreblanche (2002) asserts that unequal power structure played a critical role in South Africa's colonial period from 1652 to 1910. This is a trend that continued during segregation and apartheid from 1910 to 1994, when power was entirely monopolized by whites with devastating consequences for black South Africans. But, unfortunately, new sets of unequal power structure and unequal socio-economic outcomes have remained characteristics of post 1994 South Africa. Similar historical experience shapes the narrative of American social inequality—from slavery, segregation, institutionalized policies of state and private firms that have consequential impacts on the experiences of well being for many minority groups (Dorling and Dorling 2015; Neckerman 2004). And similar historical experiences resulting in inequality can be studied in many other regions of the world ranging from South America to Asia, from Africa to Europe. These cases of historical trajectories of inequality exemplify an aspect of why social inequality creates series of consequences that are objectionable. As Schuppert (2012) observes, what counts as objectionable inequality ranges from the observations that inequality threatens the satisfaction of basic needs, creates stigmatizing differences in status, leads to dominations, undermines people's self-respect, and leads to servile behavior. These experiences are not merely consequences of the unequal distribution of goods or high Gini coefficient inequality, but, as Anderson (1999) notes, they are consequences of unequal power relations between superior and inferior persons or groups. The *unequal power structure* creates a situation where the superior rank or class inflicts violence on the inferior class "to exclude or segregate them from social life, to treat them with contempt, to force them to obey, work without reciprocation, and abandon their own cultures" (Anderson 1999: 312). The empirical effects of social inequality moves beyond the economic narrative of consequences to the social and cultural terrains, where oppressive experiences of marginalization, domination, powerlessness, cultural imperialism, exploitations, misrepresentation, under representation, exclusion and discrimination are shaped by class, race, gender and other socially defined categories of people.

SOCIAL INEQUALITY, CONSEQUENCES, AND PRAXIS

Evans, Hout, and Mayer (2004) provide an influential typology of inequality effects (see also Neckerman and Torche 2007). They identify four categories of effects of inequality, namely: mechanical, relational, functional, and externality effects. *Mechanical* effect occurs when an individual's economic position is associated with a specific outcome. As a result an increase in economic inequality leads to an increase in inequality in that outcome. *Relational* effect occurs when a relationship between economic status and a given outcome changes. For example, if the relationship between income and voting becomes stronger, the electorate will tend toward the affluent (Neckerman and Torche 2007). *Functional* form of inequality effects occurs when there is a nonlinear relationship between economic status and an outcome. Again, Neckerman and Torche (2007) provide an example from the study of health and inequality: the increase in income is associated with a larger improvement in health for the poor than for the rich. In effect, reducing inequality improves health by the redistribution of income to those for whom it is more efficacious.

The fourth consequence is the *externality* effect. This effect is contextual, psychological, sociological and cultural. As Evans et al. (2004: 935) note, "inequality can affect outcomes even when income and outcome are unrelated." In this regard, for the low-income groups who live in a context of high inequality it may lead to or intensify feelings of relative deprivation, which may result in increased levels of violent crimes (Neckerman and

Torche 2007). The externality effect also works in a psychological context. By drawing on social comparison and relative deprivation theories, Evans et al. (2004) present arguments that people compare themselves to those who are more advantaged than them, which as a result makes people feel relatively deprived.

For cultural critics, media scholars and sociologists, the analysis of so-cial inequality is more than the economic determinist approach derived from a dominant focus on income inequality as seen in the mechanical, relational, and functional effects. Sociologists draw on the economic nar-rative of inequality and its mechanical, relational and functional effects to justify the importance of socio-economic criteria in social stratification and social inequality. For sociological analysis of inequality the focus is not necessary on the perfect distribution of goods but more about how inequality creates unequal social relationships in society, where certain group's sense of self-worth, participation, inclusion, well-being and the pursue of individual claims to happiness are hindered by unequal eco-nomic and power structures often shaped by social categorizations of people.

The work by Melvin Oliver and Thomas Shapiro (1995), *Black Wealth / White Wealth*, is an example of a sociological approach to economic in-equality. By explaining core differences between *income* - as what people receive for work -, and *wealth* - as what people own -, they are able to reveal the experience of social inequality based on economic power and race, specifically the differentials in black and white wealth holdings. They argue that a sociology of wealth seeks to situate the social context in which wealth generation occurs by identifying the 'racialization of state policy' and its impairment of black American's ability to accumulate wealth in most of American history, their relatively low level of entrepre-neurship, and how these have led to 'sedimentation of racial inequality'.

The sociological and cultural approaches provide an understanding of inequality that deepens economic narrative by revealing how a class of people with economic power creates social and cultural conditions that misrepresent other groups or hinder their ability to participate in social, cultural, and economic spheres of society. For example, the media narratives of poverty often focus on inner city and urban experiences of poverty often located in city ghettos. However, this tends to ignore the experiences of many poor people in rural areas. Because their stories are not told, their plights are unknown and state policies to address their condition are miniscule.

For communication and media scholars the consequences of social inequality are largely cultural and sociological. But this *cultural analysis* draws on socio-economic stratification, economic disparities, demo-graphic criteria, unequal power structures, and institutionalized policy actions to draw attention to the well-being of people in relation to their experiences with the media. Take for instance the "political economy" critique of the media that addresses the unequal ownership structure of the media. The effect of the ownership structure is not merely the unequal economic power imbalance, but the consequences on how this shapes stories that are told and not told in the media, and the implication on the socio-cultural well-being of large groups of people outside the ownership structure, which in some instances describes the experiences of racial and marginalized communities.

What we have discussed so far shows the *complexity* of studying social inequality and its consequences, especially considering that these consequences are diverse. For social inequality scholars, the focus is to study and measure issues of income inequality in relation to social stratification, cultural practices, access to socio-cultural resources, and how these intertwined with race, gender, geography and other categorizations that shape human demographics. The praxis of social inequality reveals the process of how issues of discrimination, power structure, and social stratification intersect with ability to participate in the economic, social, and cultural spheres of society, including their subjective experiences with media and communication cultures.

The Socio-Cultural Praxis of Social Inequality

The socio-cultural consequences of social inequality are derived mainly from the social relationship that exists between individuals based on class or ranks, and in relation to access to and location of all forms of capitals (social, cultural, material). Embedded in this description are issues of power, freedom, marginalization, exclusion-inclusion, participation, alienation, domination, agency, self-respect, and other material, social and cultural utilities that advance people's well-being.

To address this diverse nature of what we identify as the socio-cultural consequences of social inequality, Schuppert (2012) suggests focusing on two core values: freedom and autonomy. *Freedom* focuses on the ability of individuals to act freely without domination. Domination takes many forms, it can be through violence, threat, or abuse, it can also be psychological, and cultural. So when state or private institutions discriminate against groups based on gender or race, "freedom as non-domination" helps to unmask such consequences of social inequality. Amartya Sen (1999) argues this aspect succinctly by offering an approach to "development as freedom," where development is not merely measured in growth of gross national product or rise in personal income, but to focus on development as the removal of "unfreedom." This includes addressing poverty, tyranny, deprived economic opportunities, social deprivation, and the activities of repressive states in denial of political and civil liberties, which restrict ability to participate in the social, political, and economic spheres of the community. Schuppert (2012) also identifies another value, *autonomy*. "Autonomy as non-alienation" highlights the alienation in many social relationships and structures in society. As Schuppert (2012: 109) notes:

> social alienation leads to a person feeling powerless, inferior, and disrespected. Autonomy as non-alienation is concerned with securing the conditions under which each and every member of society can see herself as a legitimate source of claims and reasons. That is to say, autonomy as non-alienation cares about the social conditions for a person's proper relation to herself, which include among others the opportunities for meaningful participation and adequate recognition.

Taking the values of freedom and autonomy into account in a case of cultural domination in the media, groups and communities have come together to establish community radio as a way of voicing issues relevant to their community thereby confronting alienation and domination from commercial media institutions.

The works of Pierre Bourdieu (1984a, 1984b, 1986) exemplify the sociocultural praxis of social inequality. For Bourdieu the process of class fractions in society is best observed by engaging capital in all its forms, economic, cultural, and social. His influential analysis of cultural capital as core value of class analysis reveals socialization processes, ownership of certain cultural material objects and educational attainment as practical indexes of class fraction. Bourdieu explores how cultural competence exposed in the nature of cultural goods consumed relates to a social class. As such, the *taste* for certain cultural practices such as newspaper reading, art and museum visitation, food, drink, and music are social markers that separate distinct social classes or class fractions. Just as social capital, manifested in membership in groups and organizations, networks of influence and relationship relate to individual class location in social hierarchy.

Baron, Grusky, and Treiman's (1996) analysis of social differentiation and social inequality adopts a cultural consideration as microsocial underpinnings of status attainment. They argue that the advantages and disadvantages accruing to individuals may be disaggregated into characteristics of family origin and individual actors. They assert that "the intergenerational transmission of advantage (or disadvantage) may be seen as a reflection of the extent to which families differentially hold three forms of capital: cultural, material, and social capital" (Baron et al. 1996: 351).

Also, status attainment may be seen as a reflection of how individuals hold the same three forms of capital. The *cultural capital* of the stock of information, knowledge, skills, and education that a family holds—measured rather loosely by parental education—may contribute to class location and status attainment, not only for the parents but intergenerational to the children. This not only contributes to level of income, but also cultural practices that indicate class and status attainment. Access to *material capital*—such as income and wealth—undoubtedly provides advantages to families in status attainment, and offers various choices of education and career for children with families with a safety net of material capital. Equally *social capital*, as in interpersonal networks of influence, may provide individuals admission to universities, acquire good jobs, and other benefits that may accrue from their personal or family connections of influence, as Baron et al. note.

The consequences of social inequality in regards to media and communication relate to this cultural analysis. The "taste" for and consumption of certain media products—movies, music, newspaper, online content, opera, and theater—have been studied as evidence of class location and social inequality (Bourdieu 1984b). In addition, Chan and Goldthorpe (2005), through an empirical study of social stratification of theater, dance, and cinema attendance, mapped out and tested a typology of arguments about the relationship between social inequality and patterns of cultural taste and consumption. The *homology argument* claims that social stratification and cultural stratification map on to each other closely. Individuals in higher social class are those who preferred consuming high culture; while individuals in lower social strata are those who predominantly consume popular or mass culture. The *individualization argument* minimizes the homology argument and seeks to argue that in the modern commercialized societies individuals tend to free themselves from social conditions and form their own identities and lifestyles including pattern of cultural consumption. The *omnivore-univore argument* sees cultural consumption still closely related to social stratification, however it is not based on the elite/high and popular/mass binary. It claims that the cultural consumption of those in higher strata of society differs in that it is greater and much wilder in range. So those in higher strata have a wide range of choices of cultural consumption, they consume more elite culture, more middle-brow culture and consume more "low-brow" culture as well, while those in lower class tend to consume mainly and largely popular cultural forms. The argument is that higher status, higher educational attainment, and higher income increase individual chances of being an omnivore rather than a univore. But social inequality and pattern of media consumption is only one aspect. Broadly, social inequality in media reveals issues of power, exclusion, marginalization, economic inequality, race and gender inequalities, and how other aspects of social inequality in society shape people's media experiences. The praxis of social inequality in media reveals how racial representation and discrimination shape identity, culture, and participation in the media. It reveals how gender analysis exposes marginalization and exclusion of people in media realities. It seeks to answer questions, such as who gets to use media technologies, and who is excluded? Who owns and controls these technologies and how does the control shape economic and social participation of those outside the ownership class? In what ways do capitalism and attendant neoliberal ideologies configure patterns of exclusion and inclusion in the media? How are media and communication tools effective in addressing social concerns around issues of poverty, development, and social change?

THE PRAXIS OF SOCIAL INEQUALITY IN MEDIA

The focus of this volume is to provide global case study instances and country-specific issues of power relations, class, exclusion, marginalization, participation, economic inequality, race and gender inequalities, empowerment, social change, and other aspects that shape the media experiences of people from different regions of the world.

The volume opens with assessments of the discourse of poverty and its representation in the media. Steven Harkins and Jairo Lugo-Ocando engage the narrative of poverty in the press by examining the way the British press plays a role in articulating discourses that legitimise inequality by using rhetorical strategies that are embedded in journalistic narratives and are contextualised in the wider dominant media discourses of poverty. They observe that news reports on poverty have often ignored inequality as a rationale, rather concentrating instead on the manifestations of poverty as a way of displacing inequality from the news agenda and public debates. They suggest that this discursive regime is used by the news media to highlight the inadequacies of individuals in order to shift attention away from structural social inequality as a fundamental cause of poverty.

Through analysis of newspaper articles on poverty and homelessness from twelve English- and French-language newspapers in eight paired cities in North America and Europe, Greg Nielsen, Amanda Weightman, James Gibbons, and Mike Gasher examine the narrative of poverty in the press. They seek to imagine a form of news reporting that forges a dialogic relationship with the audience. They imagine journalism that would perceive its implied audience to include the subjects of news stories, particularly when those stories concern marginal populations such as the homeless and the poor.

Within a similar backdrop, Rebecca Wells and Martin Caraher provide another perspective of poverty in the British press through the analysis of the portrayal of food bank users in the UK national press. They observe that voices of food bank users were often unheard, with food bank volunteers and others acting as a 'proxy' voice for them. In this situation the circumstances surrounding individual cases of poverty were rarely acknowledged. In contrast, politicians and celebrities were given privileged access to the media and their views on those living in poverty were reported.

Kaan Taşbaşı examines the representation of poverty and its perception in Turkey through the study of how the *sadaka* (charitable gift) culture through the media might be linked to the lack of social policy mechanisms in Turkey, and whether the media might be seen as a bridging element in this respect. Taşbaşı examines how the *sadaka* culture has generated a postmodern *tele-sadaka* practice, which enabled people in need to be visible on the screen via a television program that called for donations and acted as a transmission mechanism that transfers these donations. This culture thus raises questions about representation of poverty in the media, and the defects of the social state mission.

The section on technology and inequalities draws on case studies from Europe and South Asia. Roberta Bracciale and Isabella Mingo examine digital inequalities by studying how social inclusion and digital inclusion have become strongly correlated concepts, such as to generate a paradigm shift whereby e-inclusion becomes synonymous with social inclusion in the knowledge society. By drawing on macro and microdata of the official statistical sources and indicators that are harmonized and standardized at the European level, they examine patterns of digital skills from an Italian case study and reveal that there is a basic and non-experts use of the net, especially among groups of people "at risk" of exclusion. The finding, as they argue, highlights the existence of digital inequalities in population groups that could be considered already included in terms of access to the Internet.

Within the backdrop of low literacy rates among Bangladesh's poor and initiatives about how information and communication technologies can effectively deliver educational content to disadvantaged Bangladeshi children, Gyuri Kepes, through extensive fieldwork in an economically-disadvantaged district of Dhaka, Bangladesh, studies underprivileged children's uses of "Hole in the Wall" computer kiosks. The study of this social experiment that provides computers on an exterior wall of a school, that neighbors several sprawling slums, highlights the argument that participation and empowerment be given greater recognition as indicators of education and development, notwithstanding the many challenges that such technology access strategy produces.

The next section deals with empowerment and participation in communication for sustainable social change and development. Attention is specifically focused on issues of gender within the context of sustainable social change. The chapter by Aparna Moitra and Archna Kumar explores empowerment and participation of women through community media. With a case study from Henvalvani Community Radio in the Himalayan region in India, they examine the role participatory media, like community radio, can play in the amplification of women's voices in the context of climate change.

Staying on the theme of women, empowerment and media, Francisco Sierra Caballero, Alice Poma, and Tommaso Gravante explore the role of "ordinary" women who were not activists or leaders of any social organization, but were female teachers, housewives, young women, female students, and unemployed women in the protests of the local section of the teachers' union in the city of Oaxaca in Mexico in 2006. In their chapter they propose an analysis "from below," which seeks to invert the look toward ordinary women who participate in media experiences in order to understand how the experience of media appropriation affects the process of empowerment. Their analysis focus on three experiences that characterized actions of these 'ordinary women': the creation of two "alternative" digital projects called *Revolucionemos Oaxaca* (Let's revolutionize Oaxaca) and *Frida Guerrera* (Warrior Frida), and the experience of occupation by Oaxacan women of radio station 96.9 FM and TV Canal 9 of the state radio and television facilities (CORTV) for almost a month.

The last section of this volume includes three contributions that explore the representations of race and gender in the media. Louise North starts off with a feminist analysis of gender inequality in the Australian news media. She observes that while female journalists in Australia are closing the gender gap in the lower ranked reporting roles, men still overwhelmingly dominate senior decision-making ranks in news organizations in Australia. Through a large survey of female journalists from all media platforms in Australia, North asserts that the patterns of gender inequality and power relations have not changed. Female journalists still experience sexual harassment by male colleagues, and struggle for career promotion—hampered by the fact that reviews of work and promotional opportunities are often decided by a single senior figure (usually male). Female journalists still struggle with the need to balance motherhood and career, and are typically excluded from certain reporting roles and news stories, which arguably stymies women's promotion opportunities.

John C. Pollock, Lucy Obozintsev, Hannah Salamone, Lauren Longo, and Stephanie Agresti examine cross-national media coverage of rape and rape culture by using the community structure approach to compare multiple national demographics with cross-national coverage of rape and rape culture in leading/accessible newspapers in twenty-one countries.

Argument is made that most media sampled worldwide declare society to be the responsible party for ending rape in their respective nations.

This volume ends with the examination of immigration and exclusion. While the positive popular discourse about immigration tends to focus on narratives about multiculturalism and diversity that immigration brings, Fay Patel argues that multiculturalism can be a disabling paradigm for new immigrants, depending on personal, socio-economic, and political circumstances and history of immigrants. The author notes that one of the most attractive aspects of Canadian immigration is the country's multicultural policy, which inspires notions of respect, dignity and a humane approach to building the strength of Canada's citizenry. However, as Patel argues, this narrative tends to obscure the practical realities of the socio-economic inequities that are present in Canadian society, which new immigrants confront.

The eclectic nature of the chapters in this volume reveals the various ways that issues of marginalization, representations, participation, exclusion, and poverty intersect with class, power and socio-economic dynamics to shape people's experiences of social inequality in relation to the media.

REFERENCES

Anderson, E.S. (1999). What is the point of equality? *Ethics* 109, no. 2, 287337.

Baron, J.N, D.B. Grusky, and D.J. Treiman. (1996). Social differentiation and inequality: Some reflections on the state of the field. In J.N. Baron, D.B. Grusky, and D.J. Treiman (eds.), *Social differentiation and social inequality: Essays in honor of John Pock.* Boulder, CO: Westview Press.

Bourdieu, P. (1984a). *Distinction: A social critique of the judgment of taste.* London: Routledge.

Bourdieu, P. (1984b). *Questions de sociologie.* Paris: Les éditions de Minuit.

Bourdieu, P. (1986). Forms of capital. In J. Richardson (ed.), *Handbook of theory and research for the sociology of education.* New York: Greenwood Press.

Chan, T.W., and J.H. Goldthorpe. (2005). The social stratification of theatre, dance, and cinema attendance. *Cultural Trends* 14, no. 3, 193–212.

Dorling, D., and D. Dorling, D. (2015). *Injustice: Why Social Inequality Still Persists.* Oxford: Policy Press.

Evans, W.N., M. Hout,and S.E. Mayer. (2004). Assessing the effect of economic inequality. Ed. K.M. Neckerman. *Social Inequality.* New York: Russell Sage Foundation.

Jencks, C. (2002). Does Inequality Matter? *Daedalus* 131, 49–65.

Neckerman, K. (ed.). (2004). *Social inequality.* New York: Russell Sage Foundation.

Neckerman, K. M., and F. Torche. (2007). Inequality: Causes and consequences. *Annual Review of Sociology 33,* 335–357.

Oliver, M.L., and T.M. Shapiro. (1995). *Black Wealth/White Wealth: A new perspective on racial inequality.* New York: Routledge.

Piketty, T. (2015). *The economics of inequality.* Cambridge: Harvard University Press.

Schuppert, F. (2012). Suffering from social inequality: Normative implications of empirical research on the effects of inequality. *Philosophical Topics* 40, no. 1, 97–115.

Sen, A. (1999). *Development as freedom.* New York: Alfred Knopf.

Servaes, J. (ed.). (2013). *Sustainability, participation and culture in communication: Theory and Praxis.* Bristol and Chicago: Intellect-University of Chicago Press.

Terreblanche, S. (2002). *A history of inequality in South Africa 1652–2002.* Pietermaritzburg: University of Natal Press.

I

POVERTY AND THE MEDIA

1

All People Are Equal, but Some People Are More Equal Than Others

How and Why Inequality Became Invisible in the British Press

Steven Harkins and Jairo Lugo-Ocando

In George Orwell's *Animal Farm* (1945), after they had overthrown Farmer Jones, the animals created a list of seven commandments which were designed to guarantee a more equal society. However, once the pigs took over, the commandments were eventually replaced with the maxim, "all animals are equal, but some animals are more equal than others." The key moral of this tale is the need of those at the top to justify inequality and their own power and wealth through a system of belief that reflects their own interests and which underlines their own right to such a privileged position. Although Orwell's story was originally intended to be an allegory of the Soviet Union under Stalinism it nevertheless reflects strikingly well the way in which British elites have articulated over the years a belief system that seems to make inequality acceptable and somehow necessary.

In this chapter we argue that the British press, as part of that establishment, plays a pivotal role in articulating discourses that legitimize inequality. They do this, we suggest, by using a series of rhetorical strategies which are embedded within journalistic narratives and that are contextualized in the wider dominant media discourses of poverty. Because of this, these narratives reflect historical ideological constructions such as Malthusianism and social Darwinism. To further explore these issues, this chapter takes a historical view on the construction of narratives of inequality within the press.

We argue that despite the fact that Great Britain experienced a sharp rise in inequality between 1974 and 2008 (Dorling 2011a: 156), this was almost completely ignored by the news media when reporting poverty during that period. This is a time often referred to by scholars as the end of collectivism and the Keynesian welfare consensus (Cockett 1994); a time which saw a massive transfer of wealth from the poorest to the richest. Nevertheless, this was a theme that was rarely picked by newspapers in Britain as a news story (Davies 2009: 36). Instead, poverty was reported—as we argue here—in a *de-contextualized* manner, where alternative rationales were offered to reinforce prevalent discourses of power. Indeed, we suggest—based on our data—that news reports on poverty have often ignored inequality as a rationale. They have concentrated instead on the manifestations of poverty as a way of displacing inequality from the news agenda and public debates.

This chapter examines the specific historical period of 1985 to 2014. It does so, because it was during this period that media discourses in Britain consolidated a fundamental shift that reflected the emerging consensus among the elites around neo-liberalism (Lugo-Ocando and Harkins 2015: 56). The beginning of this shift has been studied in detail by other scholars (Cohen 2011: xxi; Critcher 2003: 64; Deacon 1978: 1; Golding and Middleton 1982), who have highlighted some of the fundamental changes in the reporting of poverty in the British media of that time. The chapter suggests that this new discursive regime is used by the news media to highlight the inadequacies of individuals in order to shift attention away from structural social inequality and dismiss its origins as a fundamental cause of poverty.

This discursive regime, we suggest, has been characterized by a return to more classical interpretations of Malthusianism and social Darwinism as explanatory theoretical frameworks which journalists use to contextualize their work and provide meaning to their audiences by articulating a series of ideas, concepts and symbols. This discursive regime is then constantly referred to by journalists in their work, allowing them to link their stories to wider ideological constructions. In so doing, it permits news stories on poverty to be framed in a particular way that reflects the ideas of the dominant class while avoiding inequality altogether as an underpinning rationale.

Malthusianism, which consolidated as a dominant discourse during the Victorian era, was rapidly adopted by the emerging commercial press which had displaced by the end of that century the political and ideological newspapers (Briggs and Burke 2009; Conboy 2004; Curran 2002). Particularly, after 1850 the commercial press the press adopted in the public discourse a strong view on poverty as an individual issue rather than a structural social problem; this would become over the years the predominant version and reference for mainstream journalism (Lugo-Ocando and Harkins 2015: 42). Among the key theories used by the commercial press to explain poverty were social Darwinism and Eugenics. In both cases, they underpin the notion that the distribution of wealth in society reflected somehow inherited intellect and abilities to perform better or worse in society as an individual.

By placing responsibility upon those in poverty for their own condition, the elites in Britain have been able to obscure their own role and responsibility and that of the economic structures in the creation of poverty. Mainstream journalism is part of this establishment (Gibson 2006; GraduateFog 2013; Sutton Trust 2006) and therefore works within these ideological boundaries in order to further marginalize those in a state of poverty from the public discourse. They do this as a way of reconciling the *intrinsic contradictions* they face between their normative claims, the deontology they embrace and the actual superstructure and structural systems within which they operate. At the centre of this process of discursive reconciliation in the construction of social reality by journalists lays the articulation of evasive rhetorical tactics that avoid allocating inequality at the centre of the explanatory framework for poverty within the news.

There are many historical examples of this, but perhaps one of the most notorious was the way the British press reported the Irish and Indian famines of the nineteenth century. Indeed, official versions reinforced by the British press of the time, explained the millions of deaths in these colonies by returning to a Malthusian understanding of overpopulation which assigned poverty to nature, scarcity of resources and the overall inability of the poor to stop procreating. In not one single report of the key London-based newspapers was there a critical examination of the irrational structures of production and distribution imposed by colonial rule (Lugo-Ocando 2015: 22). No mention either that both countries were in fact exporting food to the United Kingdom during these famines (Ross 1998: 40). It was because of the need to obscure this paradox that the Victorian press blamed those living in poverty in the colonies for their own disgrace by using Malthusianism as a rhetorical device.

This classical interpretation of Malthusianism lasted more or less until the end of World War II when Keynesian economics and the welfare consensus emerged. It was a consensus that brought about a slightly different interpretation of poverty and inequality. One which would dominate media discourses until the macroeconomic crisis of the 1970s, which was triggered by the Yom Kippur War and the subsequent oil embargo and energy crisis of 1973. This crisis led subsequently to the UK government approaching the International Monetary Fund (IMF) for a loan of $3.9 billion in September 1976, which included additional funds from the US and

Germany. However, the IMF negotiators demanded heavy cuts in public expenditure and the budget deficit that would translate in a cut of around 20 per cent in the budget as a precondition for the loan. By the end of 1977, partly as a result of new oil revenues, there were improvements in the balance of trade. At the end, Britain did not need to draw the full loan from the IMF. Nevertheless, the IMF crisis reinforced a change in policy orientation away from full employment and social welfare and towards the control of inflation and expenditure (Cabinet-Papers 2014).

The "neo-liberal" consensus that emerged from this crisis led to a revival of classic liberalism and the individualist ideology that underpins it (Cockett 1994). Once again the press adopted a more classical Malthusian understanding of poverty although this variation was linked to neo-liberalism and its sustained critique of the welfare system. This discursive regime of Malthusianism places the responsibility for poverty solely on the shoulders of people experiencing poverty themselves thus absolving the wealthiest members of society of their responsibility, while dismissing structural factors that cause poverty in the first place. By this rationale the victims of poverty are always to blame for their own situation and this can be seen in the way the British press frames news items about poverty and social exclusion, particularly in times of great inequality.

WHAT THE DATA SAYS

To develop this argument further we have looked at a sample of stories published in the British press. Indeed, we examined a sample of articles that reported poverty in four British newspapers. This included the left leaning tabloid the *Daily Mirror* and the *Sunday Mirror* and the right wing tabloid the *Daily Mail* and the *Mail on Sunday* and the left leaning the *Guardian* and the *Observer* and the right leaning the *Times* and *Sunday Times*. We used these newspapers as they represent both the tabloid/popular market and the so-called quality press, reflecting different ideological and editorial stances. These were also the newspapers that offered better access to their archives in longitudinal terms.

We also took into consideration what other similar studies have done in the past, which have indicated that poverty in the British media is usually only covered as a secondary issue to another main story (Bullock, Fraser Wyche, and Williams 2001; Franklin 1999). Therefore, to select the articles of the sample, we establish specific criteria used in similar studies that have looked at news on poverty (Kitzberger and Germán 2009; Kivikuru 2001). This meant that the study would examine all articles in the Nexis database between 1985 and 2014. They had to contain the word "poverty' in the headline and would have had to mention the word poverty three times or more in the main body of the news. This gave us a total of 3,431 news articles across the newspapers during that period of time. We then carried out a close reading and content analysis, which we used to develop our arguments.

From the total universe of articles selected, 1,217 referred to international poverty of which 569 focussed on global poverty as a whole while 648 reported poverty in a specific region or country of the world. This left 2,214 that reported poverty in the UK. Thereafter, we coded the news stories in order to examine what the main theme of each news story was. The news stories were initially coded into three geographical categories: (1) Poverty Overseas, (2) Global Poverty, and (3) Poverty in Britain.

In this context, poverty overseas was a category used for stories about poverty in a specific geographical region, these usually focused on poverty in a particular country. However, many articles focused on poverty in a wider geographical region such as Africa or Europe. These stories focused on poverty as a global phenomenon with many of them referring to the "Make Poverty History" campaign in 2005, which in that period of time provided an unusual impetus for stories related to this theme. Nevertheless, looking at the sample, we can see that the majority of the articles in the British press focused on poverty in the UK.

Given the predominance of national news on poverty, we went then to code these stories into themes which examined the main topics being discussed in each of the articles. Figure 1.2 shows the main thematic category that each of these articles of our sample fell into. This table includes only those single themes that had a frequency of forty or more articles from the

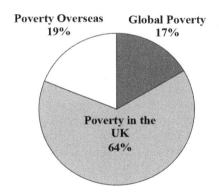

■ **Global Poverty**   ▨ **Poverty in the UK**   □ **Poverty Overseas**

Figure 1.1.   Three categories of poverty. Nexis Database.

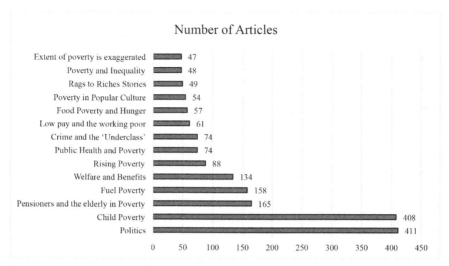

Figure 1.2.   **Number of articles on poverty. Nexis Database.**

overall sample. In so doing, we were able to focus our analysis on the key themes covered by the press. This translated into a sub-sample of 1,827 of the 2,214 articles on poverty in Britain as the following graphic shows.

It was not surprising to find that "politics" dominated the news on poverty as previous studies (Iyengar 1996) have suggested that media coverage of poverty as an issue is linked to political debates. Neither was it surprising to find that the category of "child poverty" was almost at the top in numbers of stories as children are considered to be a vulnerable group and therefore often categorized as "worthy" of charity and state support in the news (Barnett et al. 2007; Males 1996).

On the other hand, the fact that the following category is that of "pensioners and elderly" followed by "fuel poverty"—two categories that are intrinsically related—seems to be linked to both, the consideration that this age group is also vulnerable as in the case of the children but that is also very decisive in terms of electoral votes as older people tend to be more likely to vote than young people (Goerres 2009; Quintelier 2007); hence they are seen by politicians as a key constituency.

Overall, "inequality" was one of the categories that received the smallest attention from the press and was indeed below the "rags to riches stories" type stories that often portray successful business people and celebrities who were able to overcome their condition of poverty without welfare state intervention. As we suggest in our theoretical framework, "inequality" is a problematic category for most newspapers and the ideologies that underpin their editorial policy.

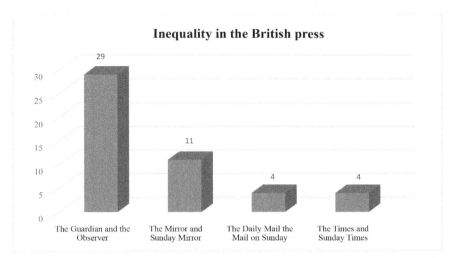

Figure 1.3.   Inequality in the British press. Nexis Database.

Therefore, one of the most interesting observations was that almost all of the stories on inequality in relation to poverty were published by the *Guardian* and the *Mirror*, which total 84 percent of all news on poverty that dealt with or mentioned inequality in our sample.

The gap in the reporting of poverty between the left-wing newspapers and the right-wing ones suggest a prevalent role of ideology in the editorial policy that informs news coverage and dissemination of inequality as an explanatory framework for poverty. This finding is paramount in our thesis that the discursive regimes that serve as an explanatory framework for the new stories on poverty are in fact underpinned by editorial approaches defined and constrained by ideology.

To explore the way ideology defines narratives, we have selected paragraphs and phrases in news stories published by part of the sample at the other side of the ideological spectrum. In an article in the *Times*, for example, the newspaper's property editor questions why academics have been putting so much emphasis on inequality,

> Seldom has there been such an outpouring of opinion on the concentration of wealth. We would, however, give more than a penny for the thoughts of the Chancellor of the Exchequer on whether the top 0.1 per cent are an example to us all of the rewards of hard work, or are fit only for more taxation? (Ashworth 2008)

To be sure, ideology defines editorial policies regarding the news coverage of poverty. It is therefore not surprising to find out from our sample that the only two newspapers which tended to pay more attention to inequality were precisely those that are often identified as left-wing; that is the *Guardian* and the *Mirror*. However, one particularly interesting observation is the way news on inequality and poverty are presented using different types of "journalism genres." This term refers to various journalism styles, fields or separate genres, in writing accounts of events, which readers have come to recognise (Rudin and Ibbotson 2002: 81). The selection of a particular genre allows journalists to introduce or not opinions in their work. For example, "hard news stories," "reportage," and "feature articles" are genres often associated with the idea of objectivity, while "open-ed" (or opposite the editorial page), "profiles" and "editorials" are linked to opinion.

The split between "objective" genres and "opinion" genres was exactly 50 percent in our sample. However, opinion was mainly used in the left wing quality press, while *the Times* had only one opinion piece on inequality in that period. The *Daily Mail* and the *Mail on Sunday*, on the other hand, only reported inequality as "hard news." An almost similar skewed distribution can be seen in the *Mirror,* in which 90 percent of the articles dealing with inequality as a contributor fact for poverty were presented as hard news stories. Finally, it is important to mention, that the *Guardian* and the *Observer* had the largest data set of opinion pieces with nineteen in total.

The preference for "hard news stories" needs to be interpreted within the wider notions of news cultures (Allan 2004) and news values (Brighton and Foy 2007), which often define not only the way news is gathered but also presented and disseminated to the public. At the centre of these two notions is objectivity as a "norm" in journalism practice (Maras 2013: 226). This norm presents journalists writing about poverty with what some authors have called "the false dilemma between hard news and opinion" (Genro Filho 1987: 48).

This false dilemma—or false dichotomy—means that journalists tend to opt for styles that offer them the ability to put across specific narratives and stories in a way that seems to be neutral and balanced. In this context, journalists feel the need to perform the "strategic ritual" of objectivity (Tuchman 1972: 661), moving within well-accepted frameworks when reporting news and using quotations from others as to reinforce their authority as impartial observers. We suggest as a *thesis* that this is because "inequality" as an explanatory framework is contested as being too ideological within their organizations and by the key stakeholders that sustain the political economy of the newspapers.

SOURCING INEQUALITY

Equally important to the language used to report inequality is the ability to identify who says what. News sources are indeed pivotal in articulating news content (Berkowitz and Beach 1993; Manning 2001; Lewis, Williams, and Franklin 2008). News sources which provide information about the events and news shapers that offer opinions, angles, or views (Soley 1992), help journalists to articulate meaning in their stories.

In our sample of articles dealing with inequality, we identified 119 different news sources. Because the reporting of inequality is mostly carried out by the newspapers at the left of the political spectrum, the great majority of the sources are either politicians identified with the left, academics often critical of the government policies on welfare and members of the public who live in poor areas in Great Britain.

Indeed, the most commonly used type of source in constructing stories about inequality came from the world of politics, with forty-three sources being politicians or political organizations. That means that 37 percent of all these sources were politicians. From this, eighteen were linked to the Labour Party, who were quoted mostly in the left wing newspapers. The next largest categories were academics and members of the public, with seventeen quotations each.

The second most cited sources were academics and members of the public. In both cases, these citations happened mostly in left-wing newspapers. Moreover, in those cases in which the *Times* cited members of the

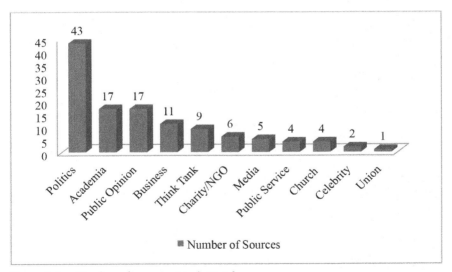

Figure 1.4.   Number of sources. Nexis Database.

public, those voices spoke in the context of very specific stories referring to the legacy of the London Olympics and the development of Canary Wharf. Think-tanks and business people are also quoted in these stories, but this happens mostly to provide "balance" to the story; that is to offer alternative views to the main sources quoted, which in the case of our sample were mostly to provide a counterbalance to the left wing views.

The *Guardian* is overall the newspaper that not only provided more articles on inequality but also that offered a wider choice in journalistic genres and more diversity in the nature of the news sources it used to articulate its stories. It was also, with the *Mirror,* one of the two titles that placed poverty within the framework of inequality as the following quote reflects,

> The signs are not promising, with a likely deterioration in the public finances over the next two years as the economy slows down making it inconceivable that the Treasury will find the extra £3.4bn needed to meet the pledge of halving the number of children living below the poverty line by 2010. Tackling child poverty is not a "sexy" issue and poor children don't have powerful friends to lobby for them in the way that the CBI acts as the shop steward for non-doms. Last week, for example, Richard Lambert, director general of the CBI, said the "rushed and confused" approach to taxing non-doms was damaging London's reputation as a global financial centre. . . . The reason the global financial markets have been suffering a collective nervous breakdown for the past eight months and caused what Rachel Lomax, deputy governor of the Bank of England, calls the world's "largest-ever peacetime liquidity crisis" is because the City's non-doms (many of them American) gorged themselves in a speculative frenzy without equal for its greed, stupidity and recklessness in living memory. In the circumstances, a long period of silence from both the non-doms and the CBI would be welcome. (Elliott 2008)

TALKING NONSENSE

All in all, the media in Britain, as in many other countries, tends to avoid the subject of inequality in the context of news stories of poverty (Lugo-Ocando 2015: 2). In our sample, inequality is in fact mentioned far more times that we have indicated here. Nevertheless, it is mentioned in other contexts such as gender, race, and even Scottish devolution. This last, paradoxically was brought up by the *Times* to argue that Scotland although hosts some of the poorest areas in the UK is getting a disproportionate amount of public money through the Barnett formula.[1]

> A decade on, the North-South divide, which characterised Scotland as a disadvantaged partner in the Union, has been reversed, according to a new

study by the Joseph Rowntree Foundation. On every key measurement of poverty looked at for the report, Scotland now outperforms the rest of the UK and enjoys among the highest wage levels. . . .The foundation says the improvements, reflecting wider economic trends and policies reserved to Westminster rather any dramatic performance by the Scottish parliament, will have been helped by Scotland's higher share of spending. While the findings are good news for Scots, they raise questions about whether the Barnett formula, which gives Scotland 20% more funding per head than England, can continue to be justified. (Allardyce and Belgutay 2010)

However, when inequality comes into play in the few stories that get to be published, it does so in a sense that undermines it as a crucial factor or—in the case of the right-wing press—dismisses it altogether. Moreover, one of the rhetorical strategies increasingly used by the right-wing media and its news sources is that of the "narrative of envy." Envy in the context of economic discourse is often linked to the so-called post-industrial societies and closely associated with individual irrationality or limited rationality (Block 1990: 25). Take for example a report of the *Daily Mail* dealing with inequality and crime,

A SCOTTISH criminologist yesterday exploded the myth that poverty and deprivation are behind soaring post-war crime. Instead, he laid the blame firmly on the breakdown of family values, envy and an emphasis on equal opportunities which have led young people to expect more than they are capable of earning. Professor David Smith said rising crime levels throughout Europe, including Scotland, had their roots in a rich society and not in poverty. He said people envious of everyday objects of wealth, such as expensive cars, accounted for much of the rising levels of vehicle theft. . . . It is the norm for bishops, sociologists, Eurocrats and politicians to assume growing crime is the consequence of inequality, poverty, deprivation or social exclusion. (Walker 1996)

"Envy" is often referred to by the media to dismiss any structural explanation of why there is poverty in the first place. It therefore stops any further discussion by assigning an irrational motivation to those who point out inequality. The narrative of envy also reinforces the "othering" of those living in poverty as different to those among the audiences of the newspaper.

By reducing the motivations of the others to "envy" and "hate" the narratives seek to invalidate the arguments made by those who are highlighting inequality as a societal problem. David Spurr traces this rhetorical strategy to the colonial times and goes to point out that it is now often used by newspapers such as *Le Monde* in France when it refers to the "avid" consumption in China, and it highlights "a feeling of envy on the part of the have-nots" (Spurr 1993: 86).

Let us not forget that these narratives of envy are historically contextualised in the Malthusian discourse on poverty in which the rich are seen as more able, more intelligent and more hardworking. Hence, the rich deserve to be rich and the poor deserve to be poor. Anthropologists have referred to this as the "discourse of desire and envy," which is part of the capitalist ethos that drives the corporatization of public life (Kapferer 2005: 285). In other words, if desire and envy—and one might add *greed*—is the explanation for the almost incessant and irrational drive to accumulate wealth, then it would seem logical to attribute similar irrationality to those at the bottom.

Envy of course is not the only rhetorical strategy used to dismiss inequality as the main driving source for poverty. However it is the most indicative in terms of the editorial approaches taken by the newspapers. Poverty, therefore, is framed in terms of emotional irrationality in several ways. It is caused—according to the dominant discourses—because those in poverty are unable to control their urges (to put it in Victorian terms), they remain in poverty because they are not sufficiently rational as to pull themselves out of poverty and, those who want what others have in terms of quality of life are suffering from irrational envy.

Labeling calls for equality as "irrational" is one of the key legacies that Malthusianism has brought upon modern journalism and the reporting of poverty. Because of this, news on poverty is not only de-contextualized from inequality but poverty itself is explained in emotional terms. What journalists do is to introduce "values"—in a way we could argue neo-Victorian values—into the reporting of poverty as an explanatory framework for poverty. In so doing, rationales about why people are in a state of poverty are obscured or limited to individual characteristics. In so doing, journalism avoids examining existing structures in the production and distribution of wealth. This rationale emerged during the post–Cold War period which brought about a widespread rejection of socialist utopias in the British public mind.

Indeed, this "invalidation" of inequality as an explanation for poverty is at the centre of current media representations. This invalidation has become increasingly more present in the post–Cold War period where narratives such as the "end of history" (Fukuyama 1989)—or end of ideologies and utopia—have come to dominate thinking in the newsroom. The invalidation also advances the equation of inequality with other areas of public life such as terrorism, where *emotional irrationality* argued through the narratives of "hate" and "envy" against "or way of life" (eMediaMillWorks 2001) are also used to dismiss deeper structural issues.

This invalidation occurs despite a huge volume of academic literature dedicated to the social impact of inequality and the effect it has a key factor in creating poverty (Dorling 2011b; Wilkinson and Pickett 2009). Overall, little focus is placed on inequality in the press in the context of reporting poverty (Davies 2009: 36). Instead, in our sample of the British press we found many "rags to riches" type stories which highlight how rich and successful people have traversed poverty through their own efforts and skills.

These stories focus on a range of current celebrities and entrepreneurs, including famous authors like J.K. Rowling, Catherine Cookson, Josephine Cox, Frank McCourt, Buchi Emecheta, Mavis Cheek. Actors such as Sarah Lancashire; Adrian Lester and politicians like Alan Johston and David Blunkett and business people such as Alan Sugar and Duncan Bannatyne. The narrative in all cases is similar; one in which talented individuals are born among the poor and manage to defeat the odds and rise to the top by themselves and without the help of the state.

This narrative constantly focuses on how rich successful people used to be poor and how they as individuals pull themselves out of poverty without the community and the state. The suggestion is clearly Malthusian; if everyone living in a condition of poverty worked hard enough and was smart enough, they could make it to the top. A view that was satirized by R.H. Tawney, when he wrote:

> Intelligent tadpoles reconcile themselves to the inconvenience of their position by reflecting that although most of them will live to be tadpoles and nothing more, the most fortunate of the species will one day shed their tails, distend their mouths and stomachs, hop nimbly on to dry land and croak addresses to their former friends on the virtue by which tadpoles of character and capacity can rise to be frogs. (Tawney 1961: 108)

Moreover, it is a worldview that J.K. Rowling, author of the *Harry Potter* saga, debunks quickly by directly addressing this paradox in an article in *the Mirror* about her own past,

> Poverty, as I soon found out, is a lot like childbirth—you know that it's going to hurt before it happens but you'll never know how much until you've experienced it. Some articles written about me have come close to romanticising the time I spent on Income Support, because the well-worn cliche of the writer starving in the garret is so much more picturesque than the bitter reality of living in poverty with a child. The endless little humiliations of life on benefits—and remember that six out of 10 families headed by a lone parent live in poverty—receive very little media coverage unless they are followed by what seems to be a swift and Cinderella-like reversal of fortune. (Goldwyn 2002)

CONCLUSIONS

Let us start by pointing out the *elephant in the room*, which we hope became evident in this chapter. That is, despite our detailed analysis of the disaggregated issues surrounding the reporting of poverty, the key problem remains. That is, the way inequality is ignored and dismissed as a cause of poverty in the reporting of the British newspapers. The fact that from 2,214 articles focusing on Britain during this period, only forty-eight news stories linked inequality, as a cause of, or explanation for poverty, shows how the media have managed these types of stories. This is by all means a terrible indictment to all the British press regardless of their political and ideological stance. Moreover in light of numerous studies that have provided unequivocal evidence of the strong association between inequality and poverty (Dorling 2011b; Lansley 2012; Mount 2010; Stiglitz 2012; Wilkinson and Pickett 2009).

Having said that, the chapter also tried to show that the *"invisibilization" of inequality* from the news agenda happens in a diversity of ways. We highlighted the different rhetorical strategies used by journalists to avoid bringing inequality into their stories. We also underlined how these strategies are underpinned by wider discourses such as that of Malthusianism. All in all, we have suggested that these rhetorical strategies are narratives of evasion. This is because inequality is perceived and seen, we suggest, as too ideological or too problematic in the context of the political economy that allow news organisations to operate in a commercial and market-driven environment.

Indeed, contrary to the normative claims that commercial journalism is objective in the way it represents reality, the news coverage of poverty and the almost absent role of inequality in explaining it as a social phenomenon suggests a strong and explicit ideological bias against this type of rationale. Additionally, while explicit references to social class and the economic structures are nowhere to be seen in these media reports, individual stories of "rags to riches" and claims of "envy" are instead all too present.

To be sure, we can reiterate that objectivity has been used in the cases we studied here as an *evasive tactic* that deprives journalism from its ability to tell the truth. We are also able to argue that by claiming objectivity, journalists covering these issues are often able to displace the responsibilities for poverty from current structures of power and wealth and place the blame instead upon the most vulnerable members of our society, just in the same way in which Thomas Robert Malthus did more than 200 years ago.

NOTE

1. The Barnett formula is a mechanism used by the British Treasury to adjust public expenditure in Northern Ireland, Scotland, and Wales based on variations in expenditure on public services.

REFERENCES

Allan, Stuart. (2004). *News culture*. Second edition. Maidenhead: Open University Press.

Allardyce, Jason, and Julia Belgutay. (2010). North South Divide: The poverty gap between Scotland and England remains, but guess which is richer. *Times*, January 10.

Ashworth, Anne. (2008). Poverty of imagination in debate over wealth inequality. *Times*, Januray 18.

Barnett, Alison, Darrin Hodgetts, Linda Nikora, Kerry Chamberlain, and Rolinda Karapu. (2007). Child poverty and government policy: the contesting of symbolic power in newspaper constructions of families in need. *Journal of Community and Applied Social Psychology* 17 (4): 296–312.

Berkowitz, Dan, and Douglas W. Beach. (1993). News Sources and News Context: The Effect of Routine News, Conflict and Proximity. *Journalism and Mass Communication Quarterly* 70 (1):4–12.

Block, Fred L. (1990). *Postindustrial possibilities : A critique of economic discourse*. Berkeley and Oxford: University of California Press.

Briggs, Asa, and Peter Burke. (2009). *A social history of the media: From Gutenberg to the Internet*. Third edition. Cambridge: Polity.

Brighton, Paul, and Dennis Foy. (2007). *News values*. Los Angeles and London: Sage.

Bullock, Heather E., Karen Fraser Wyche, and Wendy R. Williams. (2001). Media Images of the Poor. *Journal of Social Issues* 57 (2): 229–246.

Cabinet-Papers. (2014). *Sterling devalued and the IMF loan* 2014. http://www.nationalarchives.gov.uk/cabinetpapers/themes/sterling-devalued-imf-loan.htm.

Cockett, Richard. (1994). *Thinking the unthinkable: Think-tanks and the economic counter-revolution, 1931–1983*. London: HarperCollins.

Cohen, Stanley. (2011). Folk devils and moral panics the creation of the Mods and Rockers. In *Routledge classics*. London: Routledge.

Conboy, Martin. (2004). *Journalism: A critical history*. London: Sage.

Critcher, Chas. (2003). *Moral panics and the media*. Buckingham: Open University Press.

Curran, James. (2002). Media and the making of British society, c.1700–2000. *Media History* 8 (2): 135–154.

Davies, Nick. (2009). *Flat Earth news: An award-winning reporter exposes falsehood, distortion and propaganda in the global media*. Rearsby: W.F. Howes.

Deacon, Alan. (1978). The scrounging controversy: Public attitudes towards the unemployed in contemporary Britain. *Social Policy and Administration* 12 (2): 120–135.

Dorling, Daniel. (2011a). *Injustice: Why social inequality persists*. Bristol: Policy.

Dorling, Daniel. (2011b). Underclass, overclass, ruling class, supernova class. In *Fighting poverty, inequality and injustice: A manifesto inspired by Peter Townsend*, edited by A. Walker, A. Sinfield and C. Walker. Bristol: Policy.

Elliott, Larry. (2008). Poor children pay for non-doms' tax break. *Guardian*, March 3.

eMediaMillWorks. (2001). Text: President Bush addresses the nation. *Washington Post*, 20 September.

Franklin, Bob. (1999). *Social policy, the media and misrepresentation*. London and New York: Routledge.

Fukuyama, Fracis. (1989). The end of history. *National Interest* (Summer): 3–18.

Genro Filho, Adelmo. (1987). *El Secreto de la Piramide*. Caracas: Imprenta Nacional

Gibson, Owen. (2006). Most leading journalists went to private schools, says study. *Guardian*, Junw 15.

Goerres, Achim. (2009). *The political participation of older people in Europe: The greying of our democracies*. Basingstoke: Palgrave Macmillan.

Golding, Peter, and Susan Middleton. (1982). *Images of welfare*. Oxford: Robertson.

Goldwin, Claire. (2002). I counted out coppers and found I was 2p short of a tin of beans. I pretended to the girl on the till that I'd mislaid £10; Millionaire author J.K. Rowling on her days of poverty. *Mirror*, May 23.

GraduateFog. (2014). *Not posh? Good luck becoming a journalist*. Graduate Fog 2013. http://graduatefog.co.uk/2013/2528/posh-good-luck-journalist/.

Iyengar, Shanto. (1996). Framing responsibility for Political issues. *The ANNALS of the American Academy of Political and Social Science* 546 (1): 59–70.

Kapferer, Bruce. (2005). New formations of power, the oligarchic-corporate state, and anthropological ideological discourse. *Anthropological Theory* 5 (3): 285–299.

Kitzberger, Philip, and Javier Pérez Germán. (2009). Los pobres en papel. Las narrativas de la pobreza en la prensa latinoamericana. *Fundación Konrad Adenauer, Buenas Aires* 3 (3).

Kivikuru, Ullamaija. (2001). *Contesting the frontiers: Media and the dimensions of identity*. Göteborg: Nordicom.

Lansley, Stewart. (2012). *The cost of inequality: Why equality is essential for recovery*. London: Gibson Square.

Lewis, Justin, Andrew Williams, and Bob Franklin. (2008). A Compromised Fourth Estate? *Journalism Studies* 9 (1): 1–20.

Lugo-Ocando, Jairo. (2015). *Blaming the victim: How Global journalism fails those in poverty*. London: Pluto Press.

Lugo-Ocando, Jairo, and Steven Harkins. (2015). The poverty of ideas in the newsroom. In *Blaming the victim: How Global journalism fails those in poverty*. London: Pluto Press.

Males, Mike A. (1996). *The scapegoat generation: America's war on adolescents*. Monroe: Common Courage.

Manning, Paul. (2001). *News and news sources: A critical introduction*. London: Sage.

Maras, Steven. (2013). *Objectivity in journalism*. Cambridge: Polity.

Mount, Ferdinand. (2010). *Mind the gap: The new class divide in Britain*. Revised edition. London: Short.

Orwell, George. [1945] 1984. *Animal farm*. Anstey: Charnwood.

Quintelier, Ellen. (2007). Differences in political participation between young and old people. *Contemporary Politics* 13 (2): 165–180.

Ross, Eric B. (1998). *The Malthus factor: Ppopulation, poverty and politics in capitalist development*. London: Zed.

Rudin, Richard, and Trevor Ibbotson. (2002). *An introduction to journalism: Essential techniques and background knowledge*. Oxford: Focal.

Soley, Lawrence C. (1992). *The news shapers: The sources who explain the news*. New York and London: Praeger.

Spurr, David. (1993). *The rhetoric of empire: Colonial discourse in journalism, travel writing and imperial administration*: Duke University Press.

Stiglitz, Joseph E. (2012). *The price of inequality*. London: Allen Lane.

Sutton Trust. (2006). The Educational Backgrounds of Leading Journalists. http://www.suttontrust.com/wp-content/uploads/2006/06/Journalists-backgrounds-final-report.pdf.

Tawney, R. H. (1961). *Equality*. London: Capricorn Books.

Tuchman, Gaye. (1972). Objectivity as strategic ritual: An examination of newsmen's notions of objectivity. *American Journal of Sociology* 77 (4): 660–679.

Walker, Andrew. (1996). Envy and inequality not poverty, are the root of all crime; Professor blames the breakdown of family values for rising figures. *Daily Mail*, September 19.

Wilkinson, Richard G., and Kate Pickett. (2009). *The spirit level: Why more equal societies almost always do better*. London: Allen Lane.

2

Dialogic Journalism

Bringing Marginalized Communities into the Implied Audience

Greg Nielsen, Amanda Weightman, James Gibbons, and Mike Gasher

From the perspective of a critical media sociology, this chapter posits journalism as an exclusive practice and seeks to imagine a form of news reporting that forges a dialogic relationship with the audience. Such journalism would perceive its implied audience to include the subjects of news stories, particularly when those stories concern marginal populations such as the homeless and the poor. We interpret the gap between these subjects being reported on and the audience that is addressed as evidence of an interpretive contradiction where marginalized subjects might object to the ways news stories are told about them and where fuller understandings of poverty and homelessness could be articulated. We imagine a journalism in which stories do not simply speak *of* the poor and the homeless, but address them as members of the implied audience and, in so doing, anticipate their response.

The chapter combines a coded framing analysis with a thematic interpretive analysis of newspaper articles on poverty and homelessness from twelve English- and French-language newspapers in eight paired cities: New York (*Times*)/Montreal (*La Presse, The Gazette, Le Devoir*); Toronto (*Star*)/Miami (*Herald*); Vancouver (*Sun, Province*)/Los Angeles (*Times*); London (*Times*)/Paris (*Le Monde, Le Parisien*). Despite important differences, the newspapers from these paired cities are ideal for locating comparative analysis on how the topic of poverty is covered and how it raises symbolic questions about who are the uncommon against which common urban resources are named and imagined (Gans 1995; Harvey 2012; Kornberger et al. 2014; Soja 2010). We argue it is equally important to find ways to study how news is triangulated by the specifics of global, national, and urban life. Our research joins an emerging body of work in Canada that underlines the importance of urban location on forms of political exclusion, studied, for example, in audience ethnography from a second-tier city context (Clark 2014), content analysis of newspaper coverage of poverty in major Canadian cities (Richter et al. 2011), focus groups on emotional reactions to reports about inner-city homelessness (Schneider 2014), and framing analyses of urban refugee issues (Bradimore and Bauder 2011). Parallel studies on U.S. newspapers regarding poverty in specific urban locations are also increasing (see Chavez 2008, 2012; Freiburg et al. 2011; Kendall 2011; Suárez-Orozco et al. 2011).

In the first section, we present the results of a coded framing analysis that assesses how the news stories frame emotional, moral and rational orientations of haves toward have-nots, the conditions placed on levels of hospitality for their subject positions, and how the balance of sources from external experts and internal experiences lend authority and, often, affect to information and opinion. This section speculates on the ways in which have-not subjects are defined through journalism without being included in, or while excluded from, the implied audiences of the stories about them. Statistical evidence and typographic charting suggest a consistent rationalization of poverty; this moves the address away from the subject as it underwrites volitional or emotional tones and engages the issue at a structural level.

In the second section, we document the synapses between subject and addressee via thematic interpretive analysis. These dominant narratives have been identified as follows: descriptive accounts of the conditions of poverty; the voice of critique, which features an authorial voice evaluating those conditions; and responding to poverty, which features institutional responses and initiatives aimed at solving and/or managing poverty. While each of these narratives tends to feature a hospitable or positive opening to the conditions of poverty or homelessness, nuanced analysis reveals a consistent underrepresentation of the subjects themselves, as well as an explicit lack of inclusion in the audience to whom those stories are addressed.

We conclude with a discussion of the ways in which the implied audience is a determinant factor in news reporting, and how reporting could change to adopt a more inclusive audience address. If news is defined as what is newsworthy to a particular segment of the public, then editorial decisions about when and which matters pertaining to poverty become news, the particular news value of a given story, how it is to be framed thematically, what perspective is to be adopted, and the style and tone of its language, are all governed by the story-teller's imagined audience. The discursive exclusions produced by discrepant articulations of community and audience we have identified have serious repercussions for notions of citizenship in local and global terms, especially for already-marginalized groups. They undermine journalism's idealized role as a public service and a democratically oriented communications system.

URBAN POVERTY IN THE PRESS

According to the United Nations, there are approximately 100 million people worldwide living on the streets, 600 million living in shelters, and over 1 billion in precarious housing situations (UN 2011). The conventional economic definition of extreme poverty is limited to the more than 20 percent of the planet who survive on incomes of less than $1 a day, while relative poverty includes another 20 percent of the world's population who live with less than $2.50 a day. When put into this kind of global perspective, the question arises as to whether it is appropriate to calculate facts or norms of recognition for the voices of poverty in the urban North American and European context? Voices of the poor and homeless are nonetheless cited, reported, named, and framed in terms of social facts and general norms.

Several media scholars argue that comparative media analysis remains among the most productive and challenging areas of communication research (Benson 2013; Hallin and Mancini 2004, 2012; Livingston 2003; Tiffen et al. 2013). Hallin and Mancini note, for example, that although the French press in Montreal is said to be more partisan than its English-Canadian and American counterparts, it coincides better with a liberal, "fact-centered" North Atlantic model than the Continental European model in which coverage of news follows well-known political lines of established parties (Bonnafous 1991; Hallin and Mancini 2004: 208). Rodney Benson (2013) points out that while the distinct mixture of the interview format and the long narrative is said to be more American, Parisian newspapers have traditionally been more engaged in political and academic writing. His research shows how the two distinct traditions have been merging over the past thirty years.

However, our comparative focus is on the urban scene and not on national media or field analysis that would examine the complex combination of political, organizational and creative forces that struggle with and against each other to define "good" journalistic practice (see Benson and Neveu 2005; Bourdieu 2005). While we situate our analysis of the newspaper texts in concert with the sociological tensions and diversity found in each of the mainly inner-city contexts, the analysis of newspaper format, journalists" attitudes and backgrounds, media convergence, editorial consistency or professional culture (Brevini et al. 2013; Peters and Broesma 2013; Soderlund et al. 2012) are beyond the scope of our program.

Our selection of cities is based on the similarity of their sociological profiles on a North-South continental axis, on their size, their global and/or second-tier status, and their levels of poverty. For us, the crucial point of comparison is to reveal the *specificity* of each urban context and the *symmetry* in how journalists fail to address the subjects of social exclusion as their audience. Each of the cities in our selection has comparable sociological profiles regarding social divisions around homelessness and chronic poverty (Fréchet et al. 2011; HUD 2012; Nwosu et al. 2014; Statistics Canada 2011; Weismann 2013). Today, people living in, or at risk of living in poverty in Canada (including estimates of 300,000 homeless), the United States (3 million homeless) and many parts of Europe comprise up to 40 percent of the population in many regions (Fréchet et al. 2011; HUD 2012; IFRC 2013; OECD 2011; Statistics Canada 2011). This fact sharply conflicts with the news media's tendency to address Western populations as predominantly middle class.

The North American cities are among the six largest urban regions on the continent and have symmetric levels of people living under the poverty line (Noah 2012). Due to space limitations, we include London and Paris newspapers in our coding and thematic analyses, but place a sharper focus on contextualizing the pairing of the six North American cities that reveal interesting continental and national differences. For example, the *New York Times*, while a global newspaper in a global city, is also at the cultural and political centre of the United States. And yet, New York City is widely considered to be unlike the rest of the U.S. It is a premier global city (Sassen 2011) and a world media capital that is fully implicated in current debates about the expansion of poverty in the city. *La Presse* and *Le Devoir* have been considered global media for the francophone world (Abrahamson 2004), and Montreal is often at the epicenter of Canadian culture and politics as seen across its divisive debates over the "reasonable accommodation" of new arrivals (Adelman and Anctil 2011; Maillé et al. 2014). At the same time, Montreal is widely regarded as distinct from the rest of Canada.

All of the cities have comparable numbers of homeless (Relph 2013). Toronto and Miami (Diaz 2014) do not share the same history or political economy as New York (Zukin 2010) or Los Angeles (Davis 1990, 2002; Soja 2014), but both cities have among the highest number of non-native citizens in North America, and both are major corridors for Caribbean immigration. Vancouver and Los Angeles share a West Coast "sensibility" in terms of climate, lifestyle and levels of homelessness, and yet differ dramatically in terms of global city status (Sassen 2001, 2011; Vancouver 2010). For us, the crucial point of comparison is to pinpoint the specificity in each of the paired North-South urban axes and to reveal the symmetry in how it is that journalists are knowledgeable about local poverty, housing issues, shelters and the homeless, but do not address the actors themselves. Our focus on the urban newspaper and its local reporting helps overcome ethnocentric bias associated with studies of national media systems (Livingston 2003) and the limited explanations that case studies of single cities provide. But more productively, comparison reveals the degree to which hospitality and conditionally coded acceptance of marginalized groups is symmetrically constructed in each city and so provides an original complement to comparative studies of national and even global media.

CODING SUBJECTS AND FRAMING AUDIENCES

The first level of our analysis draws on news and commentary in 1,057 articles selected as relevant for analysis from a total of 3,907 published in 2010–2011. The sample was generated using keyword searches (poor, poverty, homeless, and *pauvre, sans abri*) on the Factiva search engine. Keywords were paired with the name of the newspaper's city wherever they occurred in the same paragraph. We coded the articles" framing on both procedural and substantive levels: (1) how the article framed judgments on a positive or conditional opening toward, or outright rejection of, key issues that connect the urban commons with the subjects of poverty and the contemporary phenomenon of homelessness; (2) the external or internal sources that are cited to establish authority for the stories; and (3) the rational, moral or emotional tones used in the address. Overall, a striking 90 percent of the articles we examined displayed a positive opening toward "helping" the poor and homeless, while eight percent were conditional, and a mere two percent expressed outright rejection. Although journalists, intellectuals, activists and "concerned citizens" writing in newspapers framed positive openings toward issues of poverty and homelessness, our point is that they are writing about have-nots toward haves.

To expose this conundrum further, we asked coders to determine whether the comments that support the story are framed by external sources or authorities (54 percent), such as quotes from scholarly experts or government officials distanced from the subjects of the reports, or by internal sources (46 percent), such as direct quotes from the subjects themselves or support groups, community activists, religious groups or organizations working directly with the poor or homeless. The balance between external and internal sources indicates a distance from the subjects being reported on as part of establishing credibility for the implied audience, especially given that only 16 percent of the articles use first-hand personal references or quotes. This distancing is also supported in the finding that a minority of judgments (10 percent) are expressed with emotional tones, based on personal feelings and experiences either of the subject or of the authorities being cited. Given the traditional imperatives of professional journalism—for example balance, verification of facts, a measure of editorial autonomy from purely economic interests (Curran 2005)—we are not surprised to see that the strong majority of the judgments are expressed in rational tones (72 percent), emphasizing logical or objective considerations, or broader moral tones (18 percent), offering arguments such as "this is how things should be" or "because this is the right thing to do." These results suggest a need to create new ways to practice journalism and mediate dialogue that would give recognition to those who, from generation to generation, are not part of "the super-addressee" (Bakhtin 1986). Producing narratives that address themselves back to the subjects of the reports, writing more *to*, rather than *about*, the subject position, relying on the internal rather than the external view, shifting from rational to moral and more emotional tones, taking an advocacy role for justice while remaining accurate, and shifting from balance to greater commitment to the story, could transform journalism into a dynamic act of citizenship that should have been the case all along.

Consider the following quotes randomly selected from our database:

The Montreal Gazette: "Take me to the hospital, fill me up with morphine and tie me up for a month and maybe I'll stop," McHugh says. "Till they let me out." (Linda Gyulai, March 27, 2010)

The Miami Herald: The make-shift shantytown under the Julia Tuttle Causeway—once home to more than 100 sex offenders—is finally being dismantled. "Even if I leave, how will I live? I have no job and no car to get there," said Wilson. (Julie Brown, February 26, 2010)

The Toronto Star: Renee, whose pale, lined skin and mouth full of rotting teeth make her look worn down and older than her years, doesn't much care what happens with this new baby. "I'd prefer her to come home with us," she says with a shrug. "But I'm okay with whatever happens." (Megan Ogilvie, March 13, 2010)

Ask yourself: Who are the voices in the above quotes addressing? What are the images we get about their bodies? Do any of the passages recognize the milieu the subjects are positioned in? Moreover, is each body not somehow outside the urban commons—both physically and symbolically? The reported direct speech from the Montreal man in the first quotation gives a blunt emotional definition of the fate of the addict in the street, but is his voice framed to address others in that world? In the next quotation, is the emotionally charged direct speech from the displaced Miami man who has nowhere to go addressed back to the group living in the shanty town sharing resources under the causeway, or is it directed toward the same abstract generalized other who already understands who are the most despicable, outcast, expendable or precarious in society? Is the direct speech of the homeless pregnant woman in Toronto addressed back to the voices of those in these places, or is it framed to maximize the attraction of the story for the newspaper's ideal audience and its "normal" citizens?

The gap between the coded subjects and audience framing described above helps reveal the distance or proximity between voices of urban exclusion and the implied audience, but does not situate the voices according to types of direct or indirect speech that newspapers use to maintain the distance. In order to get a better idea of the way the subjects of poverty are used thematically, we selected a narrower sample of articles.

RATIONALIZING POVERTY:
THEMATIC ANALYSIS OF AUDIENCE ADDRESS

During the quantitative coding process, articles were assigned a rating to identify the most salient stories in terms of content and our interest in audience address and tone. A thematic analysis of narrative forms was then constructed from those 2011 news stories judged the most salient 101 articles. Each article was sorted into one of three main narrative types, with seven subtypes. These *main narratives* are: descriptive accounts of poverty; the voice of critique; and responding to poverty.

While each of these narratives tends to open with a hospitable or positive opening to the conditions of poverty or homelessness, nuanced analysis reveals a consistent underrepresentation of the subjects themselves, as well as an explicit lack of inclusion in the implied audience. Statistical evidence and typographic charting suggest a consistent rationalization of poverty; this moves the address away from the subject as it underwrites volitional or emotional tones and engages the issue at a structural level.

The *descriptive accounts of poverty* accounted for 31 articles, primarily describing the *who* of poverty. These stories relay an image from the perspective of an external observer who describes a scene or summarizes statistics to illustrate the occurrence of poverty and which individuals or subpopulations constitute the impoverished. The internal authority, when featured, is employed to bring an emotional tone to otherwise rational descriptions or quantifications. Ultimately, these internal voices are represented as secondary personifications and not as legitimate authorities on their condition. The mythos of journalism dictates that journalism is concrete, clear, direct and factual (MacGregor 2009), and thus personification is a device that satisfies these criteria. Although the use of personification may be considered positive, as subjects voice their own experiences, the effect here is a means of imagining the unimaginable. These descriptive accounts of poverty do, however, have a positive opening. The tone is one of concern: a helping voice toward the individuals or groups who exemplify a systemic issue. In this sense, the story is justified in moral terms, even if the issue is neither being described to, or by, the subject of poverty. Rather, poverty is explained in rational terms of cause and effect, from an external view, toward an external audience.

"Elemental moralism" describes how we are impelled to tell the story of poverty with disturbing specificity while simultaneously ensuring that the product can "safely be ignored" (Baron 2003). It could be that the news media's elemental moralism, or documentary imperative, compels the reporting found on what has become an all too acceptable part of the urban landscape: the homeless (see Hopper 1998). Journalism's tendency toward historiography as reality, though it might help the intended audience imagine the unimaginable, excludes the subject through such rationalism, as the product is all too often an advocacy failure. In considering the various narratives that populate coverage of homelessness and poverty, it is evident that rationalism often guides the text as opposed to, one could say, the practice of advocacy or volitional reporting, as that would undermine occupational claims of objectivity. In addition to excluding the subject, social exclusion—which is a complicated formulation that includes access to housing, resources, services, social networks and assets—undergoes what has been referred to as "falsification by simplification" (MacGregor 2009).

Descriptive accounts of poverty narratives can be distinguished by two subtypes: *vulnerable groups* and *the middle class fall*. The subtype *vulnerable groups* accounts for the majority of the descriptive narratives (20 articles). These describe a specific subpopulation facing high rates of poverty due to an additional condition which predisposes them to a cycle of poverty. That is, those who are poor are more likely to have children who are vulnerable to health problems, underperform in school, and find themselves below the poverty line as adults. These doubly vulnerable subpopulations are: veterans (in the United States), seniors, foster children, LGBT, single parents, and racial or ethnic groups. The issue of poverty is framed here as a systemic, moral fault. The subject is, in a sense, being advocated for, but seemingly from a distance. This distance suggests the subject is being spoken about, not addressed. In considering the appeal to the poor, a guide to navigating the system or saving time would likely be more useful than describing the ills of the system (which the poor likely know already). This could be a means of shifting the utility, and by it, the address, of these types of stories.

The *middle class fall* (11 articles) describes the new "who" of poverty. They are the former middle class identifiable by the rising numbers of people falling below the poverty line or accessing social support. Statistics and reports are commonly relied on to validate, animate, and draw attention to these trends—for example, "Official government figures confirm the trend" ("More Poor," 2011). Community and academic experts are dominant voices; as well, those of the new poor themselves speak to the "fall" into poverty, providing an emotional hook and inspiring empathy from the reader who is, implicitly, also at risk. These stories draw attention to the macro picture of poverty as a national issue by offering descriptive accounts, not of derelict characters, but of hard-working and even educated individuals, who are unjustly struggling as a result of broader socioeconomic and political conditions. The cause is explicitly identified as the "recession," rising costs of living, job losses and the polarization of wealth (and wealth as agency) in society. Therefore, these stories do not impose personal responsibility—"through no fault of their own" ("A Guide" 2011)—so much as frame the issue of poverty as a systemic fault—"the nation's inability to create jobs" (Lee et al. 2011)—requiring a *systemic* response.

The *voice of critique* narrative consists of only eleven of the 101 articles. These stories follow closely from descriptive accounts, which point to systemic causes of poverty. This narrative type takes these causes as its focus and directly critiques those factors.

The first subtype, the *socioeconomic critique* (six stories), fits closely with the middle class fall in that it attends to the systemic causes of growing poverty rates. The systemic causes of poverty are identified as "social, political and economic injustice," "corporate greed," "corruption," "no jobs," "cultural apathy" and "market ideology." The narrative is a critique of these forces, but does not come from an internal source about the conditions of their own poverty. The journalist serves as advocate for the dominant audience of which s/he is a part, and the critique is offered as an act of advocacy. That audience implicitly remains the middle class; those who "fall" into poverty seem also to fall away from the readership, to fall out of line from any direct address.

The *call to justice*, though accounting for only five stories, is a distinct critique. The narrative relates closely to the *vulnerable groups* narrative in that it involves a moral reaction to an external action which has indirect, negative ramifications for a population already predisposed to poverty. Notably, the voice represented is an internal support group as authority and advocate for the subject of poverty against a specific act of systemic injustice. The reaction itself is morally justified.

RESPONDING TO POVERTY

Categories such as "poor" or "homeless" suggest absolutes in the social spectrum. They constitute means of describing a group to a perceived or imagined audience. This is affirmed by institutional voices that explain poverty—in this case, a response to it. In most ways this is comprised of a superficial "what" definition of the subject; this abbreviated representation of the subject is formidable given various news limitations. A "who" definition, by contrast, would probe much further, providing more detail and portraying the subjects of the stories as individuals—rather than as types—with their own particular histories.

From this, we engage with *responding to poverty* as part of our typology: fifty-nine articles. Twenty-seven articles featured internal authorities, all of them with positive openings. Twenty-four articles featured external authorities—distinguished by positive and conditional openings. The final eight articles were coded as *polemic;* these articles focus on a debate about how or whether to manage or solve homelessness. Notably, descriptive accounts of poverty and the voice of critique refer to poverty as a broad economic condition, whereas response narratives engage with the issue of homelessness as well as poverty. Homelessness, in particular, is approached not as a structural issue *of* society, or as a humanistic concern for the homeless, but as a problem *for* the community in which it appears.

Taken as a political issue, legislation that responds to poverty comes in two varieties: "solving" and "managing." Legislation is a top-down response, as the institutional means of either alleviating or solving causes of homeless. The alleviation of poverty could be framed as a benefit to the "in-group" (Bauman 1989), as either a complement to, or in contradistinction to, benefits to the homeless. The rationale given for solving homelessness is couched in an economics of assistance and not a moral imperative (i.e., because it is the right thing to do). Efforts are justified, for example, not according to their meaning for, or benefit to, the subject of poverty, but in terms of fiscal responsibility.

Jails, shelters, and hospital emergency rooms are all examples of "managing" poverty. The subject uses a variety of state resources, yet is no better off. Furthermore, the subject is likely to frequent these resources in continuity. "Solving" homelessness, on the other hand, is exemplified in Chez Soi or Housing First programs, which provide the homeless with permanent housing and access to social services. Whereas the former is thought of as a stabilizing measure, the latter is considered remedial. The following are examples of the discussion between "managing" and "solving" homelessness. Note the use of rationale as rhetoric, as opposed to the use of a moral imperative as the basis for action.

On the creation of smaller shelters in New York, which is still categorized as an emergency service: "'The city recognized it was time to readdress the way street homelessness was dealt with,'" said Douglas Becht, the director of the homeless outreach team for BronxWorks, the nonprofit group in the Bronx. "'The widespread success shows that the system that they set up is a really good system'" (Secret 2011).

The following quote addresses a religious group that provides food to the homeless on the street: "Phil Brown, general manager of Toronto's Shelter, Support and Housing department, which operates Streets to Homes, admits the work those like Burrows, Connolly and Whelan are doing is problematic for his program.

. . .

"One of the challenges we face sometimes is there are still some groups, unrelated to the city who may be helping people stay out, when we're trying to get (the homeless) to come in. We classify that service as survival support to help people stay on the street. We don't fund those anymore" (Donovan 2011).

Both of these examples feature internal authorities; the individuals are both part of support groups, and the rational tone demonstrates a positive opening toward the poor.

Not all responses to homelessness demonstrate a positive opening. Responses are often predicated on certain conditions, sometimes outright rejection. For example, with respect to "housing first" programs, there could be the condition that subjects undergo counseling or offset housing costs by offering part of their social assistance income to the program. The implied beneficiary of a response, particularly the external response to homelessness, is not the subject of poverty but the community, businesses or social programs to which the poor are framed as a threat.

Stereotypes are drawn upon to situate the problem: "homeless, derelict, and dangerous . . . the drug dealers, gang lookouts and seriously unwell" (Sutherland 2011), "roused from a beer-induced slumber" (Groves 2011). One article from the Miami *Herald* describes a move to ban the distribution of free food to the homeless in public areas (Potts and Murray 2011). The authorities pushing for the ban argue that free public distribution is unsightly and possibly unsanitary. Noting that there are existing outlets for food distribution provides only a further rationale to relegating the homeless. It is evident, though, that this variety of response represents the status quo and placates business interests. In the story, the food distribution is in proximity to both a literal and symbolic area of wealth: the commercial and business sector of Miami.

Again, these stories are not voiced from or toward the subject of poverty. Rather, the homeless are the passive beneficiaries of the programs described; none of the stories documenting the Chez Soi program, for example, discusses eligibility requirements, or how to apply for a housing unit, which would effectively shift the address from rationalizing, or imagining the unimaginable for the intended audience, toward the subjects themselves.

"ARE YOU TALKIN' TO ME?"

Can news stories be written differently, more inclusively? If so, how? We take the position that news stories about poverty and homelessness can and should speak to the poor and the homeless, and *our aim* is to develop a new dialogic form of journalism that addresses the subjects of poverty and homelessness, including them within the implied audience. This form of audience address would shift the poor and the homeless from mere objects of news reportage to internal addressees of mainstream news coverage. Historically, journalism has gradually opened its address to new audiences: the working class, women, minority groups and youth. If these shifts remain works in progress, they nonetheless demonstrate the possibility of expanding the implied audience.

We acknowledge that the poor and the homeless do not constitute a market for commercial news organizations which operate on the basis of selling audiences to advertisers, and it is for that reason that we insist upon a distinction between journalism and the news industry. We hold journalism to its idealized role as a public service and a democratically oriented communications system, a media sphere where understandings of topics like poverty and homelessness are forged and where interlocutors congregate as citizens.

All forms of communication are interlocutory and thus the implied audience is a determinant factor in every communicative act; it is paramount in news reporting. News is defined as what is newsworthy to a particular segment of the public. Thus, editorial decisions about when matters pertaining to poverty become news, the particular news value of a story, how it is to be framed, what perspective is to be adopted, and the style and tone of its language, are all governed by the imagined audience. Defining the news value of a story to a particular imagined audience can exclude the information needs and the perspective of those not imagined as part of the audience. For the most part, the stories we have analyzed in this project are characterized by an absence of information that speaks directly to the poor and the homeless. The reportage, instead, typically casts its subjects as characters in a story, occasionally given voice, more often in the background, but consistently separated from the implied audience.

The third element of our research program consists of a series of workshops, which bring together our research team, working journalists, journalism students and those who work closely with the poor and the homeless. The aim of the first set of workshops is to rewrite news stories that have already been published on the topics of poverty and homeless in an effort to bring the subjects of the stories into the implied audience. Revisions could pertain to story angle, new information, background, sourcing, style, tone, language choices, etc.

For example, a *Toronto Star* story about the conflict between church groups providing food and clothing to the homeless and outreach workers with the city's Streets to Homes program (Donovan 2011) includes the homeless as Torontonians, but largely relegates them to the background; they are talked about, not spoken to. They are given no subjectivity in what is framed as a policy dispute, but instead they are spoken *for* by members of the church groups. Similarly, they are provided no information about how to benefit from the Streets to Homes program, nor any independent information about whether the city's housing program is effective or preferable to the church groups' charity. The story could be revised from its adversarial he-said, she-said format and reframed to address the question of whether the homeless, and Torontonians in general, are well-served by the city's Streets to Homes program, supported by verifiable data and testimony from those with direct experience of the program. The two homeless individuals who are identified in the story and asked about the church groups' services could be granted subjectivity as citizens by being asked their opinion about the city's housing program. Similarly, the story could conclude, as many news stories on other topics now do, by soliciting comment from readers, including homeless readers.

News stories typically portray poverty and homelessness as a problem, but how the stories define the problem—what kind of problem it is, and for whom?—reveals a lot about their implied audience. A *Los Angeles Times* story about an "influx of homelessness" in two Los Angeles neighborhoods (Groves 2011), for example, defines homelessness as a problem for merchants, landlords, and residents, as opposed to a problem for those seeking a place to sleep. A particularly egregious instance of defining homelessness as a problem for those who are not homeless occurs in a *Montreal Gazette* story about merchants petitioning city council "to do something about the number of homeless, derelict and dangerous people" in the city's Gay Village (Sutherland 2011). The story pits "merchants and residents" against a motley collection of undesirables, which lumps the homeless in with "drug dealers," "gang lookouts" and "derelict and dangerous people," in effect criminalizing the homeless. The story clearly sides with the "merchants and residents"; they are the only people cited in the story, and their comments are taken at face value:

> An elderly man in a winter jacket comes out of a dépanneur with a white plastic bag. His toes, visible in his flip flops, are black—the toenails blacker, and not just from dirt. One eye is swollen shut. He shuffles off.

By the shape of the bag, he's picked up several cans of beer, and chips.
"He'll go somewhere and drink and in three hours he will be sitting in the middle of the sidewalk, pissing in his pants," Rousseau said.

In simply presenting one side of this story, passively and uncritically, categorizing the homeless along with gang members and drug dealers, and representing them exclusively through stereotypes, the story endorses the petitioners and speaks to the non-homeless. "Gentrification, a boom in condo building and a cleaning up of the area for the summer patio and restaurant season are all good efforts," the story asserts in the reporter's voice.

Part of the strategy we are advocating requires journalists to abandon the passive, stenographic posture that characterizes many stories on poverty and homelessness in order to become more engaged in the story. This would require: reflecting on what kind of problems for society poverty and homeless represent, abandoning the "us" vs. "them" format, broadening story sources and points of view, resisting the stereotypes that result from simple group identifications—"the poor," "the homeless"—and thinking about the information needs of the subjects of the stories.

In a pilot workshop in September, 2013, we brought together journalists with community newspaper and national radio and television experience, undergraduate students from the journalism programs at Concordia University and l'Université du Québec à Montréal, and members of a research project working with the Inuit population in Montreal. Working collaboratively, we rewrote sample stories from Montreal's English-language and French-language press, seeking to shape those stories and their forms of address toward the subjects of the stories: in one case, Inuit receiving health care in Montreal, for whom a former hospital in the Villeray district was to be converted into a hospice; in another case, the homeless in the Montreal suburb of Laval, for whom a new refuge was to open.

The workshop participants were encouraged to revise the stories as they saw fit, provided the revised story retained a measure of news value and maintained news story structure by addressing the questions of who, what, when, where, why and how. Participants were further asked to make notes of any aspects of the story they were not able to revise. Each was given a list of specific elements to consider, such as: segregating language that created an "us" and a "them'; how the topic of the story was defined as a problem, and for whom; the identification of people in the story based on *who* they were rather than *what* they were; how statistics were employed and made meaningful; information addressed specifically to the subjects of the stories, and so on.

While the participants were partially successful in revising the articles—opening up the address, changing language, giving added meaning to statistical data, providing background information and context, and adding "what to do" information for the subjects of the stories—the general conclusion was that there were significant limitations to rewriting already-published articles. It was difficult, for example, to add research material and to reach out to new sources for stories published weeks or months earlier. More importantly, participants felt the matter of audience address could not be treated as an afterthought, but must be part of the story's original conception. A second series of workshops will engage journalism students to produce original stories aimed from the outset at an implied audience that includes the subjects of the stories.

CONCLUSION

Our idea for developing fundamental research into the creation of a more inclusive internal dialogue between the journalists and the subjects of their reports is derived from the argument that *dialogue* is not limited to a conventional exchange of ideas as in a conversation between two speakers that can be decoded according to linguistic rules. It is understood, rather, as the process that takes place in the imagination of journalists and their idea of the audience (McQuail 2010). Our comparative framing analysis and workshop activities are aimed at opening the interpretive contradiction (Boltanski 2011), the way in which subjects of reports might decode the way news stories about them are told, or how they might contest other injustices excluded from the story.

Our overriding objective is to create a new, *more inclusive journalism* that would require much more dialogic work from journalists (Curran 2005; Dahlgren 2006). This would begin not just from where the actors are located, as in much of community, alternative or citizen journalism (Atkinson 2010; Atton 2002; Atton and Hamilton 2008), but in prioritizing a lively anticipated response from the subjects of reports as themselves the primary addressees. In turn, this will mean moving the mainstream press away from purely constative to more performative acts of information and opinion formation, away from a balance of objective external and subjective internal citations and sources toward a greater commitment to their stories, but with the same degree of accuracy and rigorous verification the profession demands.

NOTE

This research project is funded by a grant from the Social Sciences and Humanities Research Council of Canada. We would like to acknowledge research assistants

Haluk Dag, Desirée Hostettler, Andreea Mandache, Mircea Mandache and Anna Meshcherova, who participated in the development of the coding protocol, story coding and the rewriting workshop.

REFERENCES

Abrahamson, Mark. (2004). *Global Cities*. New York: Oxford University Press.

Adelman, H., and P. Anctil (eds.). (2011). *Religion, Culture and the State: Reflections on the Bouchard-Taylor Report*. Toronto: University of Toronto Press.

Bakhtin, M.M. (1986). *Speech Genres and Other Late Essays*. Trans. Vern W. McGee. Austin: University of Texas Press.

Bauman, Z. (1989). *Modernity and the Holocaust*. Ithaca: Cornell University Press.

Benson, Rodney. (2013). *Shaping Immigration News: A French-American*. Cambridge: Cambridge University Press.

Benson, Rodney, and Erik Neveu (eds.). (2005). *Bourdieu and the Journalistic Field*. Cambridge: Polity Press.

Bonnafous, Simone. (1991). *L'immigration prise aux mots: Les immigrés dans la presse au tournant des années 80*. Paris: Éditions Kimé.

Bourdieu, Pierre. 2005. "The Political Field, the Social Science Field, and the Journalistic Field." In Rodney Benson and Eric Neveu (eds.), *Bourdieu and the Journalistic Field*. Cambridge: Polity Press.

Bradimore, Ashley, and Harald Bauder. (2011). "Mystery Ships and Risky Boat People: Tamil Refugee Migration in the Newsprint Media." *Canadian Journal of Communication, 36*, pp. 637-661.

Brevini, Benedetta, Arne Hintz, and Patrick McCurdy. (2013). *Beyond WikiLeaks: Implications for the Future of Communications, Journalism and Society*. New York: Palgrave Macmillan.

Charles, Alec. (2014). "The Abuse of Power: Savile, Leveson, and the Internet." In Alex Charles (ed.), *The End of Journalism 2.0: Industry, Technology and Politics*. Oxford, UK: Peter Lang.

Chavez, Leo. (2001). *Covering Immigration: Popular Images and the Politics of the Nation*. Berkeley: University of California Press.

Chavez, Leo. (2012). "Undocumented Immigrants and Their Use of Medical Services in Orange County, California." *Social Science and Medicine 74*, 887–893.

Clark, Debra. (2014). *Journalism and Political Exclusion: Social Conditions of News Production and Reception*. Montreal and Kingston: McGill-Queen's University Press

Dahlgren, Peter. (2013). "Online Journalism and Civic Cosmopolitanism: Professional vs. participatory ideals." *Journalism Studies 14*, no. 2, 156n171.

Davis, Mike. (1990). *City of Quartz*. London: Verso.

Davis, Mike. (2002). *Dead Cities*. New York: New Press.

Diaz, Many. (2014). *Miami Transformed: Rebuilding America One Neighborhood, One City at a Time*. Philadelphia: University of Pennsylvania Press.

Donovan, Vincent. (2011). "Rector Finds His Own Way to Feed Homeless; Hunger Patrol Defies City's 'Housing First' Motto for Street People." *Toronto Star*, July 4, GT1.

Fréchet, Guy, Danielle Gauvreau, and Jean Poirier (eds.). (2011). *Statistiques sociales, pauvreté et exclusion sociale: perspectives québécoises, canadiennes et internationales. Publication en hommage à Paul Bernard, Centre interuniversitaire québécois de statistiques sociales (CIQSS) et Ministère de l'Emploi et de la Solidarité sociale.* Montréal: Presses de l'Université de Montréal.

Fryberg, Stephanie A., Nicole M. Stephens, Rebecca Covarrubias, Hazel Rose Markus, Erin D. Carter, Giselle A. Laiduc, and Ana J. Salido. (2011). "How the Media Frames the Immigration Debate: The Critical Role of Location and Politics." *Analyses of Social Issues and Public Policy* 12, no. 1, 96–112.

Gans, Herbert. (1995). *The War against the Poor: The Underclass and Anti-Poverty Policy.* New York: Basic Books.

Groves, Martha. (2011). "Shelter Opens Doors Early; Influx of Homelessness in Venice, Westchester Triggers Move." *Los Angeles Times*, October 31, AA1.

"A Guide to the Autumn Statement; For More Than 100 Beginner's Guides Visit thetimes.co.uk/moneyguides." (2011). *London Times*, December 3, T1 80.

Hallin, Daniel, and Paolo Mancini. (2004). *Comparing Media Systems: Three Models of Media and Politics.* London: Cambridge University Press.

Hallin, Daniel, and Paolo Mancini. (2012). *Comparing Media Systems Beyond the Western World.* Cambridge, UK: Cambridge University Press.

Harvey, D. (2012). *Rebel Cities: From the Right to the City to the Urban Revolution.* London and New York: Verso.

Hopper, K. (2003). *Reckoning with Homelessness.* Ithaca: Cornell University Press.

Hornmoen, Harald, and Steen Steensen. (2014). "Dialogue as a Journalistic Ideal." *Journalism Studies* 15, no. 5, 543–544.

U.S. Department of Housing and Urban Development (HUD). (2012). *Annual Homeless Assessment Reports to Congress.* Retrieved from https://www.hudexchange.info/resource/3297/2012-ahar-volume-2-estimates-of-homelessness-in-the-us/.

International Federation of Red Cross and Red Crescent Societies (IFRC). 2013. *Annual Report 2013.* Retrieved from http://www.ifrc.org/en/publications-and-reports/annual-report-2013/.

Kendall, Diana. (2011). *Framing Class: Media Representations of Wealth and Class in America.* New York: Rowman and Littlefield.

Kornberger, Martin, Ester Barinaga, and Christian Borsch. (2014). *The Urban Commons.* London: Routledge.

Lee, Don, Noam Levey and Alejandro Lazo. (2011). "U.S. Poverty Totals Hit a 50-Year High; More Go without Health Insurance, and Young Adults Move Home as Recession's Effects Linger." *Los Angeles Times*, September 14, A1.

Livingstone, Sonia. (2003). "On the Challenges of Cross-National Comparative Media Research." *European Journal of Communication* 18, no. 4, 477n500.

MacGregor, P. (2009). "Journalism, Public Imagination and Cultural Policy." *International Journal of Cultural Policy* 15, no. 2, 231–244.

Maillé, Chantal, Greg M. Nielsen, and Daniel Salé (eds.). (2014). *Revealing Democracy:Revealing Democracy: Secularism and Religion in Liberal Democratic States.* New York: Peter Lang.

"More Poor Turning to Food Pantries." (2011). *Miami Herald,* September 2.

Noah, Timothy. (2012). *The Great Divergence: America's Growing Inequality Crisis and What We Can Do about It.* New York: Bloomsbury Press.

Organization for Economic Co-operation and Development. (2011). *Divided We Stand. Why Inequality Keeps Rising.* Retrieved from http://www.oecd.org/document/51/0,3746,en_2649_33933_49147827_1_1_1_1,00.html.

Peters, Chris, and Marcel Broesma. (2013). *Rethinking Journalism: Trust and Participation in a Transformed News Landscape.* London: Routledge.

Potts, Maff, and Alastair Murray. (2011). "Is It Time to Outlaw Soup Runs? Westminster Council Wants to Ban Food Handouts to the Homeless." *London Times,* April 2, 83

Richter, Solina, Katharina Kovacs Burns, Jean Chaw-Kant, Moira Calder, Shirley Mogale, Lyla Goin, and Yuping Mao. (2011). "Homelessness Coverage in Major Canadian Newspapers, 1987–2007." *Canadian Journal of Communication* 36, 619–635.

Sassen, Saskia. (2011). *Cities in a World Economy.* Thousand Oaks, CA: Pine Forge Press.

Secret, Mosie. (2011). "Deal to Help Foster Youths Find Housing." *New York Times,* October 21, 30.

Soderlund, Walter, Colette Brin, Lydia Miljan, and Kai Hildebrandt. (2012). *Cross-Media Ownership and Democratic Practice in Canada: Content-sharing and the Impact of New Media.* Edmonton: University of Alberta Press.

Soffer, Oren. (2013). "The Imagined Audience of Israeli Army Radio: A Historical Perspective." *Israel Studies* 18, no. 3, 69–94.

Soja, Edward. (2010). *Seeking Spatial Justice.* Minneapolis: University of Minnesota Press.

Soja, Edward. (2014). *My Los Angeles: From Urban Restructuring to Regional Urbanization.* Los Angeles: University of California Press.

Statistics Canada. (2011). *National Household Survey.* Catalogue no. 99-014-X201100.

Sutherland, Anne. (2011). "'We Believe in this Neighbourhood'; Gay Village Is Trying to Rid Itself of Homeless People and Drug Runners. The Mayor Says He Is Aware of the Problems." *Montreal Gazette,* September 14, A8.

Tiffen, Rodney, David Rowe, Toril Aalberg, Sharon Coen, James Curran, Kaori Hayashi, Shanto Iyengar, Gianpietro Mazzoleni, Stylianos Papathanassopoulos, Hernando Rojas, and Stuart Soroka. (2014). "Sources in the News." *Journalism Studies* 15, no. 4, 374–391.

United Nations. (2011). *The Millennium Development Goals Report 2011.* Retrieved From http://www.un.org/millenniumgoals/pdf/%282011_E%29%20MDG%20Report%202011_Book%20LR.pdf.

Vancouver Economic Development Commission. (2010). *Vancouver as a City-Region in the Global Economy. A Paper by the Vancouver Economic Development Commission for the Business Council of BC's "Outlook 2020" Project.* Retrieved from http://www.bcbc.com/publications?q=Vancouver%20as%20a%20city-region%20in%20the%20global%20economy.

Zukin, Sharon. (2010). *Naked City: The Death and Life of Authentic Urban Places.* New York: Oxford University Press.

3

Britain's Hidden Hungry?

The Portrayal of Food Bank Users in the UK National Press

Rebecca Wells and Martin Caraher

Poverty in the UK is poorly understood and reported by the media (McKendrick et al. 2008) and some researchers have suggested that the media could challenge misconceptions about those experiencing poverty, instead of adding to such misconstructions (Seymour 2009). This chapter reports on the findings from a study of British print media coverage of those living with a particular aspect or form of poverty: food poverty (Dowler et al. 2001). We examine the portrayal in the UK mainstream print media of food bank users. Food is essential for life, forms a part of social and cultural relationships and is now a marker of consumer culture (Bourdieu 1984). To be without food is an issue of both public and private concern. Lack of food, compared to other products, introduces other elements to poverty.

Food banks, where supplies of food are given free of charge to people in need, have long been a feature of the informal welfare system in North America and New Zealand (Poppendieck 1999; Riches 1997). In Britain they are a relatively new phenomenon. There were two recorded food banks in the UK in 1999 (Hawkes and Webster 2000), now there are 800+ and an estimated 1600 emergency food aid providers across the country (Forsey 2014). This dramatic rise has inspired a surge in media coverage of "Food Bank Britain" (APPG 2014; Rayner 2013) that we have analyzed for a study on food banks and the UK print media (Wells and Caraher

2014). In this chapter we draw on a data set of 190 articles published in UK national newspapers between October 2008 and January 2014, to pursue a line identified in the initial research and examine in more detail the portrayal and voice of food bank users in these media reports.

Many authors have investigated the ability of the mass media to play a role in the process of defining a social problem, discussing whether they directly or indirectly influence the policy process (Buse, Mays, and Walt, 2005; Chase and Bantebya-Kyomuhendo 2014). Cobb and Elder (1972) noted that the mass media can "set the agenda" for audiences by promoting certain issues over others, or by "framing" or "angling" issues in certain ways (Entman 1993, 2007; Goffman, 1974). Iyengar (1996), for example, found that referring to "the poor" rather than "people on welfare" elicited a different response from readers. Others have built on this research by looking at the processes of media production, noting that when information is supplied to journalists from an external source, such as a press release, it often comes with an in-built frame and is unlikely to be objective (McQuail 2010). For their part, journalists themselves can explicitly or implicitly assign responsibility for the causes and solutions to social problems—these can inform the judgment and action of citizens and policymakers (Iyengar, 1996; Kim and Willis, 2007; Leader et al. 2009). The framing of food welfare and food poverty in the media is a key issue in this study, since how people think about poverty and policy options for dealing with it has been shown to be linked to how the issue is framed (Baumgartner and Jones 1993: McCombs 2013). Iyengar's (1990) study on US broadcast media portrayals of poverty noted:

> How people think about poverty is shown to be dependent on how the issue is framed. When news media presentations frame poverty as a general outcome, responsibility for poverty is assigned to society-at-large; when news presentations frame poverty as a particular instance of a poor person, responsibility is assigned to the individual. (Iyengar 1990: 19)

However, more recent studies of poverty in the UK media highlight concern at a general lack of coverage of poverty; McKendrick et al. (2008) found that reporting of poverty was largely peripheral with explanation of the causes of poverty particularly absent. They found that in news coverage *"there was a conspicuous absence of the voices of those in poverty themselves from much of the reporting"* (McKendrick et al. 2008: 31).

PORTRAYAL OF POVERTY IN THE UK PRESS

The binary portrayal of those experiencing poverty as either "deserving" or "undeserving" has been a key theme in the literature on representations of poverty in the media (Chauhan and Foster 2013; Garthwaite 2011; Golding and Middleton 1982; McEnhill and Byrne 2014). Golding and Middleton (1982) argue that while the UK printed press expanded rapidly in the late nineteenth and early twentieth century, it was largely a newspaper industry written for and by the conservative middle classes, in contrast to the early radical newspapers (Curran 1977; Golding and Middleton 1982). This emerging Victorian printed press had developed an obsession for the "dismal yet titillating" world of urban poverty (Golding and Middleton 1982: 24) and featured it regularly. However Thompson (1984) noted the way the political inclination of a newspaper and/or its editor, could shape reporting and ignore or "edit out" the voices of those at the sharp end of poverty. The rise of these early Victorian newspapers, conservative in outlook and commercial in nature, amplified the concept of "deserving" and "undeserving" poor (Himmelfarb 1985) in which those experiencing poverty were categorized into those who deserved welfare (if their circumstances were outside their control) and those who did not (for example the "workshy"). The new mass media also perpetuated the idea of welfare as a financial burden on the state. For example the *Daily Mail* leader of February 18, 1909, reporting on the Report of the Royal Commission on the Poor Laws:

> The great fault of the English poor relief in the past has been its enormous cost, which exceeds for England and Wales alone in the present year fourteen millions. Yet, though immense sums of public money are expended, there is no civilised country where the deserving poor are so severely treated, and there is none where the undeserving live in such comfort. (*Daily Mail*, 1909)

This discourse placing those experiencing poverty in a mutually exclusive category of either deserving or undeserving has perpetuated in the British media through the twentieth century (McEnhill and Byrne 2014; Seabrook 2013) and is still repeated in today's newspapers (for example "There are limits to our empathy, and George Osborne knows it" (*Guardian*, October 7 2015), "Undeserving state-funded minority will no longer enjoy the same lifestyle as hardworking people" (*Mail Online,* October 27 2012), "Sorry, Archbishop, but there IS a big difference between the deserving and undeserving poor" (*Daily Mail*, December 30 2010).

The "othering" of those experiencing poverty in which they form a separate social group outside of mainstream society is highlighted by Chauhan and Foster (2013) who see the representational absence of those experiencing poverty in the press as distancing poverty from general society. This is heightened by the media's tendency to stereotype (Gorham, 1999). Chauhan and Foster (2013), in common with other authors (Seymour, 2009, McKendrick et al. 2008) note that research frequently finds the media stereotyping those experiencing poverty as criminals, alcoholics and drug addicts who are often portrayed as workshy and lazy. Similarly, Golding and Middleton (1982), McKendrick et al. (2008), Coughlin (1989), and Clawson and Trice (2000) all outline the media's tendency to demonize particular individuals, often extreme examples such as those in receipt of welfare payments with much larger than average family sizes and/or those using welfare to fund an "extravagant" lifestyle. These are then used as media templates with which to stereotype poverty. Seymour (2009) argued that a common characteristic of these stereotypes is that those experiencing poverty are a "drain on society" (for examples from the contemporary UK popular press, see *Daily Mail,* "Vile Product of Welfare UK," March 14 2013; *Sun,* "Exclusive: Family Cashes In: £52,000 in Handouts, 12 Kids, Another on the Way . . . Now They're Getting a Superhome," October 10 2013; *Sun* (30/06/14) "Forget Demi here's Gimme Moore. Scrounger Josie Goes Nude'[1]; *Sun,* "Weeks after Having Twins . . . Twelfth Mite: I'm Pregnant Again, Boasts Benefits Mum of 11," February 1 2015). Drawing on Cohen's work (1972) Golding and Middleton (1982) see this so-called scroungerphobia as a form of "moral panic," in which the poor are defined as a threat to societal values and are therefore categorized as "undeserving." A recent theme in the UK popular press is the demonizing of those "too fat to work" (for examples, see *Daily Express,* "Benefits Couple Too Fat to Work. And YOU Paid for Their Wedding," June 1 2015, and *Sun,* "43 Stone and Shameless. Tum and Dumber. Mum and Daughter: We're Fat, on £34k-a-Year Benefits . . . and Proud," January 14 2015).

Overall and despite these examples there is a pervasive trend in the literature suggesting that coverage of poverty is peripheral in the mainstream media (McKendrick et al. 2008; Seymour 2009). McKendrick et al. (2008) found that people experiencing poverty featured in fewer than one in eight reports. Seymour (2009), in common with Chauhan and Foster (2013) argued that children and older people experiencing poverty are more likely to receive coverage, but that overall there are few success stories—the implication is that the majority of people in poverty have failed.

FOOD POVERTY AND FOOD BANKS IN THE UK

As noted above, food banks, while common for some time in New Zealand, North America and parts of mainland Europe, are a relatively new phenomenon in the UK. In 1999 there were two reported food banks in the UK (Hawkes and Webster 2000). In the face of global economic austerity the numbers using food banks are spiraling (De Schutter 2013; Lambie 2011).

There are two types of food bank currently in operation in the UK. One of the key providers of food banks in the UK is the Trussell Trust, a Christian charity. In 2013–2014, the 400+ Trussell Trust food banks in the UK gave three days' food to over 900,000 people. (Lambie 2011; Lambie-Mumford 2013; see also http://www.trusselltrust.org). The Trussell Trust is the largest single provider of food banks due to its links in the Christian community as a Christian charity and because of its franchise system of operation. Its franchised network is expanding by three food banks per week bringing the number of food banks operated by them to just over 400 with the forecast that 1,000 food banks are required to satisfy potential demand.

Another model is provided by FareShare, which collects surplus food from supermarkets and shops and distributes it through 1,711 charities and organizations to needy families and individuals feeding contributing towards more than 13.2 million meals in the last year (see http://www.fareshare.org.uk). FareShare reveal that over 82,100 people benefit from their service every day. It itself does not operate outlets but distributes to those who do, some of which might be food banks but others could be homeless charities, shelters or soup kitchens. Aside from this there are many other food banks operating on their own either as independent charities or part of existing community groups (see http://www.milestonelondon.co.uk for an example of a group setting up a food bank for the Muslim community).

This rise in food bank use and the provision of emergency food relief by charitable organizations in the UK is contextualized by a squeeze on food and fuel spending as families cut back on spending and a program of welfare reform by the current Conservative and previous UK coalition (Conservative/Liberal) Government. According to Government statistics: "Between 2007 and 2012, average households traded down to cheaper products to save nearly 6% while the lowest income households traded down to a much lesser extent, possibly as they were already buying cheaper products" (DEFRA 2014: 22). Others such as Caraher and Cavicchi (2014) have suggested that due to further restrictions on income, significant numbers of low-income households have traded down to food banks as the outlet of last resort. This occurred, between 2007 and 2013, as the effects of the global recession bit; food prices increased alongside static incomes and other costs rising such as transport and home rentals (APPG 2014; Loopstra et al. 2015).

FOOD BANKS IN THE UK MEDIA

Riches (1997) criticizes the media's role in the development of food banks in Canada, saying food banks

> play a key role in the depoliticization of hunger as a public issue, particularly when they enlist the services of the media to support them in the food drives. In this way the media come to portray hunger and the work of food banks as just another charitable cause. This is precisely what government wishes to hear and it helps them promote their argument that it is only in partnership with the community that the hunger problem can be solved. (Riches 1997: 70)

However, to the best of our knowledge our research (Wells and Caraher 2014) is the first to map the media portrayal of food banks in the English speaking literature. Our original study analysed newspaper articles in nine national UK print media titles using the news database Nexis and focused on the period since the global financial crisis in 2007. In this study, newspapers were used over online press coverage since they are published irreversibly and in an easily accessible format (Cooper et al. 2011). The sources were nine national UK daily newspapers with their Sunday counterparts: The *Daily Mail* and *Mail on Sunday*, *Daily Star* and *Daily Star Sunday*, *Daily Telegraph* and *Sunday Telegraph*, *Financial Times*, the *Guardian* and the Observer, the *Independent*, the *Independent on Sunday*, the *Mirror* and *Sunday Mirror*, the *News of the World*[2] *Sun*, the *Times* and *Sunday Times*. Our search criteria included mention of the term food bank in a UK context at least three times in the article, in order to minimize finds in which food banks were mentioned in passing or were not the main focus of the article. This resulted in 190 usable articles from the newspapers[3]. There were no articles before October 2008 and few until 2012 when the number increased dramatically. A key theme was reporting of increasing numbers of food banks and users of them. The data most often cited was from the Christian charity Trussell Trust that runs a franchise system of food banks. There were clusters of stories indicating a common source. Reporting did not often include the voice of users and where it did often focused on their "gratitude" for the service. There was a predominance of articles from the left-leaning press.

It is important to note that UK newspapers are divided into tabloid (sometimes called "populist") and broadsheet (sometimes called "serious") newspapers with distinct readership profiles. (Audit Bureau of Circulation 2015; National Readership Survey 2014; Newsworks 2014). In addition, the UK press operates across a partisan or polarized model (Rowbottom 2010) in which a range of views are provided by a number of media outlets. During election periods some newspapers openly support a particular political party. While this changes from one election to another, some newspapers consistently support the right-of-center Conservative political party (*Daily Mail, Daily Telegraph*) while others support the left-leaning Labour Party (*Daily Mirror*) or are left leaning and support either the left-of-centre Labour Party or a liberal party (*Guardian, Independent*) (Butler and Butler 2000, 2006).

Our initial research found that food bank users were not often directly quoted, with food bank volunteers and others acting as a "proxy" voice for them, reporting anecdotes or stories of food poverty. Food bank users themselves were sometimes featured in media coverage as "case studies" accompanying an appeal for donations to food banks. Personal stories of hardship were sometimes used to generate a sense of compassion—particularly at Christmas time. Food bank users rarely gave their opinion on food banks or the politics of food poverty, more often simply and briefly describing their personal situation. The complex circumstances surrounding individual cases of poverty were rarely explored in detail. In contrast, politicians and celebrities were given privileged access to the media and their views on those living in poverty were reported. These views sometimes alluded to food bank users as undeserving or opportunistic or blamed their poverty on personal failings—for example lack of self-control or financial acumen.

Methodology

In our original research one of our major themes was "stakeholder voices." While we found that there was a disparity in reporting where food bank user's voices were absent, there were some key instances in our sample of articles where current food bank users were featured and quoted directly. In order to explore further the portrayal of food bank users in our data we used the same core sample of 190 articles and reanalyzed them. Both researchers read all of the newspaper articles to identify codes (Altheide and Schneider 2013; Saldana 2013). Similar codes were clustered together to form categories, redundant codes were removed. From these clusters of codes or categories we identified themes and these formed the basis of our coding frame. We reread all the articles, working together to check and validate each other's coding and making adjustments to the coding frame. We identified 6 main categories (see Appendix for the coding frame). From the initial categorization, where voices were represented we undertook further in depth thematic analysis on the direct quotations of the food bank users.

Results

In the majority of cases, current users were not often directly quoted and sometimes they were not referred to at all. By far the biggest category was that of "users referred to." In this category current food bank users were not directly quoted but were referred to, often in very general terms. For example referring to "poor households" (Oakeshott 2013) "the desperately poor and hungry" (Kelly 2013) "people at the bottom of society" or "some of the poorest in our communities" (Morris 2013).

Ex-users were sometimes used as a proxy voice for current users. A striking example of this was prominent references to and articles by food writer Jack Monroe. Monroe, a former food bank user, rose to prominence writing on a website ("A Girl Called Jack," http://agirlcalledjack.com) that started as a blog about local politics and became a resource of budget food and recipes (Monroe 2014). Part of Monroe's prominence in our sample of articles was due to her involvement in a successful petition run jointly by the UK trade union Unite, the food bank charity the Trussell Trust and the tabloid Mirror newspaper to force a debate in the UK House of Commons on the causes of food bank use and hunger in Britain (Monroe 2014). Monroe often appears as an author writing opinion pieces about food poverty or food banks for left-leaning newspapers such as the *Guardian*, the *Observer,* or the *Mirror*. (Monroe 2013a, 2013b, 2013c, 2013d, 2013e, 2013f, 2013g). She is also mentioned several times in relation to the *Mirror* petition and campaign, predominantly in the *Mirror* newspaper itself. Other notable former users who were given a voice in the media reporting were volunteers who were interviewed in that capacity, often empathizing with current users and citing gratitude as the reason for their work:

> That was the case for Louise Andrews, 26, who used the bank when she had problems with her Jobseeker's Allowance and is now a volunteer. "Jo was so kind-hearted to start this food bank," she said. "I had nowhere else to turn when I was referred here by the Citizens Advice Bureau in town." (Merrill 2013)

> Jackie Bicknell, a recovering alcoholic and former drug user, who leads the team of volunteers, can empathise because in the past she has been in the situation faced by many of those using the food bank. Happily, the volunteering work she secured through her involvement with the church has given her a new focus. (Carter 2012)

As a group, food bank volunteers frequently referred in their descriptions of food banks to individual incidents of hardship involving users, for example:

We've had people say they can't afford the gas or electric, so we try to put in extra tins of fruit for them, food they can eat cold. One man told me he'd borrowed a camping stove from his next door neighbour because he couldn't afford the energy meters. (Cochrane 2013)

Staff at the centre in Barrow, Cumbria, told of their shock when they realised a woman in her late-50s had walked almost 10 miles in heavy rain from Ulverston to collect a handout. (Armstrong 2012)

Volunteer Ursula Gallagher said: "One man cycled 30 miles from Derry and back. A mum-of-four walked three and a half miles as she needed to keep the bus fare." These desperate scenes are repeated across the country. (Glaze 2013)

The quotes used from volunteers are largely uncritical of food banks either specifically or in general. They are portrayed as heroes, working tirelessly and unselfishly for those less fortunate than themselves. This sometimes amplifies the sense of "otherness" of those experiencing poverty:

"I just couldn't have sat at home with my kids, having a good time, knowing that there are people who are suffering. They are not that different from ourselves, they just have different circumstances." (McPhee 2013)

The food bank is open on Mondays and Fridays, so Edward normally helps out twice a week during the school holidays, sorting the food and packing boxes to be given out to families in need. He hopes to go back during the Christmas holidays. He said: "When I see people coming in, I feel sorry for them that they have no food, but I'm glad I'm able to help them." (Manger 2013)

Without her selfless work there wouldn't even be a tea bag to hand out. The mother of two started up the bank one of the first of its kind in London in June 2010, after being unable to stand the thought of local children going hungry. (Sturgis 2012)

They not only distribute food but collect it. They stand outside supermarkets all day asking strangers to buy the tinned food they need or hand out leaflets in the streets or plead with businesses to help. Sharon Cumberbatch is unemployed but she works to help others for nothing. (Cohen 2013)

Many of the articles have religious overtones, either because of a spike in articles during the Christmas period or because of the inherently Christian nature of the Trussell Trust. Many of their food banks are based in Christian churches therefore churchmen and women are frequently featured in reports. In addition, and again, perhaps because of the Christian connection to the Trussell Trust, religious language is often employed by journalists (for example, "They Saved Our Lives, We Feel Blessed," *Daily*

Mirror, December 22, 2013; "Food Samaritans; Mirror Xmas Help Appeal Hits Orkney," *Daily Mirror*, December 13, 2013; "Feed Thy Neighbour: Charting the Journey of a Food-Bank Donation," *Independent on Sunday*, July 14, 2013; "The Mum Who Works a Miracle," *Daily Mail*, October 4, 2012) and also by users, several of whom refer to the food bank as a "godsend" (*Daily Mirror* 2012; Ellicott 2011; Kellaway 2012; Shields, 2008).

In general and in contrast to the discourse around "benefit scroungers" or cheats in the UK popular press, food bank users were generally not portrayed in a negative light. They were not often stereotyped as lazy, workshy or addicts, nor was it implied that users were opportunistically using the food bank as a means of securing free food. Reports did not often criticize food bank users or blame them for their circumstances, more often describing a complex series of misfortunes or bad luck which had seen them resort to using the food bank. When food bank users were quoted, as well as giving their own circumstances they expressed feelings of both gratitude and shame:

> "I cried this morning before I came. It is so belittling, I feel so worthless. I hardly dared come today in case I knew someone," she said. "I used to get financial support from my father in Italy but he is so ill now I can't ask him. I've had to pawn my laptop and Jewellery but I'm still £1,100 in debt." She added: "This food is a miracle. I can't wait to see my kids" faces when they unpack the boxes. I am so very grateful." (Sherman 2013)

The sense of shame they felt was enhanced and accompanied by an unwillingness to be named in the reports—journalists noted in several reports that some food bank users who were quoted chose to remain anonymous or go under a pseudonym, for example: "One woman, a mother of three, asked me not to use her real name because she didn't want her neighbours to know she had been here. 'You shouldn't feel shame, but you just do,' she says" (Midgley 2012).

However, in contrast to the "othering" of those experiencing poverty outlined by Chauhan and Foster (2013) there were several examples giving the reader a sense of empathy with the food bank user; it could be you:

> There were times, not so long ago, when he wore a Gucci watch and Armani suits. Today Glen White survives on handouts of free food. "I'm one step away from starvation," he admits. And he pulls out the pockets of his £10 jeans to show he doesn't have a single penny in there. "I never imagined I would be living this way . . . and believe me, if it can happen to somebody like me then it can happen to anyone," he says. (Ellam 2012)

This empathy was strengthened in a number of examples where food bank users had formerly been food bank or charity donors:

In Hull, mum-of-two Wendy Clark found herself asking for help just a few weeks after she DONATED groceries to a food-bank collection. Wendy, 40, approached teachers at Alderman Cogan Church of England Primary School after she realised she did not have enough food to feed four-year-old Jacob and Zachariah, nearly one. She said: "It can happen to anyone. The fridge was very nearly bare by the time we got help." (Wellman 2013)

Sitting at a table in Swindon's St Aldhelm's Hall, Maria, who prefers not to give her surname, says she used to send her two sons off to school harvest festivals with gifts of tinned beans, pineapple and spaghetti hoops to donate to the needy. Since her husband, a surveyor, was made redundant and the rising cost of food ate into the family savings, she has been calling on these gifts herself. (Warrell 2011)

The shock was terrible. For years, I've given to international aid charities and to suddenly be on the receiving end was very traumatic. But what really made me cry was the fact that people were helping. We'd felt so isolated, but now everyone was rallying round. (Fryer 2011)

Again, in contrast to the "scroungerphobia" seen in other research (Golding and Middleton, 1982) food bank users were sometimes portrayed as selfless; they were quoted saying they had fed their children before themselves:

"It's not about my food," says Stanova softly, so as not to wake Beyonce. "I can eat bread and water. It's about providing for her. She's growing fast. You give her some clothes and she can wear them for two weeks, then she's too big . . . And as she grows, she eats more. I'm trying to breastfeed her, but it's not enough." (Saner, Cochrane, and Pidd 2013)

"We moved into this house in June but our funding did not come through. Our overheads are massive. We have had to go without food to feed our kids. And there have been times when we have had to choose between heating and food. Sometimes I go to the bathroom and sob because I can't make my children's lives any better."

Just six months ago Jamie, 19, worked as a bartender, Jemma was a trainee hairdresser and they were looking forward to becoming parents. Then Jamie was made redundant weeks before Jordan—now five months old—was born. Jemma, also 19, who lives locally, said: "It was the worst time for Jamie to lose his job. We were spending all the money we had on looking after our little man." (*Sun* 2012)

"We had no money left, it was snowing and we were all sleeping in one room to save on heating. Our cupboards were bare, all our money went on nappies and formula milk for Tia. It was really hard. It is so frustrating not to be able to have the essentials, to not be able to provide the basics for your child. It gets you really down." (Owen and Brady 2010)

In addition food bank users were portrayed as victims who expressed both feelings of failure and contrition:

> "You feel you shouldn't be a mother if you can't provide food for your children. You feel like you have failed. Then you don't want to tell anyone because you feel so down." (Wellman 2013)

> "It is so embarrassing to have to go to them and ask for help," she said. "You feel like an absolute failure. But I was only able to give them a jam sandwich each and their dinner was a tin of spaghetti hoops between them and hot dogs." (Wellman 2013)

> The trip to the food bank makes him feel "really guilty" and, as grateful as he is for the three-day supplies, he says: "This has got to last me nine days. I'll have to eat every other day, and drink water on the days in between." (Meets 2012)

> "Really you're begging, aren't you?" he said. "But it's bloody hard to be honest with you. I'm not too bad—I don't feel the cold as much as Julie and Matthew," he said. "He does go to bed with his clothes on sometimes. When he has a bath, he wants to have the heating on, but I have to say "no." I feel guilty. How can you tell a 10-year-old you can't keep him warm?" (*Guardian*, 2010)

Occasionally users were quoted giving a political opinion. This sometimes was used to underpin the newspaper's own political stance, as in this visit by the Daily Mirror to Prime Minister David Cameron's Oxfordshire constituency:

> Although Banbury and Chipping Norton are market towns in the same rural county, their populations lead very different lives. "Chippy," as it's known, is the gateway to the Cotswolds and the PM is often spotted shopping in local stores. The town is in a "golden triangle" where the average price of a house is around £440,000. Banbury, meanwhile, has three of the most deprived council wards in the nation. Cleaner Sara Broadbent is a single mum of two teenage daughters who was forced to use the town's food bank after her 16 hours of work were cut to just five. "David Cameron lives just down the road and he could do a lot more for us," she says. "It's like living on a tightrope for me and I know I'm not on my own." (McPhee 2013a)

Many of the case studies featured were clients of the food bank organization the Trussell Trust. This gives the Trussell Trust a role as an important gatekeeper with some control over access to food bank users and in some cases their views. For example a cluster of articles appeared in early 2011 all featuring the food bank in the town of Okehampton in the county of Devon in the South West of England. The story about a surge in clients at this food bank appeared in three articles in three different newspapers on the same day and each featured similar quotes from Mary and Nick Wonnacott, Okehampton residents and users of the food bank:

> Mary and Nick Wonnacott live in Okehampton and both worked for Polestar for more than 15 years before losing their jobs last month. They described the food bank as a godsend without which they could not have managed. Mrs Wonnacott said: We've had four weeks where we've had to manage with no income at all, so this has been a wonderful boon for us. (Ellicott 2011)

> Husband and wife Mary and Nick Wonnacott, of Okehampton, both worked for dessert manufacturers PoleStar Foods for more than 15 years before losing their jobs last month. They described the food bank as a godsend without which they could not have managed. Mary Wonnacott said: "We've had four weeks where we've had to manage with no income at all, so this has been a wonderful boon for us." (Morris 2011)

> Mary and Nick Wonnacott worked for PoleStar for more than 15 years. Mrs Wonnacott said: "We've had four weeks where we've had to manage with no income at all, so [the food bank] has been a wonderful boon for us." (de Bruxelles 2011)

DISCUSSION AND CONCLUSION

We have focused on the voices of food bank users as they appeared in our data but it is important to note that there was an under-representation of those voices with others talking for them. In line with other literature on media representations of those experiencing poverty (Golding and Middleton 1982; McKendrick et al. 2008) they were talked about often without being talked to—supporting Chauhan and Foster's (2013) work in which those experiencing poverty are "othered" by their absence. However, in contrast to the more general literature (Chauhan and Foster 2013; Garthwaite 2011; McEnhill and Byrne 2014) in which the dominant discourse in the popular press is of benefit scroungers and cheats, reporting on food bank users seems to operate under a halo effect. The food bank users quoted in our data were rarely criticized or depicted as undeserving poor and in fact were often portrayed as sympathetic and with a complex series of circumstances outside of their control that could be applied to the reader. Given the often negative portrayal and stereotyping of those experiencing poverty in the popular press as outlined by several studies (Chauhan and Foster 2013; Garthwaite 2011; McEnhill and Byrne 2014) this finding is surprising but may be explained by work looking at the construction of the voluntary sector in the news in the UK (Deacon 1999;

Deacon et al. 1995; Hale 2007; McDonald and Scaife 2011) which suggests a "surprisingly indulgent treatment of voluntary agencies in the news, but also a broad lack of interest in reflective debate about their actions, motives, opinions and functions" (Deacon 1999: 59). While these authors acknowledge that there can be negative media portrayals of voluntary organizations, with McDonald and Scaife (2011) noting a cynicism in the media for example where corporate giving was concerned, Deacon et al. (1995) in common with Rausch (2002) found that positive media portrayals of voluntary organizations could promote volunteerism but could also encourage public apathy towards social problems, since reporting did not address the political relationship between these voluntary agencies and other institutions or individuals, more often promoting the work of volunteers or asking for donations.

There may be another factor relating to the issue of the right to food and the place of food in culture. Food is a basic need along with shelter and security but it also performs a social role. Here the sense of others in the family suffering from a lack of food as well as the role of food bank users as carers and providers makes it difficult to be critical. In one of the richest countries in the world it seems shameful that some cannot access or afford food- a basic human right (de Schutter 2013). It is important to remember that here we are not talking about the ability to afford a healthy and nutritious diet but the fact that food in its most basic and even sometimes unhealthy form is not available to some.

The empathetic representation of food bank users that we found in our research contrasts with Chauhan and Foster's (2013) work in which they argue that British newspapers distance poverty from general society and portray it as a "problematic other" (Chauhan and Foster 2013: 401). This reporting trend in our study may be related to the predominantly Christian context of food bank operations in the UK and the contribution of both food bank volunteers and donors. This halo effect further extended to users' comments on food banks, which were on the whole positive and expressed gratitude for the services offered. This contrasts with the findings of in-depth research from the Netherlands with food banks users (van der Horst et al. 2014) which outlined the negative feelings and experiences of users. In our data information on food banks users was filtered in two ways: access to users was controlled and the stories reported back by the media were more likely to reflect the positive side of food banks.

The gratitude expressed by the food bank users in media reporting could lead to a perception of food banks as successful initiatives and long-term solutions to food poverty. However there is no evidence to support this and in fact Riches and Silvesti (2014) and Poppendieck (1999) show that the rise of food banks do not address underlying issues of food poverty and may in fact depoliticize food hunger. Under these terms food banks could be classified as what Siebel (1996) calls organizations of "successful failure," which engage in "symbolic problem solving" (Siebel 1996: 1011) in this instance tackling the symptoms rather than the underlying causes of food poverty or even the reasons why people end up at food banks. This lack of engagement with the wider social determinants of poverty and the crisis situations that drive people to use food banks are enhanced by the location of food banks outside of the formal welfare system. This is not to underestimate the role food banks can play in emergency food provision. By featuring food bank users as case studies for appeals on behalf of food bank organizations, newspapers explicitly endorse them and are less likely to use critical quotes from users. This further feeds into Siebel's concept of successful failures by providing a favorable environment for public concern and fundraising to ensure continuance, without a clear indication of successful outcomes. In addition it calls into question the independence of the press and their role as the so-called fourth estate (Carlyle 1921).

While the mass media see their normative role as structuring reports using a "balanced" range of voices that can provide differing views and opinions on the same subject as part of what has been called their "discursive practices" (Chalaby 1996; Mancini, 2005), how this "balance" is achieved of course depends on the views and opinions known to the reporter, or available to them via interviewees or other sources. These views and opinions can be pre-formed in press releases or other information controlled by key gatekeepers. The reporter themselves under many codes of practice are expected to adopt a neutral stance (McQuail 2013). Interviewees and contributors to reports are cast in various roles for example as experts, victims or former victims. In general we found that while food bank users were underrepresented in our data, those that were quoted were very much cast in the role of victim, albeit grateful for the service. As such their main role was to talk about the practical experience of food bank use and their own personal circumstances. Those classed as experts who were given an opportunity to comment were often drawn from the food bank organizations themselves. Notable was the lack of independent, including academic, voices offering verification of data and experiences. There were few radical or dissenting voices to offer alternative views. One notable bridge between these two roles was that of Jack Monroe (@ DrJackMonroe) who was often used as a proxy voice for current food bank users (having used food banks herself) and was elevated to the status of expert by virtue of her rising status as a celebrity. This was reinforced by her role as a published food writer, columnist and blogger. This raises two points of concern: journalists may rely on Monroe as a source, side-lining other food bank users" access to the media—and additionally limiting the reported experiences of food bank users to a lone voice.

The consistent representation of food bank users in media reports can be explained in a number of ways. The control of case studies and access to them by key organizations resulted in quotes from the same food bank users being used across multiple publications. In addition although the Trussell Trust run 54 percent of food banks in the UK (Forsey 2014) the majority of food bank users quoted in our sample were Trussell Trust clients. This has the effect of reinforcing one model of operation, in this instance with a Christian ethic, and marginalizing users of other models of food bank. This has implications for journalism and its ability, as the fourth estate to challenge the status quo. Because of changes in news production processes (many due to technological change, for example the use of the internet and emails) research has shown that time in the newsroom is shorter and resources are stretched (Lewis et al. 2008). Journalists have become increasingly reliant on press releases to write their copy (Bartlett et al. 2002; Lewis et al. 2008) and this has caused concern about the independence of the British media (Lewis et al. 2008; Davies 2009; Williams et al. 2009). Our research echoes a concern among media scholars about a reliance of journalists on public relations professionals and news agencies (Lewis et al. 2008). As Lewis et al. point out (2008) this challenges the UK press's claims to journalistic independence and the role of journalists as a fourth estate; calling into question their ability to hold policymakers to account.

The reasons for the absence of the marginalized and poor in the UK media are themselves complex. It's recognized (Seymour 2009) that NGOs and charities act as gatekeepers between those living with poverty and journalists. While time-pressed journalists may be unwilling to seek out food bank users, food bank users themselves may be unwilling to speak to the media for fear of negative portrayals or fear of "officialdom." A lack of food may introduce another dimension to poverty, different from other forms of poverty and this may contribute to the sense of shame and embarrassment that was notable in some of the quotes used in the reporting. Here interviewees were not seeking increased financial income but food as a basic human right and need. In addition, the striking lack of quotations from current food bank users may indicate that the reality of food bank users' circumstances or views may undermine the success of the food banks themselves, which as we have shown are often endorsed by the mass media. Our research has shown that when food bank users are featured in press reports their accounts are focused on hard luck and situations outside of their control—implying that they are deserving rather than undeserving recipients. Poverty can be seen by journalists as negative or bleak and avoided in favour of stories about celebrities and entertainment news. However the halo effect surrounding food banks as charitable agencies staffed by volunteers gives journalists an opportunity to frame them and the poverty associated with them in a positive, redemptive light. This results in greater coverage for this issue, particularly around Christmas time. However, despite the volume of coverage our study shows a lack of interrogation on the part of journalists of the complex causes of food bank use and a notable absence of the voices of those at the sharp end of poverty.

NOTES

1. This headline refers to the U.S. moviestar Demi Moore who posed nude while pregnant for a front cover of the magazine *Vanity Fair*. This front page of *Sun* featured a picture of welfare recipient Josie Cunningham in a similar pose.

2. The *News of the World* newspaper ceased publication July 10, 2011.

3. This gives an indication of media coverage, Nexis in common with other news databases does not provide total coverage of all articles. For further exploration of this issue see Ridout et al. (2012) and Weaver and Bimber (2008).

REFERENCES

All-Party Parliamentary Inquiry in Hunger in the United Kingdom. (2014). "Feeding Britain: Strategy for zero hunger in England, Wales, Scotland, and Northern Ireland London, Archbishop of Canterbury's Charitable Trust." https://food-povertyinquiry.files.wordpress.com/2014/12/food-poverty-feeding-britain-final.pdf.

Armstrong, J. (2012). "Families Walking 20 Miles for Food Handout; Needy Can't Afford Bus Fare." *Daily Mirror*, December 5, 11.

Audit Bureau of Circulation. (2014). "Who We Are." Available http://www.abc.org.uk/About-us/Who-we-are/.

Barnett, A., Hodgetts, D., Nikora, L., Chamberlain, K., and Karapu, R. (2007). "Child Poverty and Government Policy: The Contesting of Symbolic Power in Newspaper Constructions of Families in Need." *Journal of Community and Applied Social Psychology* 17(4), 296–312.

Bartlett, C., Sterne, J., and Egger, M. (2002) "What Is Newsworthy? Longitudinal Study of the Reporting of Medical Research in Two British Newspapers." BMJ 325(7355), 81–84.

Baumgartner, F.R., and Jones, B.D. (2010). *Agendas and Instability in American Politics*. Chicago: University of Chicago Press.

Bourdieu, P. (1986). *Distinction: A Social Critique of the Judgment of Taste*. Abingdon and Oxon: Routledge.

Buse, K., Mays, N., and Walt, G. (2005). *Making Health Policy*. Maidenhead: Open University Press.

Butler, D., and Butler, G. (2000). *Twentieth Century British Political Facts*. Basingstoke: Palgrave Macmillan.

Butler, D., and Butler, G. (2006). *British Political Facts since 1971*. Basingstoke: Palgrave Macmillan.

Caraher, M., and Cavicchi, A. (2014). Old crises on new plates or old plates for a new crises? Food banks and food insecurity. British Food Journal, 116(9); doi.org.wam.city.ac.uk/10.1108/BFJ-08-2014-0285

Carlyle, T. (1921). Sartor *resartus: On Heroes, Hero-Worship and the Heroic in History*. New York: JM Dent and Company.

Carter, H. (2012). "Dire Straits: Discreet Buzzer Opens the Door to a Helping Hand for the Hungry." *Guardian*, June 26, 12

Chalaby, J. (1996). "Journalism as an Anglo-American Invention." *European Journal of Communication* 11, no. 3, 303–326.

Chase, E., and Bantebya-Kyomuhendo, G., eds. (2014). *Poverty and Shame: Global Experiences*. Oxford: Oxford University Press.

Chauhan, A., and Foster, J. (2013). "Representations of Poverty in British Newspapers: A Case of 'Othering' the Threat?" *Journal of Community and Applied Social Psychology* 24, 390–405.

Clawson, R. A., and Trice, R. (2000). "Poverty as We Know It: Media Portrayals of the Poor." *Public Opinion Quarterly* 64, 53–64.

Cobb, R.W., and Elder, C.D. (1972). *Participation in American Politics: The Dynamics of Agenda-Building*. Boston: Allyn and Bacon

Cochrane, K. (2013). "My First Year as a Food Bank organizer." *Guardian*, December 23, 12.

Cohen, S. (2002). *Folk Devils and Moral Panics: The Creation of the Mods and Rockers*. New York: Routeldge.

Cohen, N. (2013). "Cowardly Coalition Can't Face Fact of Food Banks." *Observer*, December 29, 37

Cooper, B.E.J., Lee, W.E., Goldacre, B.M., and Sanders, T.A.B. (2011). "The Quality of the Evidence for Dietary Advice Given in UK National Newspapers." *Public Understanding of Science* 21, no. 6, 664–673.

Coughlin, R.M. (1989). "Welfare Myths and Stereotypes." In R.M. Coughlin (ed.), *Reforming Welfare: Lessons, Limits and Choices*. New Mexico: University of New Mexico Press.

Daily Mail. (1909). "The Abolition of the Work-House System." *Daily Mail*, February 18, 4.

Daily Mirror. (2012). "I Walked 16 Miles to Get Help after I Lost My Job." *Daily Mirror*, December 9, 11.

Davies, N. (2009). *Flat Earth News*. London: Vintage Books.

De Bruxelles, S. (2011). "Food Parcel Lifeline for Town Where Jobs Are Disappearing Fast." *Times*, March 15, 22.

de Schutter, O. (2013). "Freedom from Hunger: Realising the Right to Food in the UK: A Lecture by the United Nations Special Rapporteur on the Right to Food." Just Fair, http://just-fair.co.uk/freedomfromhunger.

Deacon D. (1999). "Charitable Images: The Construction of Voluntary Sector News." In B. Franklin (ed.), *Social Policy, the Media, and Misrepresentation*. London: Routledge.

Deacon D., Fenton N., and Walker B. (1995). "Communicating Philanthropy: The Media and the Voluntary Sector in Britain." *Voluntas: International Journal of Voluntary and Nonprofit Organizations* 6, no. 2, 119–139.

DEFRA. 2014. *Food Statistics Pocketbook 2013*. London: DEFRA.

Dowler, E., Turner, S., with Dobson, B. (2001). *Poverty Bites, Food, Health and Poor Families*. London: CPAG.

Ellam, D. (2012). "'I Once Wore Gucci and Armani and Now I've Got Nothing. It Happened to Me and It Can Happen to Anyone.' *Sunday Mirror* Investigates Food Bank Britain." *Daily Mirror*, December 9, 12, 13.

Ellicott, C. (2011). "Charity Hands Out Food Parcels to the Starving . . . of Devon." *Daily Mail*, March 15

Entman, R.M. (1993). "Framing: Toward Clarification of a Fractured Paradigm." *Journal of Communication* 43, 4, 5–58.

Entman, R.M. (2007). "Framing Bias: Media in the Distribution of Power." *Journal of Communication* 57, 163–173.

Forsey, A. (2014). "An Evidence Review for the All-Party Parliamentary Inquiry into Hunger in the United Kingdom." London, Archbishop of Canterbury's Charitable Trust.

Fryer, J. (2011). "Charity Does Begin at Home." *Daily Mail*, March 23.

Garthwaite, K. (2011). "The Language of Shirkers and Scroungers? Talking about Illness, Disability and Coalition Welfare Reform." *Disability and Society* 26, no. 3, 369–372.

Gentleman, A. (2012). "A Life on Hand-Outs: Food Banks Are Springing Up across Britain to Help Struggling Families. But Is Charity Really the Answer for People Being Let Down by the State?" *Guardian,* July 19, 6.

Glaze, B. (2013). "We're All Banking on YOU; Your Chance to Join Our Festive Appeal." *Daily Mirror*, December 8, 24.

Goffman, E. (1974). *Frame Analysis: An Essay on the Organization of Experience*. Cambridge, MA: Harvard University Press.

Golding, P., and Middleton, S. (1982). *Images of Welfare: Press and Public Attitudes to Poverty*. Oxford: Martin Robertson.

Gorham, B. W. (1999). "Stereotypes in the Media: So What?" *Howard Journal of Communication* 10, no. 4, 229–247.

Guardian. (2010). "In Numbers: Forced to Choose Eating or Heating, Family Burns Furniture to Keep Warm." January 18, 6.

Hale M. (2007). "Superficial Friends: A Content Analysis of Nonprofit and Philanthropy Coverage in Nine Major Newspapers." *Nonprofit and Voluntary Sector Quarterly* 36, no. 3, 465–486.

Hawkes, C., and Webster, J. (2000). "Too Much and Too Little?—Debates on Surplus Food Redistribution." Sustain: The Alliance for Better Food and Farming. http://www.sustainweb.org/publications/too_much_and_too_little/.

Himmelfarb, G. (1985). *The idea of poverty*. London: Faber and Faber.

Iyengar, S. (1990). "Framing Responsibility for Political Issues: The Case of Poverty." *Political Behavior* 12, no.1, 19–40.

Iyengar, S. (1996). "Framing Responsibility for Political Issues." *Annals of the American Academy of Political and Social Science* 546, 59–70.

Kellaway, K. (2012). "Special Report: 'We've had to go without to feed the kids. The food bank is a godsend': Three food banks open every week and 15,000 people will turn to them over Christmas. Many are in work but find it ever harder to make ends meet. For one family in Salisbury, the arrival of a seasonal hamper has made all the difference." *Observer*, December 23, 10.

Kelly, L. (2013). "Red Cross UK Food Handout Shames MPs." *Sun*, October 19, 11.

Kim, S.H., and Willis, L.A. (2007). "Talking about Obesity: News Framing of Who Is Responsible for Causing and Fixing the Problem." *Journal of Health Communication* 12, 359–376.

Lambie, H. (2011). "The Trussell Trust Food Network: Exploring the Growth of Food Banks Across the UK." Coventry University.

Lambie-Mumford, H. (2013). "Every Town Should Have One: Emergency Food Banking in the UK." Journal of Social Policy 42, no. 1, 73–89.

Leader, A.E., Weiner, J.L., Kelly, B.J., Hornik, R.C., and Cappella, J.N. (2009). "Effects of Information Framing on Human Papillomavirus Vaccination." *Journal of Women's Health* 18, no. 2, 225–233.

Lewis, J., Williams, A., and Franklin, B. (2008). "A Compromised Fourth Estate?" *Journalism Studies* 9, no. 1, 1–20.

Loopstra, R., Reeves, A., Taylor-Robinson, D., Barr, B., McKee, M., and, Stuckler, D. (2015). "Austerity, Sanctions, and the Rise of Food Banks in the UK." *BMJ*, doi: 2015;350:h1775 doi: 10.1136/bmj.h1775.

McCombs, M. (2013). *Setting the Agenda: The Mass Media and Public Opinion*. Hoboken, NJ: John Wiley and Sons.

McDonald, K., and Scaife, W. (2011). "Print Media Portrayals of Giving: Exploring National 'Cultures of Philanthropy.'" *International Journal of Nonprofit and Voluntary Sector Marketing* 16, no. 4, 311–324.

McEnhill, L., and Byrne, V. (2014). "'Beat the Cheat': Portrayals of Disability Benefit Claimants in Print Media." *Journal of Poverty and Social Justice* 22, no. 2, 99–110.

McKendrick, J.H., Sinclair, S., Irwin, A., O'Donnell, H., Scott, G., and Dobbie, L. (2008). *The Media, Poverty and Public Opinion in the UK*. York: Joseph Rowntree Foundation.

McQuail, D. (2010). *McQuail's Mass Communication Theory*. Sixth edition. London: Sage.

McQuail, D. (2013). *Journalism and Society*. London: Sage.

McPhee, R. (2013a). "Generous Helpers Dish Out Lots of Love to Needy." *Daily Mirror*, December 26, 9.

McPhee, R. (2013b). Same County, Different Worlds; Inside Food Bank on Cameron's Doorstep." *Daily Mirror*, December 5, 28, 29.

Mancini, P. (2005). "Is There a European Model of Journalism?" In de Burgh, H (ed.), *Making Journalists*. Abingdon and Oxon: Routledge.

Manger, W. (2013). "The Little Helpers; Caring Kids at Food Banks." *Daily Mirror*, December 21, 8.

Meets, B. (2012). "Hard Times." *Mirror*, April 30, 10, 11.

Merrill, J. (2013). "Hungry in Cameron's Cotswolds; Beyond the 4x4s and Classy Shops of the Prime Minister's Own Constituency, a Food Bank Is Alarmingly Busy." *Independent on Sunday*, December 22, 10.

Midgley, C. (2012). "Land of Plenty? Don't Bank on It." *Times*, April 17, 40, 41.

Monroe (2013a). "Austerity Bites: Let's Debate Our Need for Food Banks—A National Disgrace." *Guardian*, December 18.

Monroe (2013b). "We Went Hungry in the World's 7th Richest Nation. It Has to Stop; MUM'S FOOD POVERTY PETITION." *Daily Mirror*, December 3.

Monroe, J. (2013c). "Austerity Bites: Food Banks Are Testimony to the Tories' Massacre of Hope and Dignity." *Guardian*, October 16.

Monroe, J. (2013d). "If Only Eating Healthily on a Tight Budget Were That Easy, Jamie; Jack Monroe, Acclaimed Author of 'Hunger Hurts,' Tells the TV Chef to Put His Money Where His Mouth Is." *Independent*, August 28.

Monroe, J. (2013d). "How to Eat on £ 10 a Week: IT'S HOW I COPED WITH MY LIFE." *Observer*, July 21.

Monroe, J. (2013e). "'Leaders Feasted, Kids Went Hungry to Bed'; Blogger Jack Monroe Waited in Vain for Britain to Take a Lead on Hunger at the G8." *Independent on Sunday*, June 23.

Monroe, J. (2014). "About Jack." http://agirlcalledjack.com/about-jack-monroe/.

Morris, S. (2011). "Charity Food Parcels in Devon Town Rise Tenfold." *Guardian*, March 15, 15.

Morris, N. (2013). "Hungrier Than Ever: UK's Use of Food Banks Triples." *Independent*, October 16, 1.

National Readership Survey. (2014). "Latest Topline Readership Figures." httpt://www.nrs.co.uk.

Newsworks. (2014). "Market Overview." http://www.newsworks.org.uk/Market-Overview.

Oakeshott, I. (2013). "Ministers Hide Surge in use of Food Banks." *Sunday Times*, November 3, 11.

Owen, J., and Brady, B. (2010). "Breadline Britain." *Independent on Sunday*, December 12, 10.

Poppendieck, J. (1999). *Sweet Charity? Emergency Food and the End of Entitlement.* New York: Penguin.

Rausch A.S. (2002). "Role of Local Newspaper Media in Generating a Citizen Volunteer Consciousness." *International Journal of Japanese Sociology* 11, no. 1, 102–117.

Rayner, J. (2013). "Food Bank Britain: Life below the Line." *Observer*, August 18, 38.

Riches, G. (1997). "Hunger, Food Security and Welfare Policies: Issues and Debates in First World Societies." *Proceedings of the Nutrition Society* 56, 63–74.

Riches, G., and Silvasti, T. (2014). *First World Hunger Revisited: Food Charity or the Right to Food?* Second edition. New York: Palgrave Macmillan.

Ridout, T.N., Fowler, E.F., and Searles, K. (2012). "Exploring the Validity of Electronic Newspaper Databases." *International Journal of Social Research Methodology* 15, no. 6, 451–466.

Rowbottom, J. (2010). *Democracy Distorted: Wealth, Influence and Democratic Politics.* Cambridge: Cambridge University Press

Saner, H., Cochrane, E., and Pidd, K. (2013). "I Didn't Ask to Be Ill." *Guardian*, September 12, 6.

Seabrook, J. (2013). *Povertyland: Poverty and the Poor in Britain.* London: Hurst and Company.

Seymour, D. (2009). *Reporting Poverty in the UK: A Practical Guide for Journalists.* York: Joseph Rowntree Foundation.

Sherman, J. (2013). "White-Collar Workers Are Forced to Use Food Banks." *Times*, October 16, 4.

Shields, R. (2008). "Britain on the Breadline: Families Join Food Queue; More and More Working People Are Relying on Charity to Feed Their Families." *Independent on Sunday*, October 19, 28.

Siebel, W. (1996). "Successful Failure." *American Behavioral Scientist* 39, no. 8, 1011–1024.

Sturgis, I. (2012). "The Mum Who Works a Miracle." *Daily Mail*, October 4.

Sun (2012). "I'd Starve without a Foodbank." *Sun*, February 3, 38.

Thompson, E.P. (1984). "Mayhew and the Morning Chronicle." In Thompson, E.P. and Yeo, E. (eds)., *The Unknown Mayhew*. Harmondsworth: Penguin.

van der Horst, H., Pascucci, S., and Bol, W. (2014). "The 'Dark Side' of Food Banks? Exploring Emotional Responses of Food Bank Receivers in the Netherlands." *British Food Journal* 116, no. 9, 1506–1520.

Warrell, H. (2011). "Food Bank Fills Hunger Gap as Prices Soar." *Financial Times*, August 9, 3.

Weaver, D.A., and Bimber, B. (2008). "Finding News Stories: A Comparison of Searches Using LexisNexis News." *Journalism and Mass Communication Quarterly* 85: 515–530.

Wellman, A. (2013). "Starving Kids Who Survive On Just a Jam Sandwich." *Daily Mirror*, January 20, 16, 17.

Wells, R., and Caraher, M. (2014). "UK Print Media Coverage of the Food Bank Phenomenon: From Food Welfare to Food Charity?" *British Food Journal* 116, no. 9, 1426–1445.

Williams, A.J., Gajevic, S., Lewis, J.M.W., and Kitzinger, J. (2009). "UK National Newspaper Coverage of Hybrid Embryos: Source Strategies and Struggles." Project Report, Cardiff University.

Appendix   Coding form

0	Food bank users are not referred to at all
1	Current food bank users are directly quoted (using quotation marks "")
2	Current food bank users are referred to: 2a: explicitly but they are not directly quoted 2b: in general terms - as in 'Hungry Families' or 'some of the poorest children' or simply alluded to numerically (eg: '60,000 Saved By Food Bank'
3	Provider as ex-user: 3a: volunteer food bank worker also ex-user 3b: media pundit, former user
4	Case study from central organisation or source
5	Heroes

4

The Invisible
Hand Begs for "Sadaka"

Does the Media Legitimize Poverty via Islamic Alms in Turkey?

Kaan Taşbaşı

It has been over two and a half centuries since Adam Smith first used the metaphor of the *invisible hand* to describe the self-regulating nature of the market in his famous work *The Theory of Moral Sentiments*. According to Adam Smith, "for rational, self-interested individuals, supply and demand as the major forces of market together with the competitive business environment are capable of efficiently allocating scarce resources in society." This idea provides the founding justification for the laissez-faire economic philosophy.

Indeed, the world is facing the consequences of a set of economic policies and processes currently known as *neoliberalism*, consequences which can be outlined as a dramatic increase in social and economic inequality, global environmental damage, an uncurbed global economic instability.

Among these, poverty appears as the most central global social issue. The enduring inadequacy of mainstream responses to poverty has exacerbated the problem and this, in turn has increased the questionability of the main assumptions of the neoliberal policies. Though being identically capitalist in nature, different states and international organizations have approached the problem through different analytical and policy perspectives. Indeed, neoliberal economic policy implementations have ended up with local outcomes under the circumstances of several historical, social, or cultural contexts.

The general objective of this chapter is to explore how the *sadaka* culture might be linked to the lack of social policy mechanisms in Turkey, and whether media might be seen as a bridging element in this respect. Certainly, the answer to this question requires a comprehensive research that is beyond the limits of this study. However, it is hoped that by conceptualizing the related phenomena and asking the correct questions, at least the way is paved for future research.

OVERVIEW OF SOCIAL POLICIES IN TURKEY

From the Ottoman Era to the foundation of the Turkish Republic and even later on, social policies implemented in Turkey were devoid of social equity motives. The major priorities upon which the Turkish Republic was constructed included secular and nationalist values, which were meant to be introduced into every facet of life in a "top-down" manner. It would not be possible to claim that the newly established republic planned solid strategies or took action to provide the equal distribution of income, nor provided for an increase in aggregate welfare. The absence of a Ministry of Labor and regulation of labor laws, as well as the structure of the tax regime and wage policies prove that the Turkish state also did not pursue future goals to do so. On the other hand, one of the factors that impeded social justice and social welfare in Turkey was/has been the truism that a societal opposition based on class struggle did not exist in the country. As the Marxist view suggests, "correcting the injustice of poverty is not simply a question of distribution, as most discourses on poverty tend to emphasize. Not only is it a question of production, but it is very much a class question as well" (Chakrabarti et al. 2008).

As the egalitarian political and social climate of the 1960s was starting to be felt in Turkey, social policy implementations, class-based organizations and relevant movements also started to blossom. The 1961 Constitution adopted the principle of the *social state* for the Turkish Republic. To name some examples, Article 10 of the Constitution defined the Republic as a social state, Article 41 elucidated a number of social responsibilities, Article 47 guaranteed the rights of collective bargaining and striking and Article 48 charged the state with the duty of establishing or assisting social insurance and welfare organizations. In addition, Article 49 stated that it was the responsibility of the state to ensure that everyone leads a healthy life both physically and mentally, receives medical attention and that the state shall take measures to provide the poor and low-income families with dwellings that meet certain sanitary requirements. Finally, Article 50 identified providing educational requirements for people as one of the foremost duties of the state.

The subsequent 1982 Constitution, following the 1980 military intervention, also defined the Turkish Republic as a social state. Nevertheless, the Constitution contained limitations and ideological repression for several groups, which could be understood as potential actors of effective social policy implementations (Kepenek and Yentürk 2004).

At present, little is not being achieved in the name of social state, nor is a solid understanding of social equity being established. The problems of economically disadvantaged portions of society are still not recognized; instead they are treated as natural circumstances that can easily be ignored. Thus far neoliberal economic policies have been formed independently of growth objectives based on social equity.

The World Bank data show that, as of year 2010, 16.9 percent of the total population in Turkey is living below the national poverty line and almost 3 percent lives on less than $2 a day. In 2011, income share held by the highest 10 percent of the population accounted for 30.5 percent, while it was 29.3 percent in 2010 (World Bank 2015). According to the approach that sees poverty as a problem arising out of "social exclusion," in that it is a multidimensional problem that prevents members of the society who enjoy the same legal status from equal participation in society (Buğra et al. 2007), 26 percent of the total population is at risk of poverty in Turkey. This stands as the highest percentage among European Union (EU) countries.

SADAKA IN TURKISH CULTURE AND THE MEDIATION OF POVERTY

Is *sadaka* acting as a local cultural praxis that works as a substitute for the social/welfare state and/or policies in such circumstances? Emanating from the popular Islamic belief, this praxis is formed as an answer for the individuals who are in need of a voluntary basis and is one of the most prominent practices in Islam that encourages giving anonymously (as if by an "invisible hand"). Ebaugh (2010) defines it as a term that can be understood as "a charitable gift" that is given without expecting any worldly gain, but with "the sole intention of pleasing *Allah*." The return of it, according to the Islamic belief, would be a spiritual reward in the Hereafter. *Sadaka* may take varying tangible forms such as food, money, clothes etc. as well as any favor for a fellow Muslim (Ebaugh 2010: 10).

The practice of *sadaka* has taken on its own meanings in modern Turkish culture as well, where an individual's religiosity is not even relevant to one's participation in the practice. "In Ottoman times, *sadaka* was given on many occasions and placed anonymously in a number of places: including; a mosque collection box, on a 'sadaka stone' outside of a mosque, in the street, or in the hand of the representative of a *vakıf* (charitable trust) or the local government, both of which ran soup kitchens (*aş evleri*) open to the public" (Ebaugh 2010: 10). The *sadaka* practice worked as an apparatus—in a society where social justice was not a concern of the state—that contributed to meeting the needs of the poor by helping tangible goods change hands—even though in negligible amounts—and at least was an attempt to ease the inequality. On the other hand there was some level of self-interest involved: "giving *sadaka* helped to prevent trouble in this world, made one's interring into the grave easier, and served to elevate one's status in the Hereafter, according to the Islamic belief, and thus provided conscience relief" (Ebaugh 2010: 10).

One can claim that the social and cultural reflections of postmodernization can be traced in several facets of the everyday life. The *Sadaka* practice has also taken its share from this transformation. In Turkey a number of charities which were operating on the basis of *Sadaka* practice were integrated with TV shows. This way, the charities were targeting to reach masses, and the *Sadaka* was mediated, emerging as a *Tele-Sadaka*.

A typical case was the Deniz Feneri (Lighthouse) Charity[1], which originated from a television program named *Sehir ve Ramazan* (The City and Ramadan) that was broadcast during Ramadan in 1996 on Kanal 7 (Channel 7). This program acquired a legal personality/status as an association in 1998 with the name Deniz Feneri Charity. Concomitantly, Kanal 7 started to broadcast a program with the same name. Deniz Feneri initiated its operations in Istanbul and then established new branches in Ankara and Izmir, and other cities in Turkey as well. Meanwhile, Deniz Feneri E.V. was established in Germany. Hovewer, Deniz Feneri rejected the claim that there was an organic relationship with the establishment in Germany. The Deniz Feneri Charity was structured on a voluntary basis and was solely financed through donations. The charity claims that they have reached 500,000 families both in Turkey and abroad, providing them with food, shelter, health and monetary aid. In addition, the charity has a number of projects such as providing temporary accommodations, and running soup kitchens, free clothing stores and occupational training programs. The charity gained the status of Public Benefit Association (resolution no. 2004/8278). Deniz Feneri defines the decision as "Deniz Feneri, with the status it gained, reached the opportunity to develop more efficient and comprehensive projects to eliminate the poverty" (Deniz Feneri 2014). It was with this status that it also became possible for donators to qualify for tax breaks. The ruling party Adalet ve Kalkınma Partisi (AKP; Justice and Development Party) attempted twice to give the Deniz Feneri Charity the privilege of receiving donations without prior permission. However, these attempts were rejected by the Council of State. Therefore, AKP found a solution bypassing the juridical mechanisms with a law amendment (Yerdeniz 2014). As a result, in 2005, Deniz Feneri became one of the thirteen privileged associations in Turkey that have the right to receive donations without prior permission from governmental authorities.

In 2007, the Turkish Parliament granted the association the Outstanding Service Award. State-owned Turkish Airlines became the official carrier of Deniz Feneri for its charity activities abroad. It can be seen on the charity's official website that it cooperates with 50 local radio stations, and *Deniz Feneri* programs are being broadcasted on several local TV channels when Ramadan[2] begins. Besides these, 200 local TV channels, 500 local radio stations and 1,000 local newspapers are supporting the charity's projects and campaigns according to information on the website (Deniz Feneri 2008).

The neoliberal mind perceives the concepts of poverty and inequality to be an understandable "social expenditure." Economic growth, progress and development are all evaluated over set figures and kept in 'social expenditure' balance sheets as items carrying hardly any importance. A considerable amount of reluctance is demonstrated in terms of the government assuming responsibility for "social expenditure." It is somehow expected of the "invisible hand," which regulates the market, to also tackle poverty "as much as possible." "AKP, the Justice and Development Party, which seems to dominate a considerably large realm in Islamic politics, also suggests solutions that are only in line with the rationale of capitalist development rather than offering a radical appeal or a change of political approach" (Cigdem 2011: 219). Social consent is crucial in the form that these solutions are actually carried out, and in terms of ensuring social consent, the media plays a significant role.

With mass communication, it is possible to mass-produce and spread public messages in a considerably efficient manner with the technological and institutional structures of modern societies. In this process, media politics directly reflect both the structure of social relations and the institutional organizations and types of censorship applied (Gerbner 2005: 93). According to Murdock (1994), media have always been the main tool in terms of the representation and discussion of concepts in regards to the economic and political arena. Consequently, the media have also carried out a critical role in shaping the social and cultural layout as a whole (Murdoch 1994: 365).

Van Dijk (1994) underlines that both the ideology and the praxis within are mobilized and organized through socialization agents, which are identified as the state, media, education, church and the family. While it is evident that there is a close relationship between the continuation of the status quo and the attention that can be directed both individually and socially, the media play a critical role in this area. Chomsky (2012:

22) states that the media, in collaboration with the education system, also have the function of aligning individuals and society as a whole: "Media really serve a 'social purpose'; however, this is actually quite a different purpose. . . . To educate people's minds in order to ensure they display a virtuous commitment to their government, and in more general terms, the layout of social, economic and political systems." Chomsky emphasizes that the media ultimately have the interest of the dominant class at hand and creates "vigilant guardians" which protect these interests (Chomsky 2012: 22).

As Habermas further observes:

> The political public sphere of the social welfare state is characterized by a peculiar weakening of its critical functions. At one time the process of making proceedings public [Publizität] was intended to subject persons or affairs to public reason, and to make political decisions subject to appeal before the court of public opinion. But often enough today the process of making public simply serves the arcane politicies of special interests; in the form of "publicity" it wins public prestige for people or affairs, thus making them worthy of acclamation in a climate of nonpublic opinion. The very words "public relations work" [Öffentlichkeitsarbeit] betray the fact that a public sphere must first be arduously constructed case by case, a public sphere which earlier grew out of the social structure. Even the central relationship of the public, the parties, and the parliament is affected by this change in function. (Habermas 2006: 77)

A study (Iyengar 1990) conducted on the representation of poverty on TV news, focuses on the different perceptions of a caricatured poverty, which is isolated from social conditions. The study also touches upon the representations including contrary forms and how these varying perceptions affect the support for social policies. According to the study, for instance, episodes from the miserable life of a family and a portrayal of these people as victims, lead to the perception that the individuals are responsible for their own misery. The poverty and the related conditions, in which the individuals live, are seen as circumstances that result from these individuals' own deficiencies. The factors resulting in poverty are not questioned and the social and political mechanisms that can alleviate these factors are not supported strongly. On the other hand, the representations where poverty is not portrayed as a singular case, as a dramatic situation occurred to a victim or where it is shown as a social problem, the consequence is completely different. In such a representation, social responsibility is extended, the need for social state programs and that these programs should be supported are underlined.

Clawson and Trice (2000) find that the presentation of poverty in media takes place in stereotypical categories. Representing the poverty in stereotypical categories has a deep impact on the social perception of poverty. Such representation creates social layers containing individuals who deserve the difficulties befallen. In this context, perception and representation of poverty have prominent roles, if the public opinion is shaped by the stereotypes, then it is inevitable that public policies are shaped in parallel to this image. In addition, as the study conducted by Graber (Graber 1990, as cited in Clawson and Trice 2000) suggests, audio-visual messages are more efficient than written messages. This efficiency can be observed in the perception and the retention of the messages.

It is also emphasized that conveying the lives of the poor in a dramatic way to an audience and running charity campaigns using celebrities and well-known faces, develops *a kind of citizenship* within the neoliberal framework and provides a related solution. Such programs, calling on the audience to lend a hand to people in need, attempt to attract the audience support based on individual volunteerism and preference of conscience rather than questioning the lack of related public resources and mechanisms (McMurria 2008).

When analyzing the style of representation in TV programs dedicated to poverty and the destitute, which Erdogan (2007) defined as "slow-motion poverty," we are faced with a *somewhat pornographic* style of portrayal. Locked in dramatic representation, the camera zooms into the eyes of the poor who are weeping from either sadness or happiness, and for these moments to be broadcast in slow-motion, all creates an inaccurate representation/perception. According to Erdogan,

> Slow motion is the metaphorical representation of "carrying the world's weight on one's shoulders." The slowness of action acts as a visual language in order to communicate and emphasize the passivity, hopelessness and inactivity of poverty; hence, activating the compassion and charitableness in viewers. (Erdogan 2007: 310).

On the other hand, Erdogan states that the representation style of the poor on television is actually perceived by the poor in a negative way, and that the idea of taking part in charity TV programs such as Deniz Feneri, Yarınlar Umut Olsun is perceived to be dishonorable and unfavorable.

From this viewpoint, it is possible to state that the social perception shaped with the representation of the poor in media is a social reflection, which actually corrodes the necessity we feel for a social government and social policies. It has been acknowledged that the way a society, the elite or the poor, perceive poverty and the way they relate to poverty plays an important part in the prevention/annihilation policies against poverty. It argues that the only way these programs aimed at these policies can actually be "successful" is when these perceptions are taken into account (Erdogan 2001: 9; Mora 2000).

ANALYSIS OF DENIZ FENERI TV PROGRAM

Hilal TV has broadcast the TV program Deniz Feneri since 2010. Hilal TV is a conservative TV channel and this weekly program was broadcast on Thursday evenings. Thursday evenings are considered to be holy by Muslims. For this reason, this program holds a symbolic significance.

In terms of format, the program consists of two sections. The program starts with its host (Recep Koçak) in a studio, and then continues outside the studio with a person called *Ramazan Agabey* (Brother Ramazan) visiting poor people's homes. The studio host has a guest every week, and these guests are directors, representatives, volunteers, or donors of a voluntary organization.

With the opening credits, the program starts to create a world. A lighthouse visual is used in the credits, and poor people are placed on each level of the lighthouse. As the credits proceed, we see it back out to show a general plan, first the light centre of the lighthouse, then the whole lighthouse itself, and then far out to the middle of the sea, where we see the reflection of the light on the water. Finally, we see the silhouette of a town in the distance. In line with the scene, music which strengthens the dramatic portrayal is played in the background. Recep Koçak[3] greets his viewers, announces his guest and the topic of discussion for the evening. Religious rhetoric is used heavily from the very beginning of the program:

> "Every holy Friday evening[4] we gather before you, and share with you how good deeds never cease to continue." (November 20, 2014)
>
> "As we start our program, we greet you with sincerity and love. As we come to the end of another Ramazan, having been busy running around, like other organizations, we have also completed the month of Ramazan and reached Bayram, and we thank Allah for this." (August 15, 2013)
>
> "Dear friends, greetings, love and respect to you all. Allah has blessed us with yet another day. He has granted us the true blessing of greeting you. We meet again with our program Deniz Feneri on Hilal TV screens. Like every week, we have come together this evening to battle with poverty and deprivation, to make sure the light of Deniz Feneri (Lighthouse) touches upon each and every point in the darkness. As we have done relentlessly over the years, we endeavour to continue our determined march this week as well, Allah willing." (June 6, 2013)

The following sections of the Deniz Feneri program are filled with such rhetoric. For instance, on July 11, 2013, studio guest director Mehmet Cengiz stated:

> When you look at the map of Turkey, you will see that in the last 15 years, Deniz Feneri has reached the most remote of places, the poorest of the poor, orphans, waifs and strays that nobody has ever been able to reach and lend

a helping hand. They have accomplished all this and gained the prayers of many. This organisation has earned many a prayer. (July 11, 2013).

Throughout the program, viewers are constantly summoned to feel pity and compassion towards the unfortunate, and to make a donation. The section in which the homes of the poverty-stricken are visited is first announced by the host. As soon as the videotaped segment of the house visit enters the screen, a voice with a timbre very specific to programs with religious content, starts to narrate a story, accompanied with music sharing the same religious characteristics.

In spite of the harsh winter, in spite of being knee-deep in snow, we have not given up, we have not slowed down. This week, to bring the light of Deniz Feneri, to light up the darkened lives of others, the goodness ambassadors are running to the village of Cobanozu, in Afyon Sinanpasa. And now, on your screens, the unbelievable but true life story of the Ustun family, living in deprivation of all the blessings that the 21st century offers us. (January 23, 2014).

At the bottom of the screen, for almost the whole time the program is aired, texts are calling out for viewers to donate money, along with contact details of the organization's call centre, the website address; and, running on the screen most of the time: *"To donate via SMS, send a blank message to 5560 from any operator and make a 5TL donation."*

The dramatic tone of the program is composed by the Ramazan Agabey figure. His physical appearance, his clothes, the way he speaks, Ramazan Agabey is a character that has been built to be "just like you and me," and he is portrayed as the savior who the destitute are just waiting to be rescued by. These people in desperate situations express their joy and excitement when they see him, and how full of hope they now are that they will be saved from their troubles thanks to him. Some of the expressions articulated by different people from different episodes can be presented as proof of this point: "You coming to us, it's like the whole of Ankara has been given to us as a gift," "My wounds are deep, dear Uncle, very deep. Find me a remedy for my wounds," "I wasn't expecting to see you, that's why I'm so ecstatic right now."

The illusion that these poor people find Ramazan Agabey before them out of the blue, and that the viewers are actually being witness to this moment of encountering, is crafted. For example, in one episode, we see a house that is falling apart, and somebody is cooking something on a camping gas cylinder. The position of the camera is set so that this person is in the foreground. Directly opposite the camera is the front door, which suddenly opens and this poor person sees Ramazan Agabey enter. As soon as the poor person in the house—and the viewer at home—sees Ramazan Agabey, another camera shoots from behind Ramazan Agabey and shows the inside of the house from the outside. Although it's very clear that there are at least two cameras, and that the encounter was not actually the very first, the illusion that it was remains to be scripted.

Ramazan Agabey starts to have a conversation with the person he is bringing salvation to and the viewer starts to listen to a heart-breaking story. But this impoverished person is unable to tell her story as she pleases, because Ramazan Agabey determines the prominent points of her story with the questions he asks and the way he repeats these particular points. The story of an old woman who lives with her disabled daughter is an example:

> *Ramazan Agabey (RA):* What did your son say?
>
> *Old Woman (OW):* What could he say, Agabey.
>
> *RA:* This is my mother, I could never kick her out. Didn't he say that?
>
> *OW:* He didn't.
>
> *RA:* He didn't?
>
> *OW:* He didn't. I came here in the middle o' winter.
>
> *RA:* Winter?
>
> *OW:* Winter. December 24, it was, I came here.
>
> *RA:* They threw you out in winter?
>
> *OW:* Winter.
>
> *RA:* They kicked you out, you and your daughter.
>
> . . .
>
> *RA:* So didn't you ask your son? Didn't you ask him, what are you doing my son?
>
> *OW:* Oh, Agabey.
>
> *RA:* Yeah?
>
> *OW:* What could I say?
>
> *RA:* You didn't?
>
> *OW:* What could I say. What would ya say if ya did?

In this example, even though an answer has already been given to a particular question, and although it is very clear and there's nothing to be mistaken about, Ramazan Agabey asks the same questions over and over again. This way, he is holding a giant projector over the poor person's head, a projector made up of questions aiming at creating the feeling of pity in the viewer. On the one side the poor person's expressions, and on the other side the viewer's thoughts and feelings are manipulated. One of the clichés from Yesilcam cinema[5], the "I may be poor but I am honourable" myth is constantly repeated throughout the program. It is emphasized that despite all the harsh life standards they are left to deal with, they never take a step that would taint their honor. Also, despite all their hardships, they never complain or revolt against their situation. They will express their woes and sorrows, they will cry, but they will remain at peace with their status quo. The camera frames promote this notion. The holy scripture and flags on the walls are features that demonstrate this. Paint and plaster flaking off the walls compose the physical portrayal of destitution; the symbolic holy script and the flag clumsily covering the cracks on the wall add to a feeling of admiration and appreciation on top of the feeling of pity in the viewer. The state of compliance opposed to defiance, is a very important motif.

Whether it be with the questions directed at them, or the style in which their story is scripted, the situation of the impoverished is investigated in an extensive manner. Either these people's lives were perfectly okay and were suddenly turned upside down due to various unfortunate events, or they already had a harsh life and certain events turned it even more dire. The wretchedness in households where there is a family member with a disability or a fatal illness is portrayed as an individual case, and with the questions directed at them, it is revealed that they get by with limited or short-term financial support (such as municipal aid or social welfare payments). "What are the factors that cause certain people to live in such a state of destitution?" It is impossible for this question to appear in the minds of viewers or the destitute in question. On the contrary, what stands out is the implication that if organisations such as Deniz Feneri are not supported, this issue can never be solved, and that the issue of poverty that has "individual" life stories weaved into it can only be soothed with individual intervention. A deficient perspective of solidarity is crafted through the concept of charity; and with an essentialist cultural approach, it is clearly expressed that this is a value that must be cherished. A typical example of this emphasis, which also supports the core assertion of this operation, is the essence of Recep Tayyip Erdogan's speech that he made during the opening of Deniz Feneri's logistic centre when he was prime minister. This speech was broadcast during the program on July 11, 2013. Recep Tayyip Erdogan stated the following:

> I would like to thank my brothers and sisters here before you, for all the services they have continued to provide until now. This is actually a very important value that has been instilled in us by the values we uphold. Because it was impossible to sleep if our neighbour was hungry[6]. . . . We have a wealth that stems from these set of values. We have such roots. But

unfortunately, we are losing this more and more with every passing day. . .
. I am personally calling out to my country from this meeting today. As the
person in the responsible position, a position that you have assigned me to,
I say: Ramazan has arrived, unless there are extraordinary circumstances, let
us all share what we have in our neighbourhoods during Ramazan with our
poor neighbours, our brothers and sisters.

In this speech, it is yet again implied that poverty cases, which are presented as individual cases, can only be overcome with individual responsibility. *The practice of charity is clearly stated as poverty's antidote.* While
disregarding the social dimension of the poverty issue, by referencing
from a religious field, it somehow provides hope for the chance to clear
our consciences. The speech presents substantial proof that the conservative mindset and the neoliberal mind have intertwined. Erdogan continues his speech:

There's no longer a Turkey in crisis, we are overcoming all these. Bright days
have almost arrived, we can see this. Economic parameters show this. But,
we have yet to spread this completely throughout the general population.
Until we do, there are three understandings, or three actions that can make
this process even more efficient. First, the government, the first sector; two,
the private sector; third sector is organizations, foundations and charitable
institutions like Deniz Feneri. Can we all join forces to bring down our nation's hardships to a minimum? I'm asking, can we pull it down? We will
pull it down.

Poverty is not something that can be completely wiped out. It is seen as
something that can, at most, "be brought down to a minimum by joining
forces." This state of acceptance, is proof of the fact that the issue will continue to remain an issue. Accepting the fact that a certain issue cannot be
completely eliminated is, after all, proof that there is a lack of will power
to face and fight against it. Since it is not possible to completely rid our nation of poverty, what must be done is "manage it." Like Gambetti (2009)
argued, the neoliberal mind accepts all issues and offences as "manageable," as long as they do not impose a systematic threat. In fact, they see
them as opportunities to maintain the sustainability of the system. For the
neoliberal mind, the people are now seen as a population. The crumbs of
everything particular to humans and societies have been wiped away and
life has been reduced to numbers. Thanks to this, manageability emerges.
Therefore, a foreseeable and manageable amount of deaths, disappear-
ances, destitution, war, famine etc. are merely expenditures that can be
met, and are also means of maintaining the system. Another point that
Gambetti (2009) emphasizes is that despite neoliberalism's government-
minimizing rhetoric, the government is not actually minimized. On the

contrary, it has expanded in a very established fashion, setting stable roots along the way. What is meant by expansion is, the functions related with government identification in political literature (from security to social policies) are now taken on by structures called non-governmental organisations. This way, the government expands through organizations such as Deniz Feneri. Erdogan is somewhat confessing the inadequacy of the government and stating that the structures that can compensate this inadequacy is the private sector and organizations/foundations. The target of "bringing poverty down to a minimum," lies trapped between the consciences of individuals and the mercy of the capitalist. The expression used in Erdogan's speech, "a benevolent nation that feeds the hungry, clothes the poor, employs the unemployed, gives money to the penniless, and offers their strength to the weak" puts forth the individual conscience formula. In the instance of a blockage when an individual lacks the ability to open up their conscience, it can be cleared out with the strength of the capitalist. As for the government, it will "pull poverty down to a minimum" through politics that will make the capital's work easier. The adjustments that are to be made to tax legislations will make it easier for the capitalist to be the core of social/welfare policies. With tax deductions and abatements granted in the instance of the construction of buildings that are to provide public services such as health, education, etc., will ensure social politics a brand new dimension. In Erdogan's words below:

> Until now, when a school was built, 5% could be shown as expenses. What did we do? We are not here to bite the hand that feeds us. This is why we announced that 100% can be recorded as expenses, and we did. So we're not insisting that we should get all the money and we ourselves will build schools, no, we don't have such concerns. This can be done in a much shorter time by our businessmen. Hospitals can be constructed in a much shorter time. And as a matter of fact, we started to reap the benefits of this action in a very short time. The first examples are in Bingöl. We all witnessed schools being constructed in 105 days. In 105 days. If this were handled by the government, I'm talking about the old mentality, believe me there are schools that couldn't even be completed in 15 years in this country.

Foundations, voluntary organizations and so on, are the maintainers of this situation. By channeling individual consciences into an organizational structure, charity organizations are recreating poverty. A government and administration that has been besieged with neoliberalism, applauds such foundations and organizations. And Erdogan expresses this with:

> The number of families that Deniz Feneri has managed to reach in various ways is in the 70 thousands, the number of people is in the 500 thousands—

these are unbelievable figures for an organisation such as this. When I hear this number, I will come running, flying to such a place. This is definitely a wonderful illustration of humanity and solidarity.

This statement is actually acknowledging that there are at least 500,000 victims of poverty. Rather than admitting that the number of people helped by a charity organization is increasing is something to be proud and celebratory about, it should be seen as an indication that it is a serious issue that requires to be worked on. Instead of concentrating on the reasons of and solutions to this problem, poverty is being covered up with organizations such as Deniz Feneri, and possible demands for changes and development in public policies are accordingly obviated. In this sense, the government, foundations and organizations are working in complete cohesion and collaboration. The only thing that ceases to change is the existence and state of the poor.

The Deniz Feneri/Lighthouse Association adopts a position that accepts and supports this paradigm. On 11 July 2013, during the episode when Deniz Feneri director Mehmet Cengiz joined the program as a guest, he claimed that the investigation and lawsuits for corruption and fraud were "the strategy of outside forces," and that it caused a serious plummet in the organization's funds, which in turn affected the poor people of our country who could not get the help they needed. This expression indicates that he views Deniz Feneri as an organization that is one with the government and one with the public. Cengiz states the 40 percent increase of the organization's income (donations, etc.) during 2012–2013 is a good sign that things are going well. This way, Deniz Feneri is "returning to its good old days." The assertion that the investigations against Deniz Feneri were all based on a conspiracy, and that this could in turn harm the poor is actually able to be discussed in the program from time to time. One of the findings that support this fact consists of a dialogue on May 1, 2014 with a mother of two disabled children:

Ramazan Agabey (RA): Since when has Deniz Feneri [been helping you]?

Woman (W): God bless you.

RA: For how many years has it been helping you?

W: May God bless you. For 13 years it's been helping us.

RA: They come by from time to time?

W: Sometimes they come and 2–3 years pass. I mean, they give us *some*thing.

RA: How much did they use to give you?

W: They used to give a lot.

RA: They used to give a lot. So they used to come here, check up on you, look after you.

W: Yeah, they used to come, check and give stuff.

RA: They used to get you all that you need, but they haven't been coming by much for the last 3–4 years, is that right?

W: Yeah, that's right.

As can be inferred from the dialogue, Ramazan Agabey's usual style creates the idea that the judicial process is based on a conspiracy theory, and at the same time this is causing the destitute receiving less help than they could actually be getting. Once again, instead of facing the reasons why poverty exists, the viewer is swept away towards the illusion that tools such as charity can defeat and wipe out poverty. This family that has been receiving help for thirteen years, has been receiving a lot less in the last three to four years. This time-frame falls in exact correlation with the period that the director stated funds had decreased. The fact that a family has been forced to depend on outside help in order to survive for a span of thirteen years, is not questioned by the viewer whatsoever.

CONCLUSION

In line with these arguments, one can claim that there is a social reflection that depreciates the need for social policies, of the social perception of the television programs calling the audience to support the poor on an individual basis. Television, via caricatured presentations of poverty and campaigns based on individual volunteerism, is as if "begging" in a public sphere. This cannot be considered to be a blindness in analysis. The underlying ideological background can be clearly seen to be closely related to the necessary recognition of the complicated structure of the process. The misleading presentation of poverty and manipulated performance of social solidarity should not be taken as case-specific coincidence. The complicated ownership and the organizational body of the media outlets have to be analyzed as well. Neglecting the relationship between media and ideology would be like *trying to find a way in the dark wearing sunglasses*.

Pseudo-social policy implementations eventually lose their functions, leading to the increasingly apparent problems of social discontent and conflicts. These problems and conflicts are being kept under control via *sadaka,* which operates as a *gemeinschaft* type social practice, and are embedded in neoliberal policies. The *Deniz Feneri Charity* fed by the *sadaka* culture has generated a postmodern *tele-sadaka* practice. The charity has

enabled people in need to be visible on the screen via a television program, called for donations and acted as a transmission mechanism that
transfers these donations. This structuring has led the state-government
perception to be constituted on the same floor and concealed the necessity to question the defects of the social policies. The relation between
Deniz Feneri and AKP brings along a bilateral situation. On one hand, it is
perceived as if functions of the social state are being performed by Deniz
Feneri Charity. By this means, the reasons behind inequality and poverty
are not being questioned and the government is being able to reproduce
itself ideologically. On the other hand, a pro-government broadcasting organization has been the cradle of *tele-sadaka*. The illusion has been created
as if the social mission of the state is undertaken by the ideological base
of the government. The so-called invisible hand and neoliberal economic
policy has failed to properly regulate the market, not to mention the abyss
of social equity.

NOTES

1. In 2007, Turkey was shaken by the news concerning a probe into the Deniz
Feneri Charity. In the case, large sums of money donated to the charity by the
Turkish community in Germany were transferred to the conservative media in
Turkey, most prominently to Kanal 7 and *Yeni Şafak* daily, according to a statement made by one of the suspects in the case before a German court. The claims
against the charity reached as far as the head of Turkey's Radio and Television Supreme Council (Radyo Televizyon Üst Kurulu-RTÜK), who was a former executive of an Islamist media. Three people were sentenced to jail at the conclusion of
the case in 2008. In its final verdict, the German court said that out of a total of 41
million euros collected from benefactors by Deniz Feneri, some 17 million euros
were sent to Turkey through illegal means; 8 million euros of this were transferred
to a separate organization in Turkey, also named Deniz Feneri, and the rest was
used for other purposes (Yerdeniz 2014).

Aside from being the biggest charity corruption case in Germany's history, the
so-called Deniz Feneri charity fraud case revealed that there were huge amounts
of money circulating in the hands of those who act as the transmitters within the
donation process and more generally, it showed what the *sadaka* culture was capable of. Turkish stand of the case is still in process. Kanal 7 belonged to YİMPAŞ,
a holding that was known for its connections to Turkey's ruling Justice and Development Party. The AKP has been under fire from its opponents, who accuse the
government of promoting and supporting Islamist media organs to create a new
media that has an inorganic relationship with the party (Pekoz 2011).

2. Ramadan is a sacred month for Muslims.

3. The program has been hosted by Recep Kocak since July 4, 2013. Hosted by
Yusuf Ozkan Ozburun between 2010 and 2013, the program was also hosted by
an interim host, Ugur Arslan, throughout the lawsuit process.

4. As mentioned above, Thursday evenings are regarded to be holy, and because it is the evening that leads to Friday, the sacred day, it is referred to as "Friday evening."

5. Yesilcam is a metonym for the Turkish film industry, similar to Hollywood in the United States and Bollywood in India.

6. There is a *Hadith* (sayings of Prophet Mohammad) which says "whoever goes to bed while his neighbor is hungry is not a true believer."

REFERENCES

Buğra, Ayşe, Keyder, Çağlar. (2007). *Social Assistance in Turkey: For a Policy of Minimum Income Support Conditional on Socially Beneficial Activity, Report prepared for the United Nations Development Programme.* http://www.spf.boun.edu.tr/index.php/tr/arastirma-raporlari.

Chakrabarti, Anjan, Cullenberg, Stephen, and Kumar Dhar, Anup. (2008). "Rethinking Poverty: Class and Ethical Dimensions of Poverty Eradication." *Rethinking Marxism: A Journal of Economics, Culture and Society* 20, 4: 673–687. doi:10.1080/08935690802299751.

Chomsky, Noam. (1993). *Notes of NAFTA: "The Masters of Man."* http://www.chomsky.info/articles/199303--.htm.

Chomsky, Noam. (2012). Medya Gercegi (in Turkish). Istanbul: Everest Yayınlari.

Chomsky Noam, and Herman, Edward S. (2006). *Rizanin Imalati Kitle Medyasinin Ekonomi Politigi* (in Turkish). Aram Yayincilik: İstanbul.

Cigdem, Ahmet. (2007). "Yoksulluk ve Dinsellik." In *Yoksulluk Halleri—Türkiye'de Kent Yoksulluğunun Toplumsal Görünümleri* (in Turkish). Edited by Necmi Erdogan, 203–248. Istanbul: İletişim Yayınları.

Clawson, Rosalee A., and Trice, Rakuya. (2000). "Poverty as We Know It: Media Potrayals of the Poor." *Public Opinion Quarterly* 64, 1: 53–64. http://www.jstor.org/stable/3078840.

Deniz Feneri Charity. (2008). *Medya ve Internet Destegi.* www.denizfeneri.org.tr/haberlerarsiv/medya-ve-internet-destegi_2089.

Deniz Feneri Charity. (2014). *Hakkımızda.* www.denizfeneri.org.tr/kurumsal.

Ebaugh, Helen Rose. (2010). *The Gulen Movement: A Sociological Analysis of a Civic Movement Rooted in Moderate Islam.* New York: Springer.

Erdogan, Necmi. (2001). "Garibanlarin Dunyasi: Turkiye'de Yoksullarin Kulturel Temsilleri Uzerine Ilk Notlar" (in Turkish). *Toplum ve Bilim* 89: 7n22.

Erdogan, Necmi. (2007). "Agir Cekim Yoksulluk." In *Yoksulluk Halleri—Turkiye'de Kent Yoksullugunun Gorunen Halleri* (in Turkish). Istanbul: Iletisim Yayinlari.

Gambetti. Zeynep. (2009). "Iktidarin Donusen Cehresi: Neoliberalizm, Siddet ve Kurumsal Siyasetin Tasfiyesi" (in Turkish). *Istanbul Universitesi Siyasal Bilgiler Fakültesi Dergisi* 40: 145–166. http://www.journals.istanbul.edu.tr/iusiyasal/article/view/1023009355/1023008693.

Gamson, William A., Croteau, David, Hoynes William, and Sasson Theodore. (1992). "Media Images and the Social Construction of Reality." *Annual Review of Sociology* 18: 373–393

Gerbner, George. (2005). "Kitle Iletişim Araclari ve Kitle Iletisim Kurami" (in Turkish). In *Kitle Iletisim Kuramlari*. Edited by Erol Mutlu, 75–100. Ankara: Utopya Yayınevi.

Graber, Doris A. (1990). "Seeing Is Remembering: How Visuals Contribute to Learning from Television News." *Journal of Communication* 40: 134–155. doi: 10.1111/j.1460-2466.1990.tb02275.x.

Habermas, Jurgen. (2006). "The Public Sphere." In *Adventures in Media and Cultural Studies: Introducing the Key Works*. Edited by Douglas M. Kellner and Meenakshi Gigi Durham, 73–79. Hong Kong: Blackwell.

Iyengar, Shanto. (1990). "Framing Responsibility for Political Issues: The Case of Poverty." *Political Behavior* 12, 1: 19–40.

Kepenek, Yakup, and Yentürk, Nurhan. (2004). *Türkiye Ekonomisi*. Remzi Kitabevi: Istanbul.

McChesney, Robert. W. (1999). "Noam Chomsky and the Struggle against Neoliberalism." http://www.chomsky.info/onchomsky/19990401.htm.

McMurria, John. (2008). "Desperate Citizens and Good Samaritans: Neoliberalism and Makeover Reality TV." *Television New Media*. doi: 10.1177/1527476408315115.

Murdock, Graham. (1994). "İletişim, Modernlik ve İnsan Bilimleri" (in Turkish). In *Medya, İktidar İdeoloji*. Edited by Mehmet Küçük. 365–377. Ankara: Ark Yayınevi.

Pekoz, Mustafa. (2011). "Belgelerle 'Deniz Fenerleri kardeşliği'" (in Turkish). www.sendika.org/2011/12/belgelerle-deniz-feneri-soygunu-vi-savciligin-el-koymak-istedigi-mal-varliginin-kaynagi-sahte-faturalarla-dolandirilan-paraydi-mustafa-pekoz/.

Van Dijk, Teun. A. (1994). "Soylemin Yapilari ve Iktidarin Yapilari" (in Turkish). In *Medya, Iktidar, Ideoloji*. Edited by Mehmet Küçük, 271–312. Ankara: Ark Yayınevi.

World Bank. (2015). "Poverty Headcount Ratio at $1.25 a Day." http://data.worldbank.org/indicator/SI.POV.DDAY/countries.

Yerdeniz, Sibel. (2014). "Deniz Feneri'nden Ampule Yuzyilin Aydinlanma Hareketi (1)." http://t24.com.tr/yazarlar/sibel-yerdeniz/deniz-fenerinden-ampule-yuzyilin-aydinlanma-hareketi,8308.

II

TECHNOLOGY
AND INEQUALITIES

5

Social Inequalities in Digital Skills

The European Framework and the Italian Case

Roberta Bracciale and Isabella Mingo

DIGITAL AND SOCIAL INEQUALITIES: SOME THEORETICAL ISSUES

The birth of the information society has provided the opportunity to reflect on the reinforcement of social inequalities and the formation of new disparities. In theory, the Internet may contribute to a better diffusion of information and knowledge and a decrease in the distance between the social classes. In practice, the "information gaps" between different social categories are increasing (van Dijk 1999). Thus, the analysis of this digital divide has undergone progressive refinement over the years, highlighting differences between individuals not only in terms of the "possibilities of Internet access" but also including manifold variables that determine the varying abilities to acquire and manage information data (Bentivegna 2009; Bracciale 2010; DiMaggio and Hargittai 2001; DiMaggio et al. 2004; Hargittai and Hsieh 2013; Mossberger, Tolbert, and Stansbury 2003; van Dijk 2005).

There are signs of a "second-level digital divide" (Hargittai 2002), in which the focus is no longer exclusively on the differences between the information haves and have-nots, but also on the inequalities in the diversified uses of the Internet, and on the consequent inequalities in the social lives of individuals in their opportunities for personal and social empowerment (Hargittai and Hsieh 2013; Mingo 2005). There is a *growing marginalization*: the "information poor" have increasingly fewer opportunities to participate in economic, social and political life (Norris 2001).

Therefore, social inclusion and digital inclusion have become strongly correlated, thus generating a paradigm shift whereby e-inclusion becomes synonymous with social inclusion in the knowledge society (eEurope Advisory Group 2005). In fact, an "elementary" and "non-expert" use of the net emerges, especially among certain "risk" categories, which also redefines digital inequalities regarding a segment of the population that could be considered as already being included in terms of physical access (Hargittai and Hinnant 2008; van Deursen, van Dijk, and Peters 2011; Zillien and Hargittai 2009). The focal point is that "when the Internet matures, it will increasingly reflect known social, economic and cultural relationships of the offline world, including inequalities" (van Deursen and van Dijk 2013: 507).

The theoretical model proposed by Helsper (2012) hypothesizes that digital inclusion and social inclusion are related and

> proposes that the influence of offline exclusion fields on digital exclusion fields is mediated by access, skills, and attitudinal or motivational aspects. On the other hand, the relevance, quality, ownership, and sustainability of engagement with different digital resources is said to mediate the influence of engagement on offline exclusion. (Helsper 2012: 403)

Digital skills and digital literacy have become the keys to the information society (Bracciale and Mingo 2009; Servaes 2014; van Dijk and van Deursen 2014): the higher the level of the individual skills, the greater is their inclusion in the knowledge society, like a *Matthew*[1] *effect* (Merton 1973) related to e-skills (Bentivegna 2009; Bracciale 2010; De Haan 2004; Harambam, Aupers, and Houtman 2012; Hargittai 2003; Hunsinger, Klastrup, and Allen 2010; van Dijk 2009; Zillien and Hargittai 2009). In a technological environment, the Matthew effect predicts that those with more experience in the management of new technologies and a more diverse media diet, will get more benefits from the use of the Internet. In fact, they will be able to use the network in a more sophisticated way and will be able to tap into a greater range of sources from which to obtain the most useful information for their purpose.

This chapter focuses on digital skills, and its aim is to empirically assess the Matthew effect in Italy. Thus, following an empirical point of view, microdata from Italian official statistical sources (ISTAT, Istituto Nazionale di Statistica) and harmonized European indicators was used.

The chapter is structured as follows: first we assess the various measurement approaches suggested in the literature. Secondly, we present the European framework that is the operating procedures—and the recent changes—proposed by the European Commission to detect and measure eSkills. Using ISTAT microdata, Sections 4 and 5 focus on the Italian context, to identify the synthetic indices of e-skills and an Internet user's typology based on digital competence and socio-demographic characteristics. Finally, the main results are summarized and new lines of research are proposed.

WHAT ARE DIGITAL SKILLS?
DEFINITION AND MEASUREMENT APPROACHES

There is no single definition of digital skills, thus there are numerous labels used to define the relation between digital technologies and "literacy" (Bawden 2001; 2008), including "digital literacy," "multimedia literacy," "electronic literacy," "computer literacy," "e-skills," and "digital skills." The definitions reflect the continuous shift in the concept, a multifaceted moving target, determined by the evolution itself of the technology within a digital scenario in continuous rapid change (Ala-Mutka 2011; Ferrari 2012). From an operational point of view, a primary distinction can be made between "computer literacy," the basic ability to use a personal computer, and "digital literacy," the ability to process information gathered through the computer and derived from diverse sources and in different information architectures and formats (Gilster 1997).

In reality, the expression "digital literacy" has been used to define a multiplicity of aspects tied to skills, from the most technical to those that are more linked to the motivations and objectives of those people using ICTs. The theoretical effort to pin down an adequate definition has not always met with unambiguous skills indicators.

The ambiguity in the definition of the operational components of the concept induced Eshet-Alkalai (2004: 102) to maintain that "digital literacy can be defined as a survival skill in the digital era. It constitutes a system of skills and strategies used by learners and users in digital environments."

Van Dijk (2005) considers the term "literacy" to be misleading when outlining a theoretical framework able to discern at the same time the new "special skills" required for computers and networks; skills connected with the ability to manage information data procured in multimedia formats; skills in handling the large quantity of data available. Thus he suggests replacing the term "digital literacy" with the label "digital skills," which includes all three dimensions of the concept and identifies "the collection of skills needed to operate computers and their networks, to search and select information in them, and to use them for one's own purpose" (van Dijk 2005: 73).

Hargittai concentrates on the differences in online activities of individuals, to ascertain the implications of the Internet on the possibilities of changing one's life opportunities through the implementation of one's human, financial, political, social, and cultural capital (Hargittai 2008). The concept of online skills is thus defined "as a user's ability to locate content on the web effectively and efficiently" (Hargittai 2005: 372), and is inextricably bound to the "nuanced measure of use" (Hargittai 2007: 121) which can contribute to erecting barriers for some subjects, while enabling others to improve their social position.

As the concept of online skills evolves, an approach based solely on the technicalities of the use of the Internet (and computers) needs to be replaced by a multidimensional conceptualization in which the operational aspect of e-skills is linked to the cognitive abilities of users (Donat, Brandtweiner, and Kerschbaum 2009; Ferrari 2012; Gui 2013; Gui and Argentin 2011; Haddon 2004; van Deursen, Helsper, and Eynon 2014; van Dijk and van Deursen 2014; Warschauer 2002).Van Dijk and Van Deursen (2008, 2009a, 2009b, 2010, 2012) break down the concept of Internet skills as follows:

"Operational skills: the skills to operate digital media; Formal skills: the skills to handle the special structures of digital media (such as menus and hyperlinks); Information skills: the skills to search, select and evaluate information in digital media; Strategic skills: the skills to employ the information contained in digital media as a means to reach a particular personal or professional goal" (van Deursen and van Dijk 2008: 4).

Based on a new literacy debate, Helsper and Eynon (2013) propose a categorization in two areas that are both operational, with skills called "creative" and "technical," and strategic, with "social" and "critical" skills, thus focusing more on the engagement of subjects in online activities.

Recently, Van Dijk and Van Deursen (2014) also introduced two dimensions in their theoretical framework, taking into account the evolution and diffusion of information technology among the population, with greater emphasis on the participatory phase of Web 2.0. Thus referring to Internet Communication Skills and Content Creation Skills: "Communication Skills are needed for digital media such as the Internet that increasingly concentrate on communication" (2014: 6); and Content Creation Skills "have become increasingly important, as the Internet has developed from a relatively passive content consumption medium to a medium enable actively produced user-generated content" (2014: 7).

The addition of these two skill areas in the theoretical work of van Dijk and Van Deursen highlights the seamless relationship that has developed between digital life and everyday life, and implicitly puts the emphasis on the importance of the roots of technology in fostering personal and social empowerment.

This centrality of e-skills for the empowerment of everyday life had already been highlighted in several documents published by the European Commission (2007a, 2007b), which clarify how possessing such skills grants the chance to obtain decisive empowerment, enabling individuals to take part in the knowledge society, as hoped since the Lisbon strategy (European Commission 2000). A definition issued by the European Commission (2008: 4) describes *digital literacy* as "the skills required in order to achieve digital competence, the confident and critical use of ICT for work, leisure, learning and communication," all aspects strictly connected with everyday life. Today, pillar VI of the Digital Agenda for Europe (DAE) (European Commission 2010) is specifically dedicated to "enhancing digital literacy, skills and inclusion" to get the most out of digital technologies.

Thus there is general agreement among scholars, international institutions and policy makers regarding the importance of individual skills in fostering digital inclusion. However, it is not possible to identify a shared definition of digital skills, or a single operational role given to the concept.

A primary distinction can be made related to the use of "indirect" and "direct" indicators. The former are compiled using statistics on the possession of certified skills (e.g., ECDL); the latter consider the skill levels possessed by individuals (e.g., the ability to seek information online).

As regards *direct indicators,* digital skills can be collected through two different approaches based on:

1. Direct observation: Observation of level of skills through tests in controlled environments.
2. Indirect observation:
   a. Indirect evidence of skills through survey questions on Internet use, which implies the possession of certain skills;
   b. Indirect evidence of skills through survey questions on levels of knowledge reported by individuals related to particular skills.

Research using the first approach measures performance results achieved by subjects, related both to their ability to conclude certain operations on the web, and their Internet skills, determined by inspecting the surfing time needed to solve the tasks posed (Hargittai 2005). The direct appraisal of skills by laboratory testing clearly leads to an accurate recording of the online behavior of individuals and of their effective ability to carry out operations "effectively and efficiently," however it does not facilitate the evaluation of large samples of the population because it is very expensive and time-consuming.

Research following the second approach based on a *retrospective recon-struction* of operations and behavior carried out by Internet users are the most common methods to collect data on digital inclusion.

This approach, however, presents various problems (van Deursen, Helsper, and Eynon 2014), including validity in particular: "Are self-reports valid measurements of actual skills possessed?" (van Dijk 2006: 208). Self-reported measurements are context dependent and positively biased. For example, it seems that the self-perception of competence is gender dependent: women tend to underestimate their ability to interface with technology, thus impacting on their confidence in using it and there-fore on the type of use (Bunz, Curry, and Voon 2007; Hargittai and Shafer 2006; Liff and Shepherd 2004; Sieverding and Koch 2009).

To overcome this, Van Deursen et al. (2012) proposed proxy survey questions validated using performance monitoring during laboratory testing as benchmarks that reflect Operational, Formal, Information, and Strategic Internet skills. This framework was recently proposed in the report "Measuring digital skills" (van Deursen, Helsper, and Eynon 2014) in which items related to the size of the Internet Communication Skills and Content Creation Skills were added. The questionnaire was based equally on self-assessment but "furthermore, we try to limit the problems with self-assessments by using very carefully worded items and correspondingly appropriate scales for measuring Internet skills" (van Deursen, Helsper, and Eynon 2014: 11) (e.g., I know how to download files from 1—Not at all true of me to 5—Very true of me.).

The other problems in the investigation of skills are less important, although still to be evaluated in defining the measurement models of e-inclusion. The first calls into question the *speed of technological change* that often makes certain ways of detecting skills obsolete or incomplete. This is especially the case of very large and structured surveys. In fact, there may be some delays in the upgrade of detection tools. These delays are of-ten reflected in the inability to adequately monitor the skills that become progressively necessary to fully participate in the knowledge society.

One of the most common problems in the questionnaire surveys is the *overlap* between the domain of Internet use and the domain of e-skills. Indeed the relationship concerning Internet use and Internet skills is often unclear and confused because the skills questions are closely linked to Internet use (e.g., "How often do you do 'X'?" While questions on skills sound like "How good are you at 'X'?").

Although it is important to separate skills measurement from use mea-surement: "Yet doubts can be raised about whether someone can have or claim high skills on something they have never done or whether those who undertake an activity frequently would ever classify themselves as having low skills in that area. Indeed, correlations between these types of indicators are often, unsurprisingly, high" (Helsper and Eynon 2013: 697).

Despite these critical issues, using nationally representative surveys (e.g., Eurostat in Europe; Istat in Italy) is the only approach that enables extensive surveys and comparable diachronic studies on these issues to be used, and is the most widespread and appropriate way of collecting data and testing generalizable models of digital inclusion.

DIGITAL SKILLS INDICATORS: THE EUROPEAN FRAMEWORK

The increasing focus of the European Commission on the diffusion of information and communication technologies has led to an in-depth examination of digital skills and of the appropriate indicators for monitoring digital inequality.

As happens with more academic studies, also in European Commission documents, the concept of digital skills is defined in different ways: eLiteracy, digital literacy, digital skills, Digital Competence, e-Skills, eCompetence, basic ICT skills,and so on, which illustrates the difficulty in drawing the boundaries of an extremely varied concept with many possible ways of approaching (Ala-Mutka 2011; Ferrari 2012).

Despite this *jungle of definitions*, the empirical operationalization of the concept includes some of the documents that make up the current regulation framework (European Commission, No. 808/2004; No. 1006/2009) which guides empirical findings on ICTs within Europe. This framework serves as a guideline on the items needed to build a useful *regional benchmark* for a comparative analysis, which is both longitudinal and cross-sectional.

According to the European Commission, digital literacy is based on the possession of certain skills measured through basic indicators for computers and the Internet, which have changed over time.

The first question on digital skills in the questionnaire model proposed by Eurostat (Commission Regulation (EC) No 1099/2005) aims to record interviewees' abilities in terms of certain activities related to *computer use* ("Which of the following computer-related activities have you already/ever carried out?") in terms of:

1. Copying or moving a file or folder
2. Using copy and paste to duplicate or move information within a document
3. Using basic arithmetic formulae in a spreadsheet
4. Compressing (or zipping) files
5. Connecting and installing new devices (e.g., a modem)

6. Writing a computer program using a specialized programming language.

In 2011, four new items were introduced to take into account new devices and other digital skills:

7. Transferring files between computers and other devices (from a digital camera or from/to mobile phone, mp3/mp4 player)
8. Modifying or verifying the configuration parameters of software applications (except Internet browsers)
9. Creating electronic presentations with presentation software (e.g., slides), including e.g. images, sound, video or charts
10. Installing a new or replacing an old operating system.

The *skills related to the Internet* are obtained through the question "Which of the following Internet-related activities have you already/ever carried out?" in terms of:

1. Using a search engine to find information
2. Sending an email with attached files (documents, images, etc.)
3. Posting messages to chatrooms, newsgroups or an online discussion forums (e.g. on social networking websites)
4. Using the Internet to make phone calls
5. Using peer-to-peer file sharing to exchange movies, music, etc.
6. Creating a web page

In 2011, two new items were introduced to examine the Internet skills regarding the Web 2.0:

7. Uploading text, games, images, films or music to websites (e.g., social networking websites)
8. Modifying the security settings of Internet browsers

At present the items listed above are used to measure e-skills in the European Union.

It is clear that although the areas identified by Eurostat are divided into two sets of questions on the skills related to the PC and the Internet, the items provided for in the survey refer to different concepts that are relatively easy to identify.

The first area, which could be defined as *operational*, includes essential skills for "operations" using computers and the Internet, that is, the cognitive skills needed for searching, selecting and managing information. The indicators pertinent to the "operational skills" area are: Using a search engine; Copying or moving files or folders; Using copy and paste in a document (e.g., Word); Sending emails with attachments; Using basic arithmetic formulae on an electronic page; Creating electronic presentations with presentation software (e.g., slides), including for example images, sound, video, or charts.

A second area consists of more *instrumental* skills. The "instrumental area" concerns the ability to manage the "machine" and its language, that is, the skills necessary to autonomously handle activities linked to hardware and software maintenance on the computer, also through the use of the web. Indicators inserted in the context of "instrumental skills" are: Compressing files; Connecting and installing peripherals (printer, modem etc.); Searching for downloading and installing software; Identifying and solving functional problems on the computer; Using a program language; Modifying the security settings of Internet browsers; Installing a new or replacing an old operating system. Transferring files between a computer and other devices (from a digital camera or from/to mobile phone, mp3/mp4 player), Modifying or verifying the configuration parameters of software applications (except Internet browsers).

The third area relates to a more *social* dimension. The "relational area" refers to the skills for active participation in the world of the Internet, that is, those skills that are useful to fully exploit the relational and interactive potentialities offered by Web 2.0. The indicators that represent the domain of "relational skills" are: Posting messages to chat rooms, newsgroups etc.; Phone calls via the Internet; Using "file sharing" to exchange films, music, etc.; Creating web pages; Uploading text, games, images, films or music to websites (e.g., to social networking websites).

Clearly, it is useful to identify some areas where skills can be pigeonholed, however they cannot be classified in mutually exclusive areas. In fact, the same skills e.g. "using the Internet to make phone calls" can be useful for work conference calls, in the same way as a family meeting.

In the European framework, digital skills are "measured" overall by applying a cumulative index, by adding the number of skills the individuals claim to possess. Although the decision to build an index that is simply based on adding up the number of skills possessed may at first appear simplistic and limited, the cumulative nature of the skills should not be forgotten, which makes it possible to consider them as strongly correlated.

Despite the cumulative nature, "these skills can and should be measured separately (starting with instrumental or operational skills). This could provide opportunities to investigate how these skill levels are distributed among social segments in the population" (van Deursen and van Dijk 2008: 4).

Starting from the type and level of skills possessed by individuals, it is then recommended to observe their socio-economic status, broken down in terms of individual characteristics (gender, age, etc.) and social characteristics (education level, employment level, etc.); the type of physical Internet access available to them, and the autonomy of its use.

The concept of digital skills, thus formulated and described, is empirically verified by the analysis below. This analysis is not based on the distinction between computer use skills and skills related to the Internet as described above, because they strongly and increasingly overlap. Instead we focus on the objectives and outcomes that can be achieved through these diverse skills, considering the personal computer and Internet as indispensable for full participation in the digital world.

The *principal hypothesis* is that the different skill levels directly affect the "social practices" that subjects use via the web, and that these practices implement both e-skills via learning by doing, and are affected by the level of access available (more intensive use, investments in autonomy of use, etc.). This gives rise to a virtuous cycle in which skills and actual use of the net impact on the real opportunities for participation in economic, social, and political life.

DIGITAL INEQUALITIES AND E-SKILLS: THE ITALIAN CASE

Using the European framework and focusing on Italy, an analysis of the digital skills and social inequalities can be empirically carried out, processing the microdata collected by the ISTAT survey *Aspects of daily life* (ADL) 2013, which includes the harmonized Eurostat form on the use of ICTs. The sample survey of approximately 20,000 households and 50,000 individuals covered the structural and contextual characteristics of the respondents, their digital skills, the frequency with which they use the new technologies, and how/why they used the Internet (communication, work, training, transport, health, e-government, etc.).

Our analysis focuses on the segment aged fourteen to seventy-four[2] of Internet users[3] in order to analyze the different levels of digital skills and the role played by such skills as a requirement and at the same time as a "marker" of e-inclusion. The concept of e-skills was operationalized using eighteen dichotomous items identified exclusively in Internet users (61.4%). Ten items concern personal computer management and the other eight are about navigation skills.

This subsample contains information on 21,130 respondents, representing over 28.5 million individuals, prevalently men (53.1%). In relation to the corresponding age cohorts for the entire Italian population, the younger age bands are over-represented, especially subjects aged fourteen to thirty-four (39.6% of Internet users vs. 29.0% of the population). There is also a prevalence of subjects with high educational level (68.6% vs. 51.9%), of employed (59.1% vs. 47.6%), and students (14.5% vs. 9.6%). Instead, housewives (6.0% vs. 13.7%), and the retired (6.3% vs. 14.2%) are under-represented.

In short, the Italian Internet population comprises a younger and better-qualified subgroup, which is better positioned in the labor market, compared to the segment aged fourteen to seventy-four. What e-skills and how many of them are possessed by these individuals? At first glance, the distribution of digital skill indicators, among Internet users, shows highly diversified situations (Figure 5.1) and highlights some preliminary issues.

The first is that some of skills are popular among most Internet users, while others relate to a few individuals.

Overall, the data indicate that the most widely diffused skills (over 80%) comprise a beginner's skills set, the minimum cognitive requirements to operate in the Internet world: knowing how to use a search engine, to copy files and folders, copying and pasting, and sending emails. Few (<30%) seem to possess other skills and pertain to different types of users, who would be at the top of a hypothetical scale of e-skills. Between these two poles, there are two other groups, of medium-low skills (30–50%) and medium-high (50–70%).

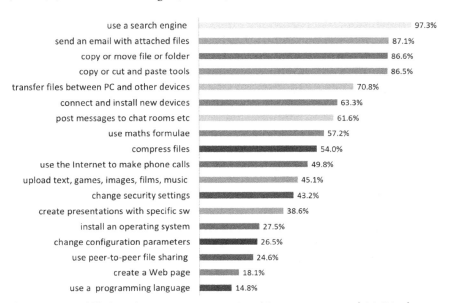

Figure 5.1. E-skills in Italy (%, year 2013): PC and Internet users aged 14–74 who can do the following operations. Created by Roberta Bracciale and Isabella Mingo, based on the Istat "Aspects of daily life" microdata (2013).

Second, on the basis of their diffusion among Internet users, the skills show an inclusivity of items: more complex e-skills—and less widely used—including the simplest and most common ones. Someone who knows how to create a web page is also likely to know how to send an email and to use a search engine. Thus, someone who knows how to write programs will also know how to copy files and folders. However, such inclusivity is less certain in other cases. For example, in order to use file sharing it is not necessary to know how to make phone calls via the Internet or to be able to remove viruses from one's personal computer. Consequently, to measure skill levels it is not enough to analyze the frequency of each of them, but rather their "co-presence," that is how they complement each other, thus constituting the personal set of digital skills.

Thirdly, the order of the items suggests a mixture of skills in relation to computers and the Internet. Computer management skills are not always the priority compared to the ability to carry out specific net operations, however in practice the distinction between the two types of e-skills is increasingly nuanced, whereby one type reinforces and completes the other.

To clarify these doubts, we need to empirically analyze the relations among the various skills in order to: (1) study the dependency structure among indicators of e-skills to condense them to a few synthetic dimensions; (2) identify groups of Internet users, diversified on the basis of these dimensions; (3) characterize these groups qualitatively and quantitatively, both in relation to their features and their internet use style.

As regards the first aim, we used Multiple Correspondence Analysis (MCA) (Benzecri 1973; Bouroche and Saporta 1983). The set of variables was divided in two categories: active variables, to find the synthetic sets of digital skills; and illustrative variables, for a supplementary analysis of these sets. Eighteen dichotomous items (36 modalities) relative to e-skills were included in the active variables. The illustrative variables are related to the structural and socio-cultural characteristics of the subjects, how much they use the net, how many activities they carry out.[4]

The results show that the non-negligible factors (with $\lambda > 1/p$, in our case $\lambda > 0.056$),[5] with which the thirty-six modalities under consideration can be synthesized are the first two; the first explaining 96.5% of the corrected inertia (Benzecri 1979).

Observation of the first factorial plan (Figure 5.2) shows that the first dimension (factor 1) synthesizes skills levels, opposing the absence and presence of e-skills. The dichotomous nature of the variables is underlined by this contraposition, while the curvilinear configuration of the points on the plane suggests a Guttman effect (Guttman 1950) and highlights the one-dimensionality of the items.

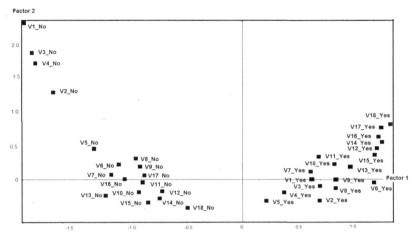

Figure 5.2. E-skills index. Created by Roberta Bracciale and Isabella Mingo, based on the Istat "Aspects of daily life" microdata (2013).

Legend for Figure 5.2

V1	use a search engine	V10	use the Internet to make phone calls
V2	send an email with attached files	V11	upload text, games, images, films, music
V3	copy or move file or folder	V12	change security settings
V4	copy or cut and paste tools	V13	create presentations with specific sw
V5	transfer files between PC and other devices	V14	install an operating system
V6	connect and install new devices	V15	change configuration parameters
V7	post messages to chat rooms etc	V16	use peer-to-peer file sharing
V8	use maths formulae	V17	create a Web page
V9	compress files	V18	use a programming language

The sets of near and juxtaposed modalities indicate an order of skills ranging from their total absence (represented by the negative semi-axis) to different positions according to levels of increasing e-skill complexity (along the positive semi-axis). Thus, the hypothesis of a prevalent additivity of the items used to detect e-skills seems to be confirmed, through the factorial representation.

Note that:

- the position on the negative semi-axis of all the "no" modalities denoting a lack of skills ordered by frequency from the origin of the semi-axis;

- the nearness in proximity to the origin of the axes of operational type e-skills, that is those simpler and basic operations most diffused among users: the ability to manage files and folders and simple applications, to conduct web searches, and use email;[6]
- the nearness of certain skills required for a full use of the relational possibilities offered by Web 2.0, that denote active participation in the world of Internet: file sharing, Internet telephone calls, uploading text or images, creating web pages, and writing programs;
- the proximity of e-skills pertaining to the technical ability to administer the "machine" in complex digital environments, to solve functional and security problems, to modify configuration parameters, to compress files.

This may be interpreted as a *synthetic index of e-skills* (skills/no skills), that enables the subjects to be evaluated on the basis of their scores in that dimension.

The second dimension (factor 2) is complementary to the first, and opposes the modalities on the basis of their frequency: less general skills are placed on the positive semi-axis, and the more frequent ones are placed on the negative semi-axis.

The skills/no skills continuum, characterized by the illustrative variables (Figure 5.3), reiterates trends already encountered in studies on exclusion, both general and digital, which identify subjects as "richer" and "poorer." Those individuals most exposed to the dynamics of exclusion, identified also during the Riga Conference by the European Commission (2006), are individuals of an advanced age (55–64 years and 65–74 years); who do not have an active employment (retired, inactive); with more limited cultural resources (lower education); and also females.

This highlights how high values on the synthetic e-skills index are associated with the younger age bands and the more highly qualified academically, but above all with frequent use and intense engagement on the net (Figure 5.3). Subjects that use the Internet daily and who carry out more than thirteen types of activities on the net (communication, e-banking, e-government, e-learning, etc.) are also those richest in digital skills.

It is thus plausible to conjecture the existence of a virtuous cycle, a reinforcement of skills and levels of activities: those who have more e-skills use the Internet more frequently and perform a large number of activities on the network. Likewise, the more frequent the use of the network and online activities is, the more skills are enhanced.

The empirical evidence underlining the importance of age, education and above all experience, of learning by doing, in the acquisition of technological know-how, is further confirmed by the results of a logistic regression model (Hosmer and Lemeshow 1989). In this model, the vari-

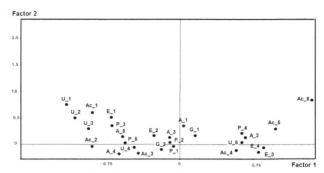

Figure 5.3. **E-skills index and social inequalities. Created by Roberta Bracciale and Isabella Mingo, based on the Istat "Aspects of
daily life" microdata (2013).**

Legend for Figure 5.3

G_1	Male	P_4	Student
G_2	Female	P_5	Retired
A_1	Age 14-24	U_1	Use Internet less than once per month
A_2	Age 25-34	U_2	Use Internet a few times a month
A_3	Age 35-54	U_3	Use Internet one time a week
A_4	Age 55-64	U_4	Use Internet a few times a week
A_5	Age 65-74	U_5	Use Internet every day
E_1	Elementary school	Ac_1	None Internet Activity
E_2	Middle school	Ac_2	1-4 Internet activities
E_3	Graduated high school	Ac_3	6-8 Internet activities
E_4	University degree or PHD	Ac_4	9-12 Internet activities
P_1	Employed	Ac_5	13-16 Internet activities
P_2	Unemployed	Ac_6	More than 16 Internet activities
P_3	Housewife		

able e-skills index, once dichotomized (higher/lower than the average)
constituted the dependent variable, while various structural variables
(gender, age, education, profession[7]) together with variables regarding
Internet experience (the frequency of use and the number of activities performed online) were introduced in the model as independent variables.
The model correctly classified 76.6% of individuals. Figure 5.4 reports the
estimated parameters (odds ratios) that identified those aspects that influence e-skills assuming other conditions remained unchanged; the low
level of e-skills index was considered as the reference category.

The analysis of the coefficients highlighted that the number of Internet
activities has a greater effect on the high level of e-skills. Performing
more than ten activities online increases the propensity for a high level of

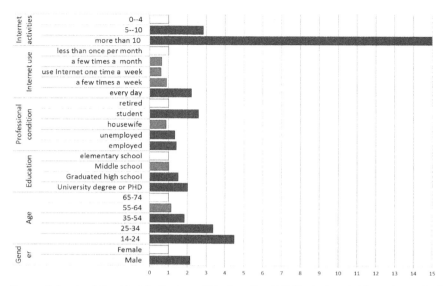

Figure 5.4. Logistic Model: Factors Affecting the E-Skills Index (odds ratios). Final Model: -2LL= 2775.727; Chi square= 8423.73; df.18; sig.<0.000; Cox and Snell=0.334; Nagelkerke= 0.445; correct classification 76.6%. Dependent reference category: Low E-skill Index. The reference categories of independent variables are in white; non-significant categories (sig->0.005) are in grey. Istat microdata: Aspects of Daily Life 2013.

digital competence by fifteen times compared to those that perform less than four Internet activities. Subjects who use the Internet every day have a greater probability of having a high index of e-skills than those who use the net less frequently.

Concerning the *structural variables*, it appears that—assuming that other conditions are kept unchanged—men have a greater propensity to have a high e-skill index level than women. For every highly e-skilled woman, there are 2.4 highly e-skilled men. Level of education positively affects the level of digital skills: increasing the level of education increases the odds-ratio values. Age group negatively affects the model: the fourteen- to thirty-four- year-old band increases the propensity for a high level of digital competence by 4.5 times compared to the sixty-five- to seventy-four-year-old band.

These results show that also within the segment of Internet users, the same *reproduction of digital inequality* subsists, which is anchored to the socio-demographic characteristics of the individuals, and to the frequency of use, which in turn reinforces the mastery of the same skills (Bentivegna 2009). In the case of the most vulnerable categories, the skills/no skills feedback mechanism risks becoming a vicious cycle, as in cases where skills are lacking or scant, feeding a gradual digital exclusion.

WHICH E-SKILLS FOR WHICH INTERNET USERS?

Using these synthetic dimensions and applying a mixed algorithm of cluster analysis, which integrates a non-hierarchical with a hierarchical technique (Lebart, Morineau, and Piron 1995), *four clusters* can be identified: Unskilled, Basic e-skilled, e-Skilled and Advanced e-skilled.[8]

To highlight the differences between these clusters, the Riga diffusion index (DI) was used. This index is based on simple penetration rate ratios (European Commission 2007c), calculated for each cluster and for each e-skill (Table 5.1), or Internet activity (Table 5.2): a value of 1 indicates an inclusion level equal to that of the population, higher values indicate higher levels of inclusion for the cluster analyzed, while values less than 1 and near 0 indicate levels of less inclusion, and thus digital exclusion.

Unskilled

Among Internet users in Italy, or at least those self-declared as such, there are individuals who lack even the basic e-skills. These comprise 10.8% of Internet users who have on average, less than three e-skills (Table 5.1) and are characterized by the prevalent lack of the simplest e-skills. Of these individuals, 41.0% (vs. 87.0% of Internet users) are able to send emails with attachments, 12.3% (vs. 86.7%) can cut and paste. These quotas decrease in correspondence to more complex e-skills: less than 4% are able to install software, create web pages, use file sharing, and compress files (Table 5.2). On average they perform four different types of Internet activities (vs. 7.5): although the percentage is lower than the total number of Internet users, the activities mainly carried out include searching for

Table 5.1.   E-Skills and Internet Activities by Clusters

Clusters	PC E-skills [a]	Internet E-skills [b]	E-Skills[c]	Internet Activities[d]
	Mean	Mean	Mean	Mean
Unskilled (10.8%)	0.76	2.07	2.83	3.74
Basic E-skilled (29.9%)	3.32	2.64	5.96	5.13
E-Skilled (35.2%)	5.88	4.57	10.45	8.04
Advanced E-skilled (24.1%)	8.76	6.83	15.59	11.41
All (N=21130)	5.26	4.27	9.52	7.52

[a]Eta squared=0.738; [b]Eta squared=0.633; [c]Eta squared=0.827;[d]Eta squared=0.349

$r_{(e\text{-skills}|Internet\ activities)} = 0.655$

Table 5.2. Internet Users and Diffusion Index by E-Skills and Cluster (% Internet Users Aged 14–74)

E-Skills	Internet users by E-Skill and Cluster %					Diffusion index (DI) by E-Skills and Cluster			
	Unskilled 10.8%	Basic E-skilled 29.9%	E-skilled 35.2%	Advanced E-skilled 24.1%	All n = 21,130	Unskilled	Basic E-skilled	E-skilled	Advanced E-skilled
Use a search engine	85.0%	98.6%	98.3%	99.8%	97.3%	0.87	1.01	1.01	1.03
Send an email with attached files	41.0%	85.0%	95.0%	98.7%	87.1%	0.47	0.98	1.09	1.13
Copy or move file or folder	14.4%	92.1%	95.5%	99.2%	86.6%	0.17	1.06	1.10	1.15
Copy or cut and paste tools	12.3%	92.6%	95.3%	99.2%	86.5%	0.14	1.07	1.10	1.15
Transfer files between PCs and other devices	16.0%	47.5%	88.4%	98.5%	70.8%	0.23	0.67	1.25	1.39
Connect and install new devices	13.3%	34.6%	79.5%	97.8%	63.3%	0.21	0.55	1.26	1.54
Post messages to chat rooms etc.	26.5%	33.2%	74.3%	93.9%	61.6%	0.43	0.54	1.21	1.52
Use basic maths formulae	3.1%	32.2%	71.1%	92.3%	57.2%	0.05	0.56	1.24	1.61
Compress files	2.5%	22.9%	67.8%	95.3%	54.0%	0.05	0.42	1.26	1.77
Use the Internet to make phone calls	22.0%	20.5%	56.6%	88.8%	49.8%	0.44	0.41	1.14	1.78

Upload text, games, images, films, music	14.1%	12.1%	52.9%	88.5%	45.1%	0.31	0.27	1.17	1.96
Change security settings	9.4%	9.0%	50.1%	90.4%	43.2%	0.22	0.21	1.16	2.10
Create presentations with specific sw	3.8%	5.5%	42.1%	89.9%	38.6%	0.10	0.14	1.09	2.33
Install an operating systems	3.1%	2.1%	21.6%	78.5%	27.5%	0.11	0.08	0.79	2.86
Change configuration parameters	3.9%	1.5%	18.5%	79.3%	26.5%	0.15	0.06	0.70	2.99
Use peer-to-peer file sharing	4.6%	2.6%	19.3%	68.4%	24.6%	0.19	0.11	0.79	2.78
Create a web page	4.8%	2.4%	10.3%	54.9%	18.1%	0.27	0.13	0.57	3.03
Use a Programming language	3.5%	1.3%	8.3%	45.9%	14.8%	0.24	0.09	0.56	3.11

Table 5.3. Internet Users and Diffusion Index by Cluster and Activity (% Internet Users Aged 14–74)

Internet Activities	% Internet Users who Performed Each Internet Activity by Cluster					Diffusion Index (DI) by Cluster and Activity			
	Clusters					Clusters			
	Unskilled	Basic E-skilled	E-skilled	Advanced E-skilled	All	Unskilled	Basic E-skilled	E-skilled	Advanced E-skilled
	10.8%	29.9%	35.2%	24.1%	n = 21,130				
Sent an email with attached files	44.0%	78.3%	89.9%	95.4%	82.8%	0.53	0.95	1.09	1.15
Used the Internet to make phone calls	18.1%	17.6%	35.8%	57.8%	33.7%	0.54	0.52	1.06	1.71
Posted messages on social media sites or instant messaging	20.8%	26.2%	56.0%	75.0%	47.9%	0.43	0.55	1.17	1.57
Participated in social networks (Facebook, Twitter, etc.)	27.6%	32.0%	61.0%	76.3%	52.4%	0.53	0.61	1.16	1.46
Expressed opinions on social or political issues	6.1%	8.6%	22.7%	43.7%	21.8%	0.28	0.40	1.04	2.01
Took part in online consultations or voting	2.8%	3.4%	9.2%	23.9%	10.3%	0.27	0.33	0.89	2.32
Consulted wikis (e.g., Wikipedia)	30.1%	40.4%	64.7%	81.9%	57.8%	0.52	0.70	1.12	1.42
Participated in a professional network (e.g., LinkedIn, Xing)	1.9%	2.5%	8.9%	30.0%	11.3%	0.17	0.22	0.79	2.65

Read/downloaded newspapers/news magazines	40.2%	53.8%	68.3%	81.8%	64.2%	0.63	0.84	1.06	1.27
Searched for health information	38.0%	45.8%	52.6%	61.6%	51.2%	0.74	0.89	1.03	1.20
Read or downloaded online e-book	3.6%	6.5%	16.0%	37.8%	17.1%	0.21	0.38	0.94	2.21
Looked for information on education, training or course offers	17.9%	29.4%	46.2%	62.5%	42.0%	0.43	0.70	1.10	1.49
Found information on goods and services	37.3%	49.3%	64.1%	77.6%	60.0%	0.62	0.82	1.07	1.29
Played or downloaded games, images, films or music	4.3%	6.5%	27.7%	61.1%	26.9%	0.16	0.24	1.03	2.27
Done an online course	2.4%	3.3%	6.0%	15.1%	7.0%	0.35	0.47	0.85	2.16
Looked for a job or sent a job application	12.1%	13.0%	21.9%	31.7%	20.6%	0.59	0.63	1.07	1.54
Used tourist services	22.7%	30.1%	45.6%	57.7%	41.4%	0.55	0.73	1.10	1.39
Sold goods or services	6.9%	7.1%	14.9%	27.5%	14.7%	0.47	0.48	1.01	1.87
Bought goods or services	4.3%	14.3%	35.9%	45.6%	22.0%	0.20	0.65	1.63	2.07
Used Internet banking	13.5%	22.6%	35.7%	52.8%	33.5%	0.40	0.67	1.07	1.58
Interacted with local government services	15.0%	25.6%	34.9%	48.3%	33.2%	0.45	0.77	1.05	1.45

information on health (DI 0.75) and services or goods (DI 0.62), and reading newspapers online (DI 0.63) (Table 5.3). The socio-cultural profile of these subjects is typical of categories at risk of exclusion, characterized by low-medium level of education and inactivity in the labor market (housewives or the retired).

Basic e-Skilled

This cluster comprises 29.9% of Italian Internet users who possess on average six of the eighteen e-skills under consideration prevalently of low complexity (Table 5.3). They are characterized with elementary digital skills that permit a limited and reduced use of the PC and the internet to use a search engine, to manage files and folders), however many have no advanced skills: only 1.3% (vs. 14.8%) know how to write programs, only 1.5% (vs. 26.5%) are able to use peer-to-peer file sharing, only 2.6% (vs. 24.6%) know how to change configuration parameters (Table 5.2). Compared to the preceding group, however, there is evidence of a more intense use of the Internet: 86.3% use the Internet every day or a few times a week (Table 5.4) and on average perform five different types of

Social Inequalities in Digital Skills: The European framework and the Italian case Roberta Bracciale, Isabella Mingo

Table 5.4.   Clusters: Socio-demographic Profiles (Column %)

			Clusters			
		Unskilled *n = 2,286*	Basic E-skilled *n = 6,313*	E-skilled *n = 7,434*	Advanced E-skilled *n = 5,097*	All *n = 2,1130*
Gender	male	46.7%	44.9%	51.2%	67.6%	52.8%
	female	53.3%	55.1%	48.8%	32.4%	47.2%
Age	14–24	7.5%	11.8%	26.5%	28.8%	20.6%
	25–34	12.2%	13.6%	20.0%	26.3%	18.8%
	35–54	52.4%	50.4%	41.0%	37.5%	44.2%
	55–64	18.1%	17.6%	9.7%	5.9%	12.0%
	65–74	9.8%	6.6%	2.9%	1.5%	4.4%
Education	Elementary school	6.6%	2.8%	1.5%	.8%	2.3%
	Middle school	45.9%	31.1%	27.0%	20.3%	28.7%
	Graduated high school	40.0%	49.9%	50.9%	50.5%	49.3%
	University degree or PhD	7.6%	16.2%	20.5%	28.4%	19.7%

		Clusters				All
		Unskilled n = 2,286	Basic E-skilled n = 6,313	E-skilled n = 7,434	Advanced E-skilled n = 5,097	n = 2,1130
Professional status	employed	52.1%	59.6%	58.7%	57.6%	58.0%
	unemployed	13.8%	12.6%	13.0%	13.2%	13.0%
	housewife	15.6%	9.2%	3.6%	1.6%	6.1%
	student	3.5%	6.7%	19.4%	24.1%	15.0%
	retired	14.8%	12.0%	5.3%	3.5%	7.9%
Familiar economic resources	excellent	0.8%	0.7%	0.8%	1.0%	.8%
	adequate	48.5%	54.9%	56.1%	58.3%	55.5%
	poor	41.0%	37.8%	36.7%	34.5%	36.9%
	quite inadequate	9.7%	6.6%	6.5%	6.2%	6.8%
Geographical location	North	49.8%	44.9%	43.3%	45.9%	45.1%
	Center	19.3%	17.9%	18.7%	19.5%	18.7%
	South	30.8%	37.2%	38.0%	34.7%	36.2%
Internet use	every day	29.3%	42.6%	73.2%	88.4%	63.0%
	a few times a week	42.7%	43.7%	23.4%	10.6%	28.5%
	once a week	7.6%	4.8%	1.2%	0.5%	2.8%
	a few times a month	14.1%	6.5%	1.7%	0.4%	4.2%
	less than once per month	6.3%	2.3%	0.6%	0.1%	1.6%
Internet activities	more than 10 internet activities	3.3%	4.9%	25.1%	59.9%	25.1%
	5-10 internet activities	30.1%	49.8%	58.1%	34.3%	46.8%
	0-4 internet activities	66.6%	45.3%	16.8%	5.8%	28.0%
All		100%	100%	100%	100%	100%

activities on the net (Table 5.1). With a lower percentage than the total number of Internet users, the activities mainly carried out by this group are relational and informational: sending and receiving email (DI = 0.95), reading newspapers and magazines online (DI = 0.84), searching for different information (on health DI = 0.89, goods and services DI = 0.84), interacting with public administration (Table 5.3). The socio-demographic characteristics of this group highlight the identikit of a user aged over thirty-five, with a middle level of education (31.1% vs. 28.7%), employed (58.6% vs. 56.9%) or inactive (housewives, retired) (Table 5.4).

e-Skilled

This cluster comprises 35.2% of Italian Internet users, characterized by 10.5 e-skills (vs. 9.5) (Table 5.1). The e-skills diffusion index shows that the prevalent skills are technical compressing files (DI = 1.25) and installing peripherals (DI = 1.26) (Table 5.2).

However, they have also some of the e-skills required for active participation in the Internet: they know how to post messages to chat rooms (DI = 1.21), upload texts, images, and music online (DI = 1.17), and make phone calls via the Internet (DI = 1.14).

Advanced skills are the most lacking in this cluster in terms of both the management of PCs and the use of the Internet (Table 5.3). They resemble people who are learning to move more easily in the world of new technologies: 96.6% use the Internet every day or a few times a week and perform over eight different types of Internet activities. These activities are relational, but also instrumental: posting messages to social media (DI = 1.17) participating in social networks (DI = 1.16), buying goods and services online (DI = 1.63), using tourist services (DI = 1.10), and using Internet banking (DI = 1.07) (Table 5.3) The profile of this cluster is comprised of young subjects (aged 14–34), with a medium-high level of education, and students (Table 5.4).

Advanced e-Skilled

This group comprises 24.1% of Italian Internet users, and represents the most advanced segment in terms of digital skills, both in quantitative terms—on average these subjects possess nearly sixteen of the eighteen e-skills—and in terms of complexity. The diffusion indices, always greater than 1 and greater than 2 for the most advanced e-skills, reveal that, compared to the average Internet user, this group has greater expertise, both in terms of managing equipment for connections and for all kind of the Internet activities, which enable them to move with ease on the net. In fact, they know both how to write programs (DI = 3.1), change PC configuration settings (DI = 2.99), install a new operating system (DI 2.86), create web pages (DI=3.03), use peer-to-peer file sharing (DI=2.78) (Table 5.2). The relation these individuals set up with the technology seems to be not only instrumental but also expressive: the net constitutes the preferred mode of relating to the world, a realm that they inhabit daily (88.4% vs. 63.0%) and in which they perform multiple tasks.

On average, they perform twelve different Internet activities (Table 5.1). With significantly higher percentages compared to the population, the subjects of this cluster use the Internet to participate in professional networks (DI = 2.67), to express their opinions in online consultations or to vote on social and political issues (DI = 2.32), to play or download games, images, films or music (DI = 2.27) (Table 5.3).

The Advanced E-skilled group are prevalently male (67.6% vs. 52.8%), young (aged 14–34, 56.1% vs. 49.6%), students (24.1% vs. 15.0%), with a high educational level (school diploma or university degree (78.8% vs. 69.0%) (Table 5.4). They seem to be the Internet users who use their digital skills in order to have a more active role in society, to enhance their social inclusion.

CONCLUSIONS

This chapter highlights the relation between e-inclusion and e-skills, start-ing with the complexity of these concepts, which are often applied with different semantic dimensions and different modalities of measurement. The different approaches to establishing indicators of e-skills inevitably introduce elements of diversification. To obviate this problem, setting up shared indicators, used in periodical extensive surveys, makes it possible to compare the results in cross-sectional and longitudinal studies. Thus, it seems appropriate to use indicators harmonized in the European Union.

The results of this study, which was based on using data collected by the Italian official statistical sources (Istat), reveals the convergence of skills pertaining to computer use with those linked to the Internet use. A diversification of skills in terms of complexity and the different types of ability is clear, depending on a prevalently instrumental or prevalently relational use of the technology.

Digital inequalities are thus reiterated, also within a segment of the population that represents the youngest, better qualified subgroup, bet-ter positioned in terms of the labor market and which can consider itself "included," on the basis of the simple criterion of net access.

Even within the connected group, *the dynamics of the Matthew effect can be seen*: those with the "richest" personal resources activate a cumulative multiplication of advantages that follows the logic of "those who have, will be given more." Instead the "poorest" are victims of a cumulative multiplication of disadvantages according to the logic of "those who have nothing, will have even that taken away."

What is surprising is that, amongst this group, there are individuals who completely lack even the basic skills. This raises the question as to whether these data reflect unreliable answers from some subjects, who erroneously claim to be users, or whether these subjects perform operations online unwittingly: for example, they use search engines but they are not aware of doing it (i.e., they use Google but do not know that it is a search engine).

Some apparent anomalies in the numbers of Internet users who do not have even basic skills -but say they use the Internet to perform functions that require precisely the skills that they lack - could reside in the fact these subjects interface with the Internet using devices other than PCs, such as tablets and smartphones. For these users, the devices have the sole role of connection drivers, they are "lazy machines" that allow them to go online by clicking on an icon that appears on the screen. It is one of the aspects that should be investigated in the future, also to understand what skills and uses are implemented by Internet users who use the network mainly through personal and mobile devices with friendly interfaces, without the need for specific skills related to the PC. Unfortunately, at present, there are no extensive surveys that specifically take account of the use of content through these types of devices and that are able to return more precise information on the consumption of network in mobility. Updating the framework for the detection and measurement of e-skills, at a European level, should therefore introduce new items that consider this aspect.

In any case, users who are less capable of handling technical connection tools are likely to be those for whom the incorporation of new technologies in everyday life becomes more "provisional." The connection through mobile devices often makes the enjoyment of content online more simple and immediate, and has certainly encouraged the diffusion of new technologies, while a PC is still a tool where one needs to perform a series of operations effectively and efficiently. It is clear that for these segments of the population, *the dangers of digital marginalization are likely to worsen*. For example, a lower capability in the management of the "machine" could result, in a less varied mix of networking activities and a more cautious online behavior and less oriented to experimental "trial and error" use typical of learning new technologies through learning by doing. It should however be recognized that it is the need to perform daily living activities online (e.g., filling in and submitting a form to enroll in a school, arranging low cost holidays, paying taxes without queuing) that may impact positively on digital skills and on the empowerment of marginal users.

Thus, there are categories of subjects who are "richer" and "poorer" in e-skills, who again present the customary inequalities of gender (men/women), generations (young/old), and culture (low/high education). These elements reiterate the old, but not negligible, inequalities, heightened by the new technologies: *"The rich get richer, and the poor get poorer."*

NOTES

1. It was applied initially to celebrity mechanisms amongst the scientific community (Merton 1973). The effect takes its name from a verse in the Gospel of Matthew: "For whomsoever hath, to him shall be given, and he shall have more abundance; but whomsoever hath not, from him shall be taken away even that he hath" (13:12).

2. In the microdata ADL 2013, the age of the respondents is grouped into classes: young people from fourteen to seventeen years are classified in a single category, thus it is not possible to consider only young people from sixteen years, as done for the European context.

3. According to Eurostat, the "Internet user" is considered as the individual who claims to have used the Internet over the past twelve months.

4. The illustrative variables are the following: gender, age, professional status, education level, use of Internet, level of Internet activity.

5. λ is the ith factor eigenvalue, and p is the number of active variables.

6. The origin of the axes coincides with the average profile of the matrix; the distance of a modality from the origin is inversely proportional to its relative weight.

7. The variables "Familiar economic resources" and "Geographic location" were eliminated from the analysis because they were not statistically significant.

8. To select the number of clusters, different partitions were considered using the method of mobile centers to identify stable groupings. These groupings were the input for the hierarchical method (Ward algorithm). Inspection of the dendrogram produced by the hierarchical procedure, alongside an evaluation in substantial terms of the groups, identified four clusters. The package used to apply the cluster analysis was Spad 5.6.

REFERENCES

Ala-Mutka, Kirsti. (2011). "Mapping Digital Competence: Towards a Conceptual Understanding." Seville. ftp://ftp.jrc.es/pub/EURdoc/EURdoc/JRC67075_TN.pdf.

Bawden, David. (2001). "Information and Digital Literacies: A Review of Concepts." *Journal of Documentation* 57 (2): 218–259.

Bawden, David. (2008). "Origins and Concepts of Digital Literacy." In *Digital Literacies: Concepts, Policies and Practices,* edited by Colin Lankshear and Michele Knobel, 17–32. New York: Peter Lang.

Bentivegna, Sara. (2009). *Disuguaglianze Digitali. Le Nuove Forme Di Esclusione Nella Società Dell'informazione*. Rome and Bari: Laterza.

Benzecri, Jean-Paul. (1973). *L'analyse Des Données, Tome 2: l'Analyse Des Corrispondences*. Paris: Dunod.

Benzecri, Jean-Paul. (1979). "'Sur Le Calcul Des Taux D'inertie Dans L'analyse D'un Questionnaire Addendum et Erratum À [bin.mult.] [taux Quest.].'" *Cahiers de L'analyse Des Données* 4: 377–378.

Bouroche, Jean-Marie, and Gilbert Saporta. (1983). *L'analisi Dei Dati*. Naples: CLU.

Bracciale, Roberta. (2010). *Donne Nella Rete. Disuguaglianze Digitali Di Genere*. Milan: FrancoAngeli.

Bracciale, Roberta, and Isabella Mingo. (2009). "La E-Inclusion E Le Competenze Digitali: Il Contesto Europeo E Il Caso dell'Italia." In *Concetti E Quantità. Percorsi Di Statistica Sociale*, edited by Isabella Mingo, 179–214. Rome: Bonanno.

Bunz, Ulla, Carey Curry, and William Voon. (2007). "Perceived versus Actual Computer-Email-Web Fluency." *Computers in Human Behavior* 23 (5): 2321–2344.

De Haan, Jos. (2004). "A Multifaceted Dynamic Model of the Digital Divide." *IT and Society* 1 (7): 66–88.

DiMaggio, Paul, and Eszter Hargittai. (2001). "From the 'Digital Divide' to 'Digital Inequality': Studying Internet Use as Penetration Increases." Center for Arts and Cultural Policy Studies, Woodrow Wilson School, Princeton University. http://www.maximise-ict.co.uk/WP15_DiMaggioHargittai.pdf.

DiMaggio, Paul, Eszter Hargittai, Coral Celeste, and Steven Shafer. (2004). "Digital Inequality: From Unequal Access to Differential Use." In *Social Inequality*, edited by Kathryn M. Neckerman, 549–566. New York: Russell Sage Foundation.

Donat, Elisabeth, Roman Brandtweiner, and Johann Kerschbaum. (2009). "Attitudes and the Digital Divide: Attitude Measurement as Instrument to Predict Internet Usage." *Informing Science: The International Journal of an Emerging Transdiscipline* 12: 37–56. http://www.inform.nu/Articles/Vol12/ISJv12p037-056Donat229.pdf.

eEurope Advisory Group. (2005). "E-Inclusion: New Challenges and Policy Recommendations." http://www.umic.pt/images/stories/publicacoes/kaplan_report_einclusion_final_version.pdf.

Eshet-Alkalai, Yoram. (2004). "Digital Literacy: A Conceptual Framework for Survival Skills in the Digital Era." *Journal of Educational Multimedia and Hypermedia* 13 (1): 93–106.

European Commission. (2000). "Lisbon European Council 23–24.03.2000: Conclusions of the Presidency." http://www.europarl.europa.eu/summits/lis1_en.htm.

European Commission. (2007a). *E-Skills for the 21st Century: Fostering Competitiveness, Growth and Jobs*. COM(2007) 496 final.

European Commission. (2007b). *European i2010 Initiative on E-Inclusion. "To Be Part of the Information Society."* COM(2007) 694 final.

European Commission. (2007c). "Measuring Progress in E-Inclusion. Riga Dashboard." http://www.umic.pt/images/stories/publicacoes2/rigadashboard.pdf.

European Commission. (2008). "Digital Literacy Report: A Review for the i2010 eInclusion Initiative." http://www.ifap.ru/library/book386.pdf.

European Commission. (2010). *A Digital Agenda for Europe*. COM(2010)245 final.

Ferrari, Anusca. (2012). "Digital Competence in Practice : An Analysis of Frameworks." Seville. http://ftp.jrc.es/EURdoc/JRC68116.pdf.

Gilster, Paul. (1997). *Digital Literacy*. New York: Wiley.

Gui, Marco. (2013). "Indagine Sull'uso Dei Nuovi Media Tra Gli Studenti Delle Scuole Superiori Lombarde." Edited by Marco Gui. Regione Lombardia. http://www.formalavoro.regione.lombardia.it/shared/ccurl/733/622/REPORT_Indagine_Bicocca.pdf.

Gui, Marco, and Gianluca Argentin. (2011). "Digital Skills of Internet Natives: Different Forms of Digital Literacy in a Random Sample of Northern Italian High School Students." *New Media and Society* 13 (6): 963–980.

Guttman, Louis. (1950). "The Problem of Attitude and Opinion Measurement." In *Measurement and Prediction (Studies in Social Psychology in World War II)*, edited by Samuel A. Stouffer, Louis Guttman, Edward A. Suchman, Paul F. Lazarsfeld, Shirley A. Star, and John A. Clausen, 60–90. Princeton: Princeton University Press.

Haddon, Leslie. (2004). *Information and Communication Technologies in Everyday Life: A Concise Introduction and Research Guide*. Oxford: Berg.

Harambam, Jaron, Stef Aupers, and Dick Houtman. (2012). "The Contentious Gap. From Digital Divide to Cultural Beliefs about Online Interactions." *Information, Communication and Society*: 1–22. doi:10.1080/1369118X.2012.687006.

Hargittai, Eszter. (2002). "Second-Level Digital Divide: Differences in People's Online Skills." *First Monday* 7 (4): 1–17. http://firstmonday.org/htbin/cgi-wrap/bin/ojs/index.php/fm/article/viewArticle/942.

Hargittai, Eszter. (2003). "The Digital Divide and What to Do about It." In *New Economy Handbook*, edited by Derek C. Jones, 821–841. San Diego, CA: Academic Press.

Hargittai, Eszter. (2005). "Survey Measures of Web-Oriented Digital Literacy." *Social Science Computer Review* 23 (3): 371–379.

Hargittai, Eszter. (2007). "A Framework for Studying Differences in People's Digital Media Uses." In *Cyberworld Unlimited*, edited by Nadia Kutsher and Otto Hans-Uwe, 121–137. Wiesbaden: Fachverlage.

Hargittai, Eszter. (2008). "The Digital Reproduction of Inequality." In *Social Stratification*, edited by David Grusky, 936–944. Boulder, CO: Westview Press.

Hargittai, Eszter, and Amanda Hinnant. (2008). "Digital Inequality: Differences in Young Adults' Use of the Internet." *Communication Research* 35 (5): 602–621.

Hargittai, Eszter, and Yuli Patrick Hsieh. (2013). "Digital Inequality." In *Oxford Handbook for Internet Research*, edited by William H. Dutton, 129–150. Oxford: Oxford University Press.

Hargittai, Eszter, and Steven Shafer. (2006). "Differences in Actual and Perceived Online Skills: The Role of Gender." *Social Science Quarterly* 87 (2): 432–448.

Helsper, Ellen Johanna. (2012). "A Corresponding Fields Model for the Links Between Social and Digital Exclusion." *Communication Theory* 22 (4): 403–426.

Helsper, Ellen, and Rebecca Eynon. (2013). "Distinct Skill Pathways to Digital Engagement." *European Journal of Communication* 28 (6): 696–713.

Hosmer, David W., and Stanley Lemeshow. (1989). *Applied Logistic Regression*. New York: Wiley and Sons.

Hunsinger, Jeremy, Lisbeth Klastrup, and Mattew Allen, ed. (2010). *International Handbook of Internet Research*. London and New York: Springer.

Lebart, Ludovic, Alain Morineau, and Marie Piron. (1995). *Statistique Exploratoire Multidimensionnelle*. Paris: Dunod.

Liff, Sonia, and Adrian Shepherd. (2004). "An Evolving Gender Digital Divide?" *OII, Oxford Internet Institute* (2): 1–17. doi:10.2139/ssrn.1308492. http://www.ssrn.com/abstract=1308492.

Merton, Robert K. (1973). *The Sociology of Science: Theoretical and Empirical Investigation*. Chicago: University of Chicago Press.

Mingo, Isabella. (2005). "Tra Inclusi Ed Esclusi: Gli Italiani Nella E-Society." In *E-Society. Strumenti E Percorsi Di Analisi Della Società in Rete*, edited by Patrizio Di Nicola and Isabella Mingo, 215–240. Milan: Guerini e Associati.

Mossberger, Karen, Caroline Tolbert, and Mary Stansbury. (2003). *Virtual Inequality*. Washington, DC: Georgetown University Press.

Norris, Pippa. (2001). *Digital Divide: Civic Engagement, Information Poverty, and the Internet Worldwide*. Cambridge, MA: Cambridge University Press.

Servaes, J. (ed.). (2014). *Technological Determinism and Social Change. Communication in a Tech-Mad World*. Lanham, MD: Lexington Books.

Sieverding, Monika, and Sabine C. Koch. (2009). "(Self-)Evaluation of Computer Competence: How Gender Matters." *Computers and Education* 52 (3): 696–701.

Van Deursen, Alexander J.A.M., Ellen Helsper, and Rebecca Eynon. (2014). "Measuring Digital Skills. From Digital Skills to Tangible Outcomes Project Report." www.oii.ox.ac.uk/research/projects/?id=112.

Van Deursen, Alexander J.A.M., and Jan A.G.M. van Dijk. (2008). "Measuring Digital Skills. Performance Tests of Operational, Formal, Information and Strategic Internet Skills among Duth Popolation." Paper presented at the Conference of the International Communication Association, ICA, Montreal, Canada, May 22–26 2008. http://www.utwente.nl/gw/mco/bestanden/ICA2008.pdf, 1–25.

Van Deursen, Alexander J.A.M., and Jan A.G.M. van Dijk. (2009a). "Improving Digital Skills for the Use of Online Public Information and Services." *Government Information Quarterly* 26 (2): 333–340.

Van Deursen, Alexander J.A.M., and Jan A.G.M. van Dijk. (2009b). "Using the Internet: Skill Related Problems in Users' Online Behavior." *Interacting with Computers* 21 (5–6): 393–402.

Van Deursen, Alexander J.A.M., and Jan A.G.M. van Dijk. (2010). "Measuring Internet Skills." *International Journal of Human-Computer Interaction* 26 (10): 891–916.

Van Deursen, Alexander J.A.M., and Jan A.G.M. van Dijk. (2013). "The Digital Divide Shifts to Differences in Usage." *New Media and Society* 16: 507–526.

Van Deursen, Alexander J.A.M., Jan A.G.M. van Dijk, and Oscar Peters. (2011). "Rethinking Internet Skills: The Contribution of Gender, Age, Education, Internet Experience, and Hours Online to Medium- and Content-Related Internet Skills." *Poetics* 39 (2): 125–144.

Van Deursen, Alexander J.A.M., Jan A.G.M. van Dijk, and Oscar Peters. (2012). "Proposing a Survey Instrument for Measuring Operational, Formal, Information, and Strategic Internet Skills." *International Journal of Human-Computer Interaction* 28 (12): 827–837.

Van Dijk, Jan A.G.M. (1999). *The Network Society. An Introduction to the Social Aspects of New Media*. London: Sage.

Van Dijk, Jan A.G.M. (2005). *The Deepening Divide: Inequality in the Information Society*. Thousand Oaks: Sage.

Van Dijk, Jan A.G.M. (2006). "Digital Divide Research, Achievements and Shortcomings." *Poetics* 34 (4–5): 221–235.

Van Dijk, Jan A.G.M. (2009). "One Europe, Digitally Divided." In *Routledge Handbook of Internet Politics*, edited by Andrew Chadwick and Philip N. Howard, 288–304. London and New York: Routledge.

Van Dijk, Jan A.G.M., and Alexander J.A.M. van Deursen. (2014). *Digital Skills. Unlocking the Information Society*. New York: Palgrave Macmillan.

Warschauer, Mark. (2002). "Reconceptualizing the Digital Divide." *First Monday* 7 (7): 1–14. http://firstmonday.org/htbin/cgiwrap/bin/ojs/index.php/fm/article/viewArticle/967.

Zillien, Nicole, and Eszter Hargittai. (2009). "Digital Distinction: Status-Specific Types of Internet Usage." *Social Science Quarterly* 90 (2): 274–291.

6

Breaching the Divide

"Hole in the Wall" Computer Kiosks for Education and Development in Urban Bangladesh

Gyuri Kepes

Obstacles to obtain a standard education, including financial constraints, child labor, lack of access to government services, and high dropout rates continue to drive low literacy rates among Bangladesh's hard-core poor (Hosen, Khandoker and Islam 2010; Jalil and Islam 2010). However, recent governmental and non-governmental initiatives have shown that information and communication technologies (ICTs) can effectively deliver educational content that is affordable, accessible, and stimulating for disadvantaged Bangladeshi children. Through extensive fieldwork in an economically disadvantaged district of Dhaka, Bangladesh, this study has gathered a range of perspectives on the impact of underprivileged children's uses of "Hole in the Wall" computer kiosks. Interview data and on-site observations revealed connections between Hole in the Wall learning activities and children's level of interaction and participation, empowerment, creativity, and curiosity, which have increasingly been recognized as key factors in human development and education (Sen 1999; Servaes 1999; Servaes, White, and Jacobson 1996). In thinking beyond inequalities in access (between the "haves" and "have-nots") this study gives greater recognition to *socio-psychological components* of the digital divide (i.e., between the participation and non-participation). Bringing together multiple theoretical traditions from sociology, psychology, education and development studies, such as critical pedagogy, the multiplicity paradigm, and the capabilities approach, this study takes an interdisciplinary approach to understanding the multifarious causes of inequality—and through inquiry into the impacts of Hole in the Wall computer kiosks proposes that participation and empowerment be given greater recognition as indicators of education and development.

HOLE IN THE WALL:
PARTICIPATORY LEARNING FOR EMPOWERMENT

With increasing integration of ICTs into everyday life, digital literacy has become an essential requirement for social and economic inclusion. Yet, the digital divide both between and within nations in terms of ability to access and use ICTs persists—with those unable to use ICTs to their advantage in danger of being deprived of essential twenty-first century skills. Without the ability to access the wealth of information and communication resources available on the Web, digitally excluded communities in both the developed and the developing world risk being pushed further into the margins. As educated and trained professionals in developing economies such as India, reap the economic benefits of the information revolution, digitally illiterate populations are left behind. As IIT Delhi researchers Jha and Chatterjee (2005: 2) point out: "India's emergence as a superpower in Information Technology (IT) has also led to an increase in inequalities in digital literacy within the country. While IT has improved the quality of life of the digitally literate population, it is still beyond the reach of the underprivileged."

Despite this trend in places like India, a variety of innovative ICT-based educational projects have been implemented through non-profit and government initiatives to enhance not only digital literacy, but also increase access in general. One of the most efficient ways of providing ICT access to economically disadvantaged and isolated regions is through community sharing-of-computer programs. One of the first computer-sharing programs designed to extend computer access to poor and isolated communities was implemented in the 1980's in Sweden. Physical centers equipped with computers, or so-called telecottages were set up to provide education and technology services to remote communities (Qvortrup 1991).

Since the "telecottages" of the 1980s, community computer-sharing programs have been developed across the world. Through these sharing programs an array of services are made available to a large number of users, with little or no cost to the user. This model presents one of the most promising approaches to closing the gap between the 'information rich' and the 'information poor,' and supporting social development and poverty alleviation among marginalized groups (Qvortrup 1991).

It is not surprising then that computer sharing programs have been expanding rapidly in the developing world. Some examples include the "telecenters" in Peru, village information centers in India (Larson and Murray 2006), and GrameenPhone community information centers in Bangladesh (Sein, Ahmad, and Harindranath 2008). In collaboration with UNDP's Access to Information (A2I) Programme, the Bangladeshi Government has established 4,500 Union Information Service Centers (UISC) across the country, which are small entrepreneurial run computer centers that provide services such as Internet access, email, printing, scanning, etc. for a small cost. UISCs give approximately three million rural Bangladeshis access to important e-services, and help save time and money by reducing the need to travel long distances to access information or services. At the same time, UICSs provide sustainable income to self-employed operators (UNDP 2011b). According to 2011 UNDP statistics 9,002 people were self-employed as UISC operators, jointly generating 150,000 US dollars a month in revenue (UNDP 2011a). This computer-sharing program has the potential to narrow the divide between those who have access to computers and those who do not and at the same time promote sustainable economic and human development by providing access to important social, governmental, and commercial services via ICTs.

Yet, one of the most innovative approaches to community level sharing of computers has come under the leadership and direction of the Indian scientist and professor, Sugata Mitra. In 1999, Sugata Mitra, carried out a unique and innovative social experiment. He placed a computer on the exterior wall that abutted a large slum in New Delhi, India and observed as children began to play with the computers that were embedded into the wall. After detailed analysis of activity on the computers (now referred to as "hole in the wall" computers), Mitra found that children with no previous computer experience were able to acquire basic computer skills without adult intervention, in a matter of a few days (Mitra et al. 2005). The absence of adult supervision and guidance in the pedagogical process led Mitra to call this method Minimally Invasive Education (MIE). Mitra et al. (2005: 2) have defined MIE as "a pedagogic method that uses the learning environment to generate an adequate level of motivation to induce learning in children." In the "hole in the wall" (HITW) experiment it was collaborative interaction with the computers, which generated the curiosity and motivation in groups of children to acquire knowledge. This innovative, participatory approach to pedagogy allows education to become a fun, collaborative process, which can be complimentary to education in more structured environments (Pratapchandran 2009).

Most early investigations of HITW focused on *what* children could learn without adult supervision. However, in recent studies increasing importance has been placed on understanding *how* children acquire knowledge of complex concepts without the intervention of adults (Dangwal and Kapur 2008). In one study, HITW researchers observed that knowledge was shared among children through the transfer of new ideas and information across informal social networks. The participatory, collaborative, and self-directed approach to learning facilitated the horizontal diffusion of ideas and innovation to the groups of children, without any expert guidance—a process which has been referred to as, "playground kiosk democracy" (Aurora 2010: 698). According to Jha and Chatterjee (2005: 2), children with access to HITW kiosks "acquired collaborative behavior by learning how to work together, by forming their own learning groups and by transferring knowledge from one child to another, from one group to another group and from present users to new ones." Jha and Chatterjee (2005) have also noted that frequent users of HITW computer kiosks played key roles in facilitating the transmission of knowledge and information to new and infrequent users. In other studies, children have also been observed forming informal learning networks organized around exploring and sharing computer-based knowledge (Dangwal and Kapur 2008) and forming impromptu classes to teach one another (Mitra and Rana 2001). HITW researchers Ritu Dangwal and Preeti Kapur (2008: 347) have noted that, "Gradually a fluid and flexible group emerges that operates on the computer learns through any one or combination thereof – through the methods of trial and error, exploration, incidental learning, observation or seeking computer information knowledge from others." Dangwal and Kapur also found that children formed ad hoc social networks, and were self-motivated to learn information and skills from more knowledgeable participants. Through this social arrangement children acted simultaneously as teachers and students. Dangwal and Kapur (2008: 347) discovered that, "Each child learns from the others, whether a friend, brother, sister or even a stranger, and also tutors and guides these very same others." It was also noted that these dialogical relationships allowed information to filter "in all directions from one child to the other" creating a "snowballing effect," which multiplies the number of children that the information reached (Dangwal and Kapur 2008: 347).

Dangwal and Kapur's (2008) findings were partly based on diaries completed by children using the HITW computers, which give a first-hand account of the cooperative learning process that occurs. The following account written by an eleven-year-old boy illustrates how learning occurs in the informal social networks.

I like to work with Malaiah, Nagarathana and Avinash. We share our time with each other and while one of us works the others watch. I play many games like: shoe matching, skeleton game, electricity connecting game, and I have also done painting and saved it. I opened newspaper and music of Kannada film; this comes from opening the Internet. I taught the skeleton game to Nagarathana, which I learnt it from Naveen. From Prashanth, I learnt to open Internet. While, Avinash learnt painting from me. (Dangwaal and Kapur 2008: 345)

This account shows how the boy simultaneously acted as a learner and a teacher. It also illustrates how learning a process of collaborative construction and scaffolding of collective knowledge, rather than linear instruction.

Based on the promise that children can achieve learning through peer collaboration and dialogue, HITW can also be analyzed from Paolo Freire's critical pedagogical perspective. In his 1970 manifesto, *Pedagogy of the Oppressed*, Freire advocated for a system of schooling that emphasized the use of dialogic communication, participation, and action to promote conscious empowerment. Freire has suggested that replacing linear, top-down education models for more dialogical and transactional pedagogy can liberate marginalized peoples from the fetters of the traditional education system.

The underlying principle of HITW is that disenfranchised children take ownership of their own learning through individual and collaborative exploration, in the absence of a teacher. Similarly Freire has proposed unorthodox student-centered approach to education, including informal peer-collaborative learning, self-organized learning, and networked learning as alternatives to the traditional institutionalized learning. These alternatives are presented as means for liberating disenfranchised peoples from the oppressive structures of institutionalized learning. In the same way, HITW is presented as tool for increasing opportunities for underprivileged children that can encourage exploration, creation, collaboration, and at the same time bridge the digital divide (Arora 2010). As HITW researcher Arora (2010: 689) has pointed out:

The concept of free learning is not simply concerned with liberation from long-standing inequitable access to education. It entails the transformative capacity of learning that is more dialogic and less didactic (Freire, 1998). It disregards hierarchies and formal structures and promotes the alluring proposition that learning can take place anywhere and with anyone. It does not take much stretch of the imagination to draw linkages between such advocacies and the HiWEL experiment in trying to provide education without dependency upon the teacher and the school.

Dialogic communication requires community participation, and community participation is deeply connected to power and how it is distributed in society (Servaes 1999). According to Servaes (1999: 76), "Participation involves the more equitable sharing of both political and economic power, which often decreases the advantage of groups in power." Servaes has advanced a new paradigm of research and knowledge that gives greater recognition to the role of community participation and dialogic communication, often referred to as the Multiplicity Paradigm or the Participatory Approach (Servaes 1989). According to Servaes (1999: 88), "It stresses the importance of cultural identity of local communities, and the democratization and participation at all levels—international, national, local, an individual. It points to the strategy that is not merely inclusive of, but emanates from the traditional 'receivers.'"

Thus, the participatory approach does not view development communication in terms of a one-way transmission between an active sender and a passive receiver, or in terms of the subjective Western values of progress and modernization. Instead, the participatory approach can be thought of as a networked, omnidirectional, transactional, emancipatory process, whereby ground-level collaboration, community, and dialogue are facilitated.

The participatory approach also has strong connections to educational theory and praxis, as it is highly influenced by Paolo Freire's work on critical pedagogy, which challenges the traditional didactical relationship based in linear, top-down transfers of knowledge from teacher to student. In terms of knowledge production, Freire advocated for praxis oriented, horizontal, dialogical pedagogy that fosters critical interrogation of oppression and inequality. From Freire's perspective, the empowerment and liberation of marginalized peoples starts with transforming traditional educational institutions characterized by strict hierarchy between teacher and student. Through the multiplicity paradigm, the principles of horizontal communication and dialogue proposed by Freire are extended to a development context (Huesca 2008).

Servaes (1999), like Freire, sees empowerment as a process that is linked to participation. For Servaes (1999) social inequalities cannot be reduced without local grass-roots actors being involved and participating in decision-making practices—empowerment occurs through democratized, participatory structure of communication, restricting dependency on outside development resources and interests, and moving towards economic and social self-reliance. However, White (2004) questions whether empowerment is really the answer. According to White (2004: 21) "The concept of empowerment as it has been developed, so far, is, at best incomplete and possibly dangerous if not oriented towards the service of society." The danger for White (2004) is that empowerment can lead to the amplification of "one set of interests to the exclusion of other groups," thereby exacerbating inequalities. White (2004) proposes locating empowerment within a broader framework of human rights, which would move discussions beyond 'subjective' well-being, and towards a legally binding definition. Recent empirical studies, however, have shown that empowerment and freedom are associated with individual welfare and well-being. Amartya Sen's (1985) capability approach, for example, employs multidimensional measures to link individual welfare to the quality of life people are capable of achieving if they empowered to do so. In his articulation of well-being, Sen differentiates between "functionings," which represent various states of being or doing, and "capabilities" or one's ability, currently or in the future, to navigate various combinations of functionings to achieve a desired quality of life. One's capability, from this perspective is dependent upon freedom to choose from available functionings, or a "process of expanding the real freedoms that people enjoy" (Sen 1999: 2).

To use an ICT example, functionings may represent using or placing value on a computer (rather than material access to the computer alone), while capability might refer to the freedom to employ various combinations of digital literacies to achieve a preferred lifestyle. More narrowly, applying Sen's capability approach to HITW might not help to guide understandings of how and why children use the public computer kiosks (functionings), but also how new possibilities are formed through the development of ICT related skills and literacies (capabilities). In order to survey the functionings of HITW it is important to understand who uses the computer kiosks and how the user participates in the learning process, and to what effect.

The present study therefore first asks:

RQ1: Who uses the computer kiosks and for what functions?

Together with the multiplicity paradigm, the capabilities approach provides a dynamic, multidimensional framework for understanding how humans can participate in their own development and social well-being. Freire (1970), Sen (1999), and Serveas (1999) all offer explanations for how participation can lead to empowerment and freedom. When their contributions are considered in relation, we can begin to better understand how potentials or capabilities are created when people participate in their own development and education. Given the grass-roots, collaborative nature of HITW learning activities, it is important to consider how participation can empower users to consider new potentialities and capabilities beyond their current circumstances. This study therefore asks:

RQ2A: How do users participate in their own education and learning?

RQ2B: Can participation empower users to consider new potentialities and capabilities beyond their current circumstances?

METHODOLOGY

The current study examines a replication of the HITW model in Dhaka, Bangladesh. This HITW project has been implemented by a small youth-run non-profit organization that promotes poverty reduction through education. Although not an official undertaking of HITW founder Sugata Mitra, this project has deliberately replicated the innovative model popularized by Mitra. Like the HITW computers kiosks found in India, the ones examined in this study have been set into an exterior wall of a school that neighbors several sprawling slums in Dhaka, Bangladesh, home to approximately 200,000 inhabitants. The computers are equipped with Broadband Internet, mouse, keyboard, and processor, are available from 9:00 AM to 6:30 PM and are located outside of the main gate of a school, along a busy walkway. The children typically come from families that earn less than two dollars a day and are often deprived of a standard education.

Research for this project was carried out using the case study method (Yin 1994). Case studies have long been used in the social sciences as a method of inquiry that provides rich description, explanation and exploration of complex social phenomenon. Case study research involves detailed analysis of the beliefs, values, and practices of an organization, project, or group of people based on observation, direct interaction, or participation (Gillham 2000). According to Gillham (2000: 1), case studies can be used to examine the following;

- a unit of activity embedded in the real world;
- which can only be understood in context;
- which exists in the here and now;
- that merges in with its context so that precise boundaries are difficult to draw.

The case study method highlights the importance of cultural specificity, and thus involves the examination of the subject in relation to its context or setting. This means that the researcher can gain a better sense of contextuality by immersing his or her self in the social milieu of the specific case being studied (Gillham 2000).

Qualitative forms of inquiry are most commonly associated with the case study method. While quantitative approaches are useful in measuring efficacy and comparing results from different samples, statistical evidence can be inadequate in capturing the nuances and specificities of the human experience within a social context. Qualitative methods, specifically interviews and focus groups allow people to collectively and individually define problems and identify possible solutions to them (Gillham 2000).

With the central purpose of this study being the exploration of local perspectives and experiences, interviews were thus chosen as the most appropriate method of inquiry. Through extensive dialogues with teachers, administrators, and guardians, local perspectives and knowledge were illuminated and highlighted. From the dialogical process, important information was revealed about how HITW was being used by disadvantaged urban Bangladeshi children, and to what effect.

This study also employed covert observational techniques—meaning that the researcher observed subjects from a distance. This method was chosen so that the presence of the researcher did not influence the behavior of the subjects. This approach was used to observe children using the HITW computer kiosks, and served as a reference for which claims made through interview reports and previous research could be measured against.

This study is exploratory in nature—going beyond descriptive analysis of the context, to attempt to look at how, when, and why certain phenomena occur. Although results may not be generalizable for a larger context or population, this study provides rich heuristic analysis located within a specific context.

The research is also informed by epistemological framework of the participatory approach, and operates from a *participatory research* (PR) perspective (Servaes and Arnst 1999). Kemmis and McTaggart (2005: 337) identify three characteristics of participatory research that differentiate it from conventional forms of inquiry. They include: (1) "shared ownership of research projects," (2) "community-based analysis of social problems," and (3) "an orientation towards community action." Rather than serve the interests of the powerful and the elite, this approach is highlighted by a "commitment to social, economic and political development responsive to the needs and opinions of ordinary people" (Kemmis and McTaggart 2003: 337). During the course of the study at hand, the principles of participatory research were applied and every effort was made to put them into practice. Through this research, ordinary people were given the chance to collectively define, and evaluate the issues that impact them, delineate the causes, and identify and analyze possible solutions. The involvement of the community in dialogues allowed for shared assessment of the problems and opportunities encountered, and at the same time allowed the community to self-determine the best possible solutions.

In the present study, cultural differences and the "outsider" positionality of the researcher were the most challenging obstacles. As an "outsider" it was recognized that it was imperative to gain acceptance, trust and respect of the group, and equally important, strive to understand and appreciate the intricate and complex system of values of a heterogeneous culture. Although this process posed an enormous challenge, it also provided opportunities for learning and reflection, on the part of both the researcher and the community. As Servaes and Arnst (1999: 124) point out:

> Interaction fosters a pedagogical environment for all participants. The researcher, as a newcomer, contributes in that he or she requires the membership to give account of how things are done, which fosters an atmosphere where participants may better know themselves, question themselves, and consciously reflect on the reality of their lives and their sociocultural milieu. Through such interaction, a fresh understanding, new knowledge, and self-confidence may be gained. Furthermore, awareness confidence, and cohesiveness are enhanced not only for group members, but also among and between those members and outsiders who may participate, thereby increasing their understanding of the context and obstacles under which people strive.

Therefore, rather than thinking of the insider-outsider relationship as an impediment to honest and open communication, the dialogical process that occurs can be seen as an opportunity for mutual self-discovery (Servaes and Arnst 1999).

Participants

A total of thirteen participants were interviewed for this project. In-depth interviews regarding the HITW experiment and the online school were conducted at a small elementary school in a socioeconomically disadvantaged section of Dhaka City. Participants included the founder and director of the school, a communication officer, two online teachers, one face-to-face Instructor, and one community liaison. In addition, four guardians of children that regularly use the HITW computer kiosks were interviewed in their homes. Over a period of one week, numerous children from the community were also observed first-hand using the HITW computer kiosks.

Procedure

Participants were recruited non-randomly, and selection was based on organizational affiliation with programs that have integrated ICTs in their educational approach. Administrators and Teachers at a small school in the Rayer Bazaar district of Dhaka were selected for interviews, as they have the most direct knowledge of how children in the community use HITW learning stations. Through snowball sampling the researcher was directed to additional participants including a Community Officer and guardians of children that regularly use HITW computer kiosks. In addition, the researcher was introduced to an employee of a prominent NGO, who directed the researcher to four guardians of children that regularly use the HITW computer kiosks. By interviewing Teachers, Administrators, a Community Officer, guardians, and an NGO worker, multiple perspectives were accessed—allowing for the comparison of data from different sources. Through this process the accounts of stakeholder groups with substantial investment in positive program outcomes could be measured for consistency against perspectives of non-organizational stakeholders.

Participants in the study had the choice of conducting the interview in either English or Bengali, the national language of Bangladesh. Eight of the thirteen participants chose to conduct the interviews in English. For the remaining five participants, interviews were conducted in Bengali. For these interviews, questions and answers were interpreted through a Bangladeshi translator fluent in both English and Bengali. All interviews were open-ended and semi-structured. In addition, detailed observations about the physical settings, and human interactions, and behaviors of children using the "hole in the wall" learning stations were also made.

RESULTS

RQ1 asked: *Who uses the computer kiosks, and for what purpose?* From personal observation it was found that the HITW kiosks were well utilized by children from the community. The computers were almost constantly being operated, while groups of about six or seven children looked on. According to one participant approximately fifty children use the computers per day, but there are leaders who come and occupy it for one hour or more. As groups often congregate to observe peer-leaders, the impact extends beyond just the children that use the computers. Over the course of a normal day, hundreds of children from the community had some type of exposure to the computers, either through direct interface or through peer observation.

It was also found that the kiosks are used for a variety of purposes. According to one administrator, about 50 percent of the children use the technology for paint, about 25 percent use it for interactive spelling and reading games, about 15 percent use it for Internet, and the rest, about 10 percent, do not know what to do. The easy accessibility of multiple computer applications translates into high operational capacity. However, given the size of the community, and the high degree of need, introducing more kiosks could be a step towards further capacity building.

Through interviews with respondents, it was revealed that through the use of HITW computer kiosks the children were able to acquire multiple literacies, including important competencies in computer operation and English language. The program director explained:

> Right now there's two things that can make a difference in a person's life. One is communication skills, which is basically right now in English in Bangladesh. Because a lot of people don't know English. Even an office assistant need to know English because when there's a letter, the person needs to know which table the letter has to go to. That's one thing, English, they're learning it, and second is if you know how to operate a computer that definitely a plus point. And here they are learning it from a very small age, and not only in the job market, they can actually find jobs here.

Through interviews and observations it was established that children could identify the basic components of the computer. On a number of occasions children were observed turning on the computer, opening a program, using the mouse, as well as opening and closing files. The children proved to be particularly adept at web browsing. Not only were children connecting to the World Wide Web, they were also successfully searching the web by using the Google search engine and using complex software such as Skype and Google Earth. Over course of the observation period, the children were seen going to specific URLs—most often game sites.

The following anecdote given by the director gives indication of the speed at which the children were able to acquire basic computer skills.

> On the seventh day [after implementing HITW], I was coming inside, you saw the two computers outside the door. I was going inside the door, and one boy was talking and said in Bangla, "sir can I have your phone number" I said why do you need my phone number?" and he's like, "I'm trying to download a game and it requires an email address, which I don't have, so I guess I can give your phone number and email." So I looked into it, I said, "How did you go there," because we didn't even tell them there was Internet, but we set it up. So he said "Sir, on the television I saw that thing's in *Googli.*" He can't even pronounce Google . . . *"Googli."* There is a lot of Indian television and there are a lot of ads about Google. So he found out that things can be found on Google. He came here, he opened the browser, he typed "Google," he typed "fast car games" and then he started downloading NFS-Need for Speed. But it wouldn't allow him to download because there was an email address required for the confirmation. So these are the stories that basically make us go "okay, it's interesting,"

Here, after one week of having access to computers the child had learned how to open the Internet, use English search terms to browse, and download games.

The children also taught themselves how to use Skype without any direction from adults, and were able to make calls to people outside of Bangladesh. As the director explained:

> We installed Skype, which we also deleted because when we installed Skype, so we were testing it with this computer, they learned how to use it. We wanted to show them that there is something like that, and we gave advertisement in Facebook, saying you can talk to our kids you can add them. A lot of people added them. They started calling everyone, so we literally had to stop it, because people would get annoyed. But see the interest they are getting. They talking "hi, hello," you can see what's going on.

This shows that if children are given communication technology they will quickly learn how to use it. The fact that the children were able to independently learn how to use Skype is particularly intriguing since it allows children from an economically disadvantaged community to connect to a much wider world. But perhaps even more impressive was the children's ability to learn how to use Google Earth. As the Director stated:

> Last interesting story was two or three weeks ago. What we do is basically at night we install things, make an icon on the desktop and we vanish. We don't want to tell them. Let them explore. So we installed Google Earth and they tracked themselves here [at the school]. So these are the small stories you can see.

RQ2A asks: *How do users participate in their own education and learning?* Through personal observation and interviews it was revealed that participation and collaboration were very much of the learning process, with HITW computers playing an important role in how children engaged with their community and how they envisaged their futures. It was observed that children were not only actively participating in their own learning but were also motivated to participate in the learning of others. Children for example were observed picking up new skills and ideas through direct interaction with the computers (self-learning), and at the same time learn through observing and imitating the behaviors of peers (peer-learning). As one respondent explained.

> What happens in the entire system, is self-learning is involved. They will do a mistake, they will learn. Another one is peer learning. For example the scenario is usually like this. There is one boy, controlling the mouse and the computer, there are four of his friends, who are giving him fifty percent right directions, do this, do that, there is ten to fifteen behind that group giving

complete wrong directions, but they are learning at the same time, because they are seeing what that boy is doing. See you don't have to keep a teacher, that friend. That one boy becomes a teacher, they become the leader, and that's how they learn.

This peer learning process was confirmed through direct observation. On one occasion, a small group of children was observed navigating the web. One child was controlling the mouse, while another child who seemed to be the leader of the group was giving oral instructions, and a third child was operating the keyboard. The "teacher" appeared to have a high social standing within the group based on his superior knowledge of English and computers. The "teacher" would read out English words on the screen, and instruct the child controlling the keyboard to type words in English in the web browser, and direct another child controlling to cursor to click on different links and tabs. Although the leader often gave his peers wrong instructions, learning was involved throughout the process, as the children were all collaboratively learning how to read, write, and speak in English. At the same time they were learning to browse the web. While the "teacher" may be giving wrong information or directions, everyone is seeing and learning from these mistakes. To illustrate, the "teacher" gave the boy controlling the keyboard the wrong spelling of a URL, and when the URL did not work, directed the other boy to click on the "bookmark this page" tab. After a series of unsuccessful trials the children were eventually able to find the web page that they were looking for. Through the collaborative construction of knowledge, learning becomes a participatory process that is distinct from the traditional, linear education model. These observations support previous research on HITW (Dangwal and Kapur 2008; Jha and Chatterjee 2005; Mitra and Rana 2001).

Interviews with a Community Officer and guardians of children indicated that information was not only being transferred from peer-to-peer, but also from child to parent. The community officer explained:

When the kids go and discuss what they learned with their parents, they realized they learned something new that will help them get a better job in the future, and they also get encouraged that this will help them get a better job. They think that it is better for them that they learn the computer from the school, because there is no such facility at home, so whatever they learn it should be from the school.

It was found that the knowledge and information gained from the computers connected to a wider global network, was transferred interpersonally through contact with parents, many of whom had never used or seen a computer before. The community officer who works closely with both children and adults in the community noted:

What the kids learn in the hole in the wall, they discuss with their parents, and some of the parents are changed by this discussion. Then the parents realize the child has learned something from the computers, and they discuss this with their parents, the parents change their way of thinking. The first batch of students, that are little more developed, now know how to email, and how to get connected with the outside world from this computer. When they go home and share this thing with their parents, their parents get so happy, that wonderful thing they have learned.

This demonstrates how knowledge is distributed through connections with multiple nodes and networks. As the children are able to traverse multiple networks; one being a vast knowledge network of the Internet, and the other being friends and family from the local community, they become important agents through which information travels from network to network and node to node. In the process of connecting to the World Wide Web, and sharing the information acquired through this connection the children bring themselves and others into the so-called information society.

This can be thought of not only in terms of community participation and collaboration, but also empowerment, which relates to RQ2B (*Can participation empower users to consider new potentialities and capabilities beyond their current circumstances?*). By participating in their own learning and in the learning of others the children are empowered to share knowledge, and at the same time gain skills that allow them to participate in the wider global economy. Besides acting as a delivery tool for general educational material, HITW also provides direct access to important employment information. The ability to connect to the outside world, brings with it many opportunities, which includes the possibility of finding jobs and tapping into the knowledge-based economy. A community officer that works directly with families of children that use the HITW kiosks also confirmed that there is a strong perception within the community that computer literacy will lead to a better job in the future. The community officer explained:

When the kids go and discuss what they learned with their parents, they realized they learned something new that will help them get a better job in the future, and they also get encouraged that this will help them get a better job. They think that it is better for them that they learn the computer from the school, because there is no such facility at home, so whatever they learn it should be from the school. The first batch of students, that are little more developed, now know how to email, and how to get connected with the outside world from this computer. When they go home and share this thing with their parents, their parents get so happy, that what wonderful thing they have learned [translation].

This perception was also shared by an educational coordinator:

> We are actually trying to install a lot of software, where they can learn English and everything, I thinks it's going to work out very well for the kids. I think they are going to learn something good from this, change their lives, I think it will because if you have those educational things or you know those kind of games, skillful games, they can use those skills at home as well. Whatever they hear from the computer, and you know tell those to their parents, so you know I think it's going to effect them in a very positive way.

The perception that computer skills lead to better opportunities in the future also extend to parents of children that regularly use the HITW kiosks. One mother expressed that the skills her son is learning from the computers will improve his future job prospects. She explained, "I am quite hopeful that the computer will bring a change in the lifestyle and help him get a good job in the future. I am very happy about it [translation]." Another mother who admitted that she had never seen a computer in her life also expressed optimism that the computers skills her son has learned will help improve his social position in the future. She commented, "I believe it will help him because the teacher does explain this aspect of computer learning, which is very necessary. I am very confident the kids will be doing something very big. I myself do not know how to operate a computer. I have not even seen a computer in my life [translation]." A third parent explained, "I believe that if the computers can give a basic training my kids will grow up in a good fashion and I hope that it will give them more and more support [translation]." These testimonials from parents confirm that HITW can provide an important impetus for self-empowerment, by expanding the children's and parents' hope for a better economic future.

Interviews also brought light onto the fact that HITW encouraged the children to "broaden horizons," change the state of mind associated with poverty, and to envision a better future for themselves According to a community officer, through their experience with computers the children's aspirations have changed from expecting to work in whatever profession their mother or father works in to wanting of becoming a doctor, engineer, or pilot. The community officer explained:

> When they first came to us, and we used to ask them about their future dreams, usually they used say they would follow their parent's profession, but now after knowing the computer they can think in a better way and their dreams are changing. So I think the foundation is playing a good role. Now if we ask the kids some will say, "I will become a doctor," some will say, "I will be an engineer." Then if we asked them how they will get the money to become a doctor they say they are learning English from the computer, and

will make money by doing a private tuition to teach others about how to run a computer. Even some kids previously use to say, "I will become a rickshaw puller," now they say, "I will become a pilot." They feel that their fathers had a tough time to teach them and give them an education so, "I will help them by becoming a pilot."

In addition, to the extent that HITW allows children to learn on their own without the need for teachers, which at times are not properly trained or qualified, public computer kiosks may prove to be a tool for empowering and liberating socioeconomically disenfranchised peoples to take their education into their own hands. As one participant pointed out:

> Even Sometimes you'll see that the teachers, they're teaching the wrong stuff. They're teaching kids you know wrong information they're giving them wrong guidance, stuff like that. Well, what the hole in the wall project would do is kind of overcome those things by encouraging children to learn on their own, right. So, one of the main aims is to push government bodies to take steps to implement this, in more rural communities where people don't have access to that. Also you'll notice that in our country the education system is really bookish, so the natural creativity, and you know the ideas that you wouldn't get they are often stifled, due to the system, and the hole in the wall project actually allows them to explore more with their own creativity, with their own ideas.

Therefore, by empowering young people through their own curiosity and creativity, by encouraging participatory and collaborative learning, and by increasing knowledge and skills that are essential for success in today's knowledge-based economy, such as digital literacy, and English proficiency, users can harness the power of HITW technology for generating new capabilities. These insights serve to bring greater recognition to not only direct observable skills acquired through computer use, but also the less tangible psychic effects.

DISCUSSION

Since the majority of the children living in urban slums often lack access to standard education, self-learning and peer-learning may represent viable option for improving education and human development. HITW thus has the potential to be part of dramatic shift in pedagogy in Bangladesh, from traditional rote learning to open collaboration and participation. This transformation involves moving from a deeply entrenched system, in which the learning process is monopolized by teachers to an educational arrangement in which students are actively involved and participating in their own learning. Through this rearrangement power, over the learning process that was once centralized is being dispersed amongst learners. As an educational model that encourages dialogue, interaction, community participation, and self-driven exploration of knowledge, HITW can open users to new forms of empowerment. At the same time interview data suggests that there were strong perceptions amongst community members that new combinations of skills related to English language acquisition and computer literacy would present users with needed opportunities in the future. Following Sen's (1985) capabilities approach, it could be suggested that the new opportunities imagined by children and adults, originated from the freedom to choose from a combination of newly available functionings, such as computer literacy and English language skills.

Interviews and observations also suggested that children from the community were motivated to learn not by a system of rewards set by authority figures, but by their own curiosity and interest in the technology. As a result learning, is structured not by teachers, but by the learners themselves through a process of self-organization. The fact that children were able to learn vital skills and perform complex computer-based tasks without any adult intervention raises important questions about the role of teachers and experts in the information society. If children can educate themselves in an informal learning environment, this may signal a decline in the preeminence of the role of the traditional teacher. As children do not possess the same cognitive processing faculty and critical thinking skills possessed by adults some would argue that young learners need to be taught how to process and evaluate messages. Sociologists and educationalists have long pointed to the necessary role adults play in cultivating critical problem solving and decision-making skills in children. Prominent social constructivist Lev Vygotsky proposed that children have a "zone of proximal development," or the difference between what a child can do without help and what a student can do with the help of an adult. According to Vygotsky's theory, there are some things children cannot do without the help of an adult—that are outside of the child's zone of proximal development—and there are other tasks that do not require any adult guidance. In this model, the role of adults in education is to help children achieve learning tasks that are within their zone of proximal development so that these tasks can be achieved independently in the future. From this perspective children using HITW computers will eventually reach a "ceiling" in terms out what they can learn on their own without the intervention of adults.

Although HITW can be seen as an example of what Freire had envisioned as emancipatory pedagogy, given its ability to support dialogic communication, community participation and collaboration, there was no evidence of it producing critical literacies. Critical literacy involves receivers conscientiously evaluating messages, and it is not clear that learning basic operation of computers and English language skills can be constituted as such. Therefore, more research is needed to explore how learning designers can improve the HITW experience to support critical conscious-raising pedagogy.

CONCLUSION

Despite recent contributions to development theory from scholars such as Servaes and Sen the bulk of mainstream western development literature has prescribed wholesale economic and social interventions for poverty and lack of education in the developing world, and concomitantly ICT-based poverty alleviation efforts are typically approached from the neoliberal market perspective that direct capital investment in technology, education, infrastructure, and so on. will promote development. These development interventions carry the tacit assumption that infrastructure, technological access, and skills will automatically stimulate economic growth, without considering the effect of psycho-social dimensions, such as participation, empowerment, and well-being. For example, most mainstream development surveys employ standardized modes of analysis, such as the *Human Development Index*, which measures the concrete dimensions of health, education, and living standards, based on life expectancy at birth, mean/expected years of schooling, and gross national income per capita to generate a ranking for each country (HDI 2011). While these dimensions are useful, perspectives collected in this study gave greater recognition to both participation and empowerment as important dimensions of education and development.

This study has gathered diverse perspectives on the role of HITW in education and development in the context of urban Bangladesh. Interviews and observations revealed that HITW can provide an interface that supports collaborative and participatory behaviors, and at the same time encourage self-empowerment, creativity, and curiosity for users. Though it is not possible to make correlative links between interaction, participation, and empowerment and established indicators of human and economic development, anecdotal evidence suggests that use of HITW played a large role in empowering children to envision better future opportunities, such as becoming a doctor, lawyer, or pilot. As ICTs proliferate in Bangladesh, there will be greater opportunities for children to supplement their own education through exploration of digital content. For the underprivileged, informal learning on shared computers can provide a path to empowerment through civic engagement and knowledge creation. However, more research is needed to further understand the relationship between psycho-social dimensions of development, like "empowerment" and "well-being" and actual material conditions.

REFERENCES

Arora, Payal. (2010). "Hope-in-the-Wall? A Digital Promise for Free Learning." *British Journal of Educational Technology* 41, no. 5, 689–702.

Dangwal, Ritu, and Preeti Kapur. (2008). "Children's Learning Processes Using Unsupervised." *Australasian Journal of Educational Technology* 24, no. 3, 339–354.

Dangwal, Ritu, Swati Jha, Shiffon Chatterjee, and Sugata Mitra (2005). "A Model of How Children Acquire Computing Skills from Hole-in-the-Wall Computers in Public Places." *Information Technologies and International Development* 2, no. 4, 41–60.

Freire, Paulo. (1970). *Pedagogy of the Oppressed*. 30th anniversary edition. New York: Continuum.

Gillham, Bill. (2000). *Case Study Research Methods*. London: Continuum.

Hamel, Yves. (2010). "ICT4D and the Human Development and Capability Approach: The Potentials of Information and Communication Technology." Human Development Research Paper.

HDI. (2014). "Human Development Index." May 1, 2010. http://hdr.undp.org/en/content/human-development-index-hdi.

Hosen, Md. Alouad, Mohammad Sogir Hossain Khandokar, and S.M. Mujahidul Islam. (2010). "Child Labor and Child Education in Bangladesh: Issues, Consequences and Involvements." *International Business Research* 3, no. 2, 1–8.

Huesca, Robert (2008). "Radio for Development." In *The International Encyclopedia of Communication*, vol. 9, 4085–4089. Malden, MA: Blackwell.

Islam, Md. Saidul, and M.A. Jalil. (2010). "Towards a Long Term Development Vision for Bangladesh: Some Socioeconomic and Legal Aspects." *Asian Culture and History* 2, no. 2: 58–70.

Jha, Swati, and Shiffon Chatterjee. (2005). "Public-Private Partnership in a Minimally Invasive Education Approach." *International Education Journal* 6, no. 5: 1443–1475.

Kemmis, Stephen, and Robert McTaggert. (2005). "Participatory Action Research: Communicative Action and the Public Sphere." In *The SAGE Handbook of Qualitative Research*. Third edition. London: Sage.

Mitra, Sugata, and Vivek Rana. (2001). "Children and the Internet: Experiments with Minimally Invasive Education in India." *British Journal of Educational Technology* 32, no. 2: 221–232.

Pratapchandan, Sarat. (2009). "Inspired by the Slum." *Educational Facility Planner* 43, no. 4: 1–2.

Qvortrup, Lars. (1991). "Community Teleservice Centres and the Future of Rural Society." *Community Development Journal* 26, no. 2, 124–130.

Sein, Muang K., Irtishad Ahmad, and G. Harindranath (2008). "Sustaining ICT for Development: The Case of Grameenphone CIC." *Telektronikk*, no. 2.

Sen, Amartya. (1985). *Commodities and Capabilities*. Amsterdam: Elsevier Science.

Sen, Amartya. (1999). *Development as Freedom*. New York: Knopf.

Servaes, Jan. (1996). *Participatory Communication for Social Change*. New Delhi: Sage.

Servaes, Jan. (1999). *Communication for Development: One World, Multiple Cultures*. Cresskill, NJ: Hampton Press.

Servaes, Jan, and Randy Arnst. (1999). "Principles of Participatory Communication Research: Its Strengths (!) and Weaknesses (?)." In *Theoretical Approaches to Participatory Communication*. New York: Hampton Press.

United Nations Development Programme (UNDP). (2011a). "Bangladesh: Access to Information (A2I) Evaluation." Prepared for United Nations Development Programme Bangladesh. erc.undp.org/evaluationadmin/downloaddocument.html?docid=5398.

United Nations Development Programme. (2011b). "The Millennium Development Goals: Bangladesh Progress Report." http://www.bd.undp.org/content/dam/bangladesh/docs/MDG/MDGs%20Bangladeh%20Progress%20Report_%20PDF_Final_September%202015.pdf.

Yin, Robert K. (1994). *Case Study Research: Design and Methods*. Second edition. Thousand Oaks, CA: Sage\.

III

WOMEN, EMPOWERMENT, AND THE MEDIA

7

✛

Hill Women's Voices and Community Communications about Climate Change

The Case of Henvalvani Community Radio in India

Aparna Moitra and Archna Kumar

Climate change is one of the gravest threats that the world is facing today, intimidating human freedoms and limiting choice. Occurring at a faster pace than it has in centuries, climate change with its potential to stall developmental efforts is capable of causing major human development reversals in the lifetime of humanity (UNDP 2007). According to scientists, melting of glaciers is among the first observable signs of human-induced global warming. Glacier melting is said to affect the global climate, raise sea levels, trigger regional flooding, threaten water availability, endanger lives and alter the habitats of many plant and animal species (Mastny 2000).

The Himalayan Glaciers are among the fastest retreating glaciers in the world. Expected to shrink by one-fifth in the next three decades they are predicted to cause massive economic and environmental problems in the Himalayan region and the whole of Northern India (Mastny 2000; Rai 2005). The Garhwal Himalayan region in India, known for its rich natural wealth, is particularly facing severe social and ecological stress due to rising population and increased exploitation of natural resources. Longitudinal studies conducted in the region indicate that in a span of twenty-five years, the region has seen a decrease in the intensity of rainfall, increase in the range of maximum temperature and decrease in the rate of snowfall (Singh 2010). Climatic changes and increased instances of natural calamities have led to reduced employment opportunities and a sharp reduction in agricultural incomes and livelihoods of people, resulting in high rates of male migration (Kollmair 2010), thus further intensifying the struggles and hardships of people residing in the region.

Societal vulnerability to the risks associated with climate change exacerbate ongoing social and economic challenges, particularly for marginalized societal groups who are most dependent on resources that are sensitive to changes in climate (Adger et al. 2003). Women are particularly affected by the combination of climatic and environmental stresses, as their economic and social roles intrinsically link them to natural resources and the environment. Environmental degradation deeply entangles women in a vicious spiral of poverty, high fertility, poor health, and limited opportunities. Degraded environments increase women's drudgery and the time they must spend to find water and fuel and produce food (UNFPA 2001), intensifying their struggle to balance their productive and reproductive roles and their quality of life.

Addressing the climate change challenge requires communities and stakeholder groups collaborating for both climate change mitigation (taking steps to reduce or avoid changes in the climate) and adaptation (adjusting to the climate as it changes by anticipating or responding to climate impacts) so that any threats to community wellbeing are reduced. Hence, community participation and social learning processes involving various levels of knowledge and different stakeholder groups is vital to successful adaptation and mitigation of climate change efforts (Acunzo and Protz 2010). Any solution to the environmental crisis must provide for a new consciousness and link together the subjugated knowledge of the oppressed and marginalized people, especially women and should respect and reflect their identities, specific struggles and position (Braidotti et al. 2004). However, women's specific needs and ideas for adaptation are less likely to be heard or acted upon as their voices largely remain marginalized in the environmental debate (Jennings and Magrath 2009).

WOMEN AND ENVIRONMENT

In the last two decades scholar activists from different schools of thought have recognized and underscored the need for mainstreaming women's voices in the global environmental debate. Further as the notion of sustainability has broadened, emphasizing the balancing of environmental, economic, political, social and cultural processes under a systemic, multidimensional view of development that incorporates intergenerational solidarity, social equity and long-term considerations as essential element, the need for center-staging women's voices has gained momentum worldwide. The interconnection between gender, environment, and sustainability is increasingly being recognized for realizing the goal of sustainability and women's voices have emerged as a potent force not only in support of adequate environmental management, but also in demanding better quality of life and greater social equity (Rico 1998).

Varying viewpoints and approaches about women and environment reiterate the intrinsic link between women, environment and development. Eco-feminism conceptualizes the relationship of women with nature, maintaining that there is a strong link between the two. According to Vandana Shiva (1989) women are naturally closer to nature because of their socio-biological roles and activities. Thus, the exploitation of women and environment are directly correlated as and both need to be seen as "victims" of development where harm to nature equals harm to women. Eco-feminism contends that control over nature and over women has been perpetuated historically (Shiva and Mies 1993). Due to the patriarchal structure and the perceptive dualism that subordinates nature to culture and the feminine to the masculine, women are socially perceived as being close to nature. As a result there are connections between the oppression that they experience and the exploitation of the natural system (Shiva 1989).

While highlighting women's vulnerability to environmental change due to their dependence on natural resources, the "women and environment" approach proponents the potential of women in the management of natural resources (Dankelman and Davidson 2013). They emphasize the need for development initiatives to support the contributions made by women for managing and preserving the environment in order to reduce their vulnerabilities (Collins 1991). Thus, women are perceived as "custodians of the environment," while at the same time they are regarded as the "most valuable resource, and the most neglected one" (Linggard and Moberg 1990). Women's involvement in environmental projects and programmes is emphasized as they are perceived as important "instruments" of environmental protection (Dankelman and Davidson 2013).

The "gender, environment and sustainable development" approach provides a more holistic understanding and reiterates that the gender structure in communities (the division of labour; access to productive resources and their benefits; participation in decision-making processes and access to public power) (Rico 1998) act as critical intermediates in the relations that women and men have with the environment. Thus, the vulnerabilities faced by women are a result of the inequalities in social relationships of production and power in respect of differential access to resources, specific cultural characteristics and gender identities. Environmental conservation and development would require addressing the inequalities women and other marginalized groups face.

CHALLENGES OF CLIMATE CHANGE ADAPTATIONS

Despite increased awareness and attention on the projected impacts of climate change, a range of barriers prevent communities from seeking the most logical and appropriate form of adaptation. However, dealing with the many barriers not only requires a comprehensive and dynamic approach covering a range of scales and issues but must also be based on a consensus among all stakeholders, policymakers, and scientists (Howden et al. 2007). Studies suggest that appropriate mechanisms need to be created that enable communication of scientific research in ways that is appropriate to specific needs of communities (Gauthier 2005), their socio cultural practices (Ensor and Berger 2009), prevailing knowledge systems and meaningfully engages existing local institutions (Agrawal and Perrin 2009). For communities to be able to negotiate the challenges of climate change, scientific knowledge needs to be amalgamated with indigenous ecological knowledge to create valuable source of adaptive practice and pathways to integrating new approaches to adaptation (Berkes, Folke, and Colding 2000).

According to Harvey (2011) the key barriers to meeting the challenges include the failure to create effective local-level forums for dialog and exchange between different stakeholder groups; having a top down approach to knowledge sharing; engaging mostly those already familiar with the discourse and failure to actively engage with those at the margins of this discourse. Consequently, these initiatives have frequently failed to engage vulnerable community groups, especially women and create appropriate spaces for stakeholder mediations and interactions for communicating adaptation actions (Fahn 2009; Godfrey, Pauker, and Nwoke 2008; Ochieng 2009).

Jones (2010) notes that an informational approach remains inadequate in overcoming barriers to climate change adaptation. Apart from knowledge, individuals and communities need to be motivated and the social, cultural and institutional barriers (Tompkins and Adger 2004) they perceive need to addressed through communications, that use diverse means and fulfill several different functions.

Acunzo, Mario and Maria Protz (2010: 28) compiled the types of communications in support of adaptation that are mentioned as follows.

- *Educational communication* is about sharing proven know-how, including support (for) training and technology transfer. The trend is to move from simply delivering the message to engage the users in applying the information.
- *Policy communication* informs on policies and laws. This typically involves mass media and campaign formats, but further audience engagement is necessary when significant changes in policy take place.

- *Participatory communication* can help stakeholders come together, innovate and negotiate. Interactive group media are most often used to support such exchanges.
- *Organizational communication* improves coordination among and within groups and agencies.
- *Advocacy communication* helps people lobby for changes in policies and programmes. Very often, this function is implemented through a combination of campaigns and face-to-face interaction.
- *Conflict management communication* uses methods and media to encourage negotiation and to media conflicts. Video has been used successfully to allow each party to explain their interests, with the other side then able to view the recording. This is a form of structured listening.
- *Risk communication* informs people about hazards and supports people's participation in decision making on risk management, as well as encouraging behavior change that will enhance mitigation.

Overcoming the range of factors impeding adaptation to climate change hence requires multipronged communications that provide relevant information to appropriate stakeholders. (Acunzo and Protz 2010; Masters and Duff 2011). Using a Communication for development approach can play a catalytic role in enabling people to adapt to climate change. Fraser and Restrepo-Estrada (1998: 63) observe that

Communication for development is the use of communication processes, techniques and media to help people gain a full awareness of their situation and their options to change, to resolve conflicts, to work towards consensus, to help people plan actions for change and sustainable development, to help people acquire knowledge and skills they need to improve their condition and that of society, and to improve the effectiveness of institutions.

COMMUNITY RADIO
AND CLIMATE CHANGE COMMUNICATIONS

Community radio, often referred to as the "independent" or "third media," is seen as a means for community empowerment through peoples participation in the creation and dissemination of local content and is popularly considered as the "Voice of the Voiceless." Like democracy, Community Radio is, for the people, by the people and of the people. Truly a medium for grassroots communication, community radio strengthens the democratic system, amplifies the voice of the people and is considered a significant tool for participatory and democratic communication (Buckley 2000).

Community Radio stations can enable more people to participate in the process of creating content, thus enhancing the diversity of voices participating in the process, enabling the expression of divergent ideas and values, center-staging local issues as well as localizing issues of mainstream media (Bala 2013). Gauthier (2005: 1) elucidates that

> with its lower production costs and extreme versatility, radio lends itself just as well to rapid interventions as to the broadcasting of in-depth reports, and is just as suitable for the dissemination of information as it is for entertainment or educational purposes. Radio allows villagers to make their voices heard directly, regardless of their level of education or social standing.

Especially appropriate in areas where access to other channels of communication is inadequate, and where language, transportation, and poverty present major barriers to popular expression, participatory radio programming and broadcasting can be an effective means of learning and influencing behaviors (Harvey 2011; Monyozo 2008).

Active participation of different stakeholders forms the key mechanism by which community radio is said to empower the community. By offering a voice through pluralism and diversity in ownership and content (Pavarala and Malik 2007), community radio encourages dialog and transparency of administration. The core of community radio is not just the content or information, but the act of producing and sharing that content which is empowering. Thus, community radio showcases promising potential for engaging marginalized communities (Saeed 2009) in local discussions about the various dimensions of climate change adaptations (Harvey 2011).

This chapter explores the role participatory media like Community Radio can play in amplification of women's voices in the context of climate change. It endeavors to understand the processes synergized by a community radio in hill communities for women's participation and empowerment toward micro level adaptations in their communities in the face of changing climate.

HENVALVANI COMMUNITY RADIO

Henvalvani Community Radio (HCR) is located in Chamba, a small township in the Middle Himalayan region of Garhwal in the state of Uttarakhand in India. HCR is one of the oldest community radio stations in the country and has been operating in the region since the year 2000. The station received a broadcast license from the government only in the year 2012. Consequently for over a decade HCR has adopted a combination of narrowcasting and alternative broadcasting options and devised a multitude of innovative activities to create spaces for community groups, especially women, to voice their ideas and issues.

Interestingly, the region where the station is located has been home to major environmental movements such as the Chipko Movement and *the Beej Bachao Aandolan* (Save Indigenous Seeds Movement) that have brought national and international attention to environmental issues and natural resource management. Spearheaded by local women these movements have helped center-stage the stress on women's lives due to natural calamities and environmental degradation in the region.

Due to the association of founder members and early mentors of the station with local movements, environmental issues and their interplay with community struggles, people's concerns have been a major focus of the station's programming since its inception. Local women being a part of station's core founding team, the station has maintained an affirmative approach to women's active participation and representation in its programs and activities. In over a decade of its functioning, the HCR team has been replete with instances about climate change issues mediated by the station and the positive impact on communities, especially in the lives of local women. However, these remained notional and undocumented with little systematic evidence to ascertain their claims.

Therefore, our study attempted to comprehend HCR's functioning and the consequent influence on local issues and adaptation to climate change by communities from the viewpoint of women and their lives. The following objectives guided the study.

- To understand the perceptions of women about the changes in the climate and its effect on their lives
- To map the programs and activities of HCR and understand their scope in addressing climate change issues
- To study the perceptions of women about the role of HCR in helping them negotiate the challenges of climate change they face

RESEARCH METHODS AND TOOLS

For the research, a qualitative approach was adopted to provide in-depth insights about the nuances and multidimensional aspects of change perceived by the women. A mix of participatory methods was used to ascertain perspectives about different dimensions of climate change issues and the role HCR was playing in enabling communities to adapt to the threats they faced.

Participatory Learning and Action (PLA) exercises were done with women from the Community Based Organizations (CBO) of the villages to understand their perceptions about the changing climate and the challenges they face due to it. Seeds ranking method was used and a ten year timeline analysis was done in villages that HCR reached out to. The villages were purposively selected to allow for geographical variation within the area to enable a holistic understanding of the area HCR covered through its broadcasts and activities.

The Most Significant Change (MSC) technique was also used for the study. MSC is a dialogical, story based, participatory monitoring and evaluation technique that enables an understanding of values of different stakeholder groups about programs and contribute to organizational learning. The technique essentially involves a form of continuous values inquiry whereby designated groups of stakeholders search for significant prograe outcomes (reported in "significant change" [SC] stories) and then deliberate on the value of these outcomes in a systematic and transparent manner (Davies and Dart 2003, 2005). MSC especially lends itself to participatory processes because it relies on people to make sense of their own and other people's experiences and environments (McClintock 2003). MSC technique, hence, is a qualitative technique that endeavors to capture the nuances and the multi-dimensional aspects of change that cannot be captured through a quantitative process. Further, the MSC process creates mechanisms of communication among different stakeholders and enables them to systematically voice their ideas, dialog and develop consensus about outcomes and results most valued by them. The flexible nature of the techniques allows for its adaptation to suit local circumstances and can involve participation from as wide a range of stakeholders as is appropriate for the project situation. Stories of significant change were collected from women that were later subjected to two levels of selection—community (village level) and organizational level. Community level selectors included men and women, village level functionaries and local leaders and organizational level selectors included the core team members, staff, and volunteers of the station. For the fifty stories collected ten village level selections and three organizational level selections were done.

Additionally, analysis of HCR produced programs was done to map the extent of climate change issue based programming done by the station. Listing and analysis of programs produced on the issue of climate change between 2009 and 2012 was done. Documentation of activities and organizations HCR was affiliating with on issues of climate change was also done.

WOMEN'S PERCEPTIONS ABOUT CLIMATE CHANGE

Climate change was a term that was not within women's vocabulary. Participatory Learning and Action exercises provided a mechanism for creating a common understanding about climate change among women, which led to a common ground emerging and consensus about climate change as a term.

Women perceived climate change as an amalgamation of three broad aspects namely *variation in weather patterns (climatic aspects)* such as rainfall, heat, cold and fog; *incidence of natural disasters and calamities* such as droughts, landslides, cloud bursts, earthquakes and; *the hardships* that women face as a consequence. To understand women's perceptions about temporal variations in these aspects, three broad time periods were decided upon—the *present* being the current situation; *recent past* being four–five years ago and *past* being more than ten years. Table 7.1 shows how Seeds ranking method was used to understand both the aspects and the variation they perceived.

Women felt that over the years, rainfall pattern has become very erratic, varying between extremes, being either excessive or scanty. Further they felt that the intensity of heat in summer and cold in winter has increased with sustained periods of fog in winter. Women also perceived natural disasters such as landslides, cloudbursts, and earthquakes were much more frequent. The region was also facing severe droughts in summer. Women linked these aspects to shortage of water, reduced fodder availability and agricultural productivity along with a marked increase in attacks by wild animals. Consequently, women's drudgery in doing household chores has increased as they face immense difficulty in provisioning for drinking water; have to travel greater distances in search of fodder; reduced agricultural productivity and destruction of agricultural produce by wild animals deprived of their natural habitats has led to loss of livelihoods. These aspects significantly contributed to intensifying women's hardships and they linked these to their understanding of climate change.

Climate change, hence, for the women is a complex term having varying dimensions that juxtapose and cumulatively impact women's lives exacerbating the vulnerabilities and challenges they have to face due to it.

CLIMATE CHANGE PROGRAMMING

Documentation of radio programs produced by HCR for a span of four years found more than 390 minutes, that is, six and a half hours of program recordings to be directly related to the issue of climate change. Detailed analysis of randomly selected eight programs, totaling 240 minutes

Table 7.1. Aspects of Climate Change and Their Variations as Perceived by Women

Aspect		Past (10 years ago)	Recent Past (5 years ago)	Present (Last 1-2 years)
Variation in Weather Patterns	Rainfall	◆◆◆◆ ◆◆	◆◆◆◆	◆◆◆◆ ◆◆◆ ◆◆◆
	Intensity of Heat and Cold	✿✿✿✿✿	✿✿✿✿✿ ✿	✿✿✿✿✿ ✿✿✿ ✿✿✿
	Fog	None	■■ ■■	■■ ■■
Natural Disasters and Calamities	Drought	+++	+++++ ++	+++++ + +++
	Landslides			
	Cloudburst	None	●	●●●● ●●●●
	Earthquakes	★★	★★★★	★★★★★ ★
Hardships	Water Shortage	⊙⊙	⊙⊙⊙⊙⊙ ⊙⊙	⊙⊙⊙⊙⊙ ⊙⊙⊙
	Fodder Availability	✻✻✻✻ ✻✻✻	✻✻✻✻✻	✻✻✻ ✻✻
	Agricultural Productivity	◆◆◆◆ ◆◆◆◆ ◆◆	◆◆◆◆	◆
	Attacks by Wild Animals	◯◯	◯◯◯◯	◯◯◯◯◯ ◯◯◯◯

(four hours) of recordings were found to be mostly using entertainment-education approach and a radio magazine format for the programs. Focusing on a range of interrelated aspects of climate change, the programs revolved around issues of natural and man-made disasters, degradation and erosion, social cultural practices, livelihood issues and health. Programs glocalized the content, demystified scientific knowledge and maintained a local context in their discussions of issues. Twenty-five percent of the program content connected the issues faced at the local level to its prevalence at the national level or international context; 88 percent programs presented at least two viewpoints about the issue and in 63 percent programs women were either experts or their views were presented. The programs highlighted perspectives of marginalized groups and women in particular, out of which 75 percent of the program content explicated the impacts of climate change on women's lives. Interestingly, 87 percent program content had action suggestive content focus that provided women and families insights about measures they could use to negotiate and protect themselves from hardships they faced due to changing climate. With a strong focus on issues of climate change, HCR programs center-staged the issues local communities were facing with definitive emphasis on women's perspectives and issues.

HCR Activities

In the absence of a broadcasting license for more than a decade of its existence, HCR has used multiple methods for community outreach of which *Narrowcasting* of programs among village listener groups has remained a key strategy. Done in small groups by permitting flexibility of scheduling, narrowcasting has enabled listeners to actively participate in discussions about climate change issues raised in programs and built motivations of people to engage with HCR program and activities. Efforts to broadcast their programs led to HCR exploring the mainstream channel—state-owned All India Radio (AIR) and later World Space Satellite Radio. However these efforts proved to be unsustainable due to issues of funding and ideological clash and were discontinued. With emerging cable network in rural communities and small townships, HCR explored *cablecasting*- making digital stories of radio programs and playing them on the local cable channel network. Recently, since the last few years HCR has actively started blogging and also has an active Facebook page for engaging with people beyond its geographical limits by sharing its programs and activities online. In the year 2012, HCR received their Community Radio broadcasting license and began broadcasting its programs. It remains on air for at least four hours of live broadcast in a day with weekend broadcast time going up to 6 hours of live broadcast.

Mapping the activities of HCR found the station associating themselves with a range of organizations. Analysis of HCR activities around issues of climate change revealed a network of relationships with a range of organizations that resonated geographically. Figures 7.1, 7.2, and 7.3 illustrate the temporal changes in HCR networks of association and broadcasting systems in context of climate change issues.

Perceiving themselves not just as a radio station, HCR was found not limiting themselves to program production activities. HCR also actively associated themselves with activities of NGOs, government departments, educational institutions and people's movements, at local, regional, national and international levels. Actively participating and at times spearheading campaigns and other activities, HCR leveraged their program production, narrowcasting and broadcasting processes for center-staging the ideas of the groups they aligned with and amplifying the voices of especially women and grassroots communities, at various levels. With years of experience and changing transmission potentials the organization has spread its network and deepened its engagement with issues of climate change.

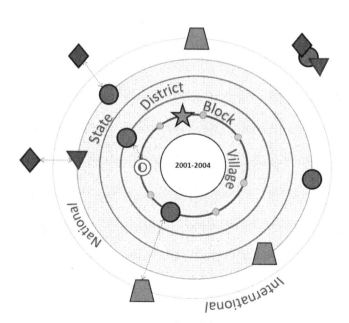

Figure 7.1.   HCR networks of association and broadcasting systems for years 2001–2004. Created by Aparna Moitra and Archna Kumar.

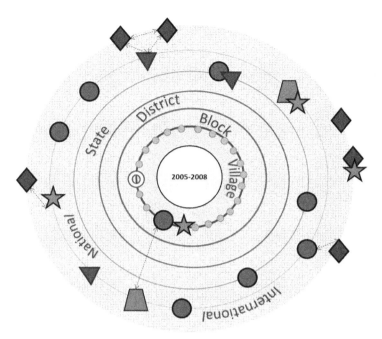

Figure 7.2.   HCR networks of association and broadcasting systems for years 2005–2008. Created by Aparna Moitra and Archna Kumar.

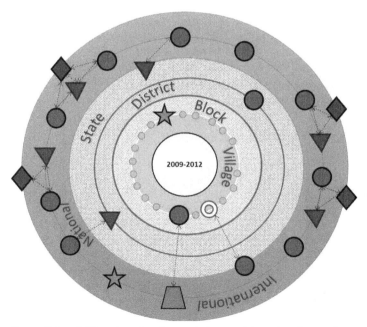

Figure 7.3.   HCR networks of association and broadcasting systems for years 2009–2012. Created by Aparna Moitra and Archna Kumar.

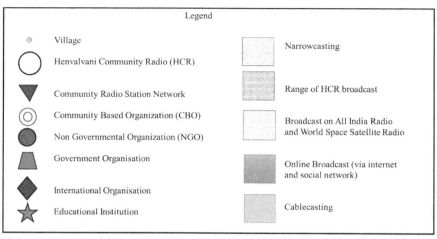

Figure 7.4. Legend for HCR networks of association and broadcasting system figures. Created by Aparna Moitra and Archna Kumar.

HCR Mediating Adaptive Change

Analysis of the significant change stories provided insights about women's articulations on HCR and its efforts to help them adapt to the changing climate. Women's stories not only focused upon the changes they perceived but also highlighted the catalytic processes mediated by HCR that enabled them to adapt to climatic variations. The emerging factors were seen to have a dynamo like effect, each energizing the other, and consequently influencing the process of women negotiating the climate change related challenges they faced.

Awareness, Information and Knowledge

The core to women being able to negotiate the challenges they faced was their enhanced awareness and knowledge about various dimensions of climate change. Stories were replete with examples of enhanced awareness about diverse aspects such as understanding of scientific facts, nuances of laws and policies, details and clarifications about government programs and schemes, alternate employment opportunities, improved agricultural practices, health risks, therapies, and remedies for health management, and so on. Kunti Devi of Hadam village highlights this aspect in the context of agricultural practices in her narrative.

> We are essentially a farming community, we were facing a lot of trouble with
> a particular weed we called Tipatti. The changes in climate in recent years

has provided favourable conditions for the growth of this weed, which is growing four times the actual crop is supposed to grow, thereby destroying our entire produce. Whatever practices we used to traditionally follow for controlling the weeds are now not effective, so the weeds keep cropping up and multiply. One day we happened to discuss about this issue in one of the listener group meetings with the Henvalvani team and it was decided that they would produce a programme on this issue as a lot of listeners from other villages were also facing similar issues with the weed. Thereafter, HCR team members took our interviews on the specific aspects of the issue. After a few weeks during the narrowcast session in the village they brought a programme on the issue of weeds. The programme was very interesting. Apart from our interviews, the HCR team had also interviewed people from other villages and a scientist from the nearby agricultural university researching on this weed. The scientist suggested some remedies we could try out. The remedy was really simple and we could easily follow. We tried it out and to our joy, the solution worked. We were able to control the weed this year and have a better yield.

By providing relevant and appropriate information, in accordance to the local context and needs, HCR filled a crucial gap and provided the basic precursor for women to be able to negotiate the challenges they faced. For women, lack of knowledge remains a root cause of their powerlessness and the marginalization they face in communities (Nellemann et al. 2011). The opportunities that HCR provided to the women for enhancing their awareness and knowledge were crucial to help them adapt and respond to the challenges they faced, further improving the quality of their lives.

NATURE AND CONTENT OF PROGRAMS

Likeability and appeal of HCR programs emerged repeatedly from the narratives of women. The programs produced in the local dialect, using local artists and oral traditional forms coupled with an entertaining format made them immensely appealing, enjoyable and popular. Their narratives repeatedly acknowledged the relevance of the issues discussed in the programs to their lives. The integration of modern and traditional knowledge, presentation of alternative viewpoints and a glocal analysis of issues contributed to making the issues pertinent to their context and circumstances. This connect women had with the content and presentation of HCR programs motivated them to prioritize listening to HCR programmeover other media forms and negotiate their time constraints. Geeta Bhandari from Chhota Syuta village discusses the glocal aspect in her story.

Being a regular listener of HCR, I have always felt that their programmes try to simplify the phenomenon of climate change suited to our levels of understanding. This premise forms one of the many reasons why I enjoy listening to their programmes very much. I am able to relate to the issue being discussed in the programme instantly and have found even the most complex issues such as global warming, very easy to understand. Apart from this, I have also heard a lot about their activities on environmental issues such as seminars, discussions and padyaatra (walking long distances on foot) to generate awareness about changing climate and taken part in a few. I am very proud to note that young girls of the village are getting involved with HCR in these activities thereby not only being equipped with the knowledge to deal with climate change issues but also be empowered to voice their concerns in the future.

Platform for Amplification of Voice and Initiation of Dialog

Narratives of women elaborated on the multiple forums they found via HCR for articulating and dialoguing about their ideas and priorities. HCR's participatory bottom up approach to program production created a preliminary platform for women to articulate their ideas and perspectives. The HCR team followed an iterative process for researching and comprehending different perspectives of program issues as well as assembling and editing the programs. Women and other stakeholders actively engaged in dialog about issues and provided their views at various stages of radio program production. This participatory nature of program production prevented the content from becoming prescriptive and skewed in any one way, consciously integrating the voice of various community groups and women about issues. Women were considered as experts in their own right. Their ideas were recognized and were given value to and their comments were corroborated with those of men, scientists, bureaucrats, local leaders and other people in position of power. The production process and the subsequent airing of these programs gave women's ideas and struggles new levels of acknowledgment.

Narratives of women also accredited the broadcast and feedback systems of the station for providing them opportunities to voice their perspectives. Phone in during live programs, voice messages, SMSs as well as sending letters created a second level platform for women to voice their ideas about issues. Women were pleased that their feedback and responses found space and acknowledgement in HCR programs. Women's stories recognized the multiplicity of activities that HCR was part of, not limiting themselves only to station based activities. HCR thereby opened up opportunities for women to participate in different activities and forums that they aligned with. This resulted in the creation of a third level platform that exposed women not only to new groups and ideas, but also to new forums for voicing their thoughts.

The various platforms HCR created, provided a freely available arena for women to learn, share and dialog issues with different stakeholder groups. These new opportunities enabled women to not only develop sensitivity about others viewpoints but enhanced the depth of their own understanding. Hamelink (2002) notes that for communities to be the agents of their own social change there needs to be an emphasis on promoting dialog among their members. Dialoguing forms an important aspect of understanding the perspectives of others and helps people reach a consensus (Figueroa et al. 2002; Waisbord 2007).

As gender based inequalities hamper women's abilities to adapt to climate change challenges (UN Women Watch 2009), participatory functioning and innovative spaces HCR created for women to voice and dialog about their ideas, problems and concerns provided strength to women's voice and created a conduit for articulating and negotiating the climate change challenges they are facing.

Adaptation and Coping Strategies

The significant change stories revealed a range of adaptations women adopted, to reduce their vulnerabilities and cope with the challenges they were facing due to changing climate. One such narrative by Mamta Rawat from Shrikot village elucidates on the water related challenges they faced and HCR's role in helping them negotiate the issue.

Our village is situated at the top of a hill and there is one village named Jugadgaon at the base of the hill. Some time back both villages faced extreme water shortage. Supply from the tap water became very erratic and less. Women had to wait hours for water lest they miss the meagre supply. Most walked long distances to get a few pots of water. Our village blamed the foothill village of Jugadgaon for water shortage and they us. The animosity reached such high levels that a few times people landed up having fist fights. Hurling abuses at each other was common. Troubled, the HCR village volunteers of Jugadgaon discussed this matter with the rest of HCR team and requested them to take up the matter. HCR team members held meetings at both the villages and recorded bytes of the villagers. They shared these with the people of the other village. To further the matter, they approached the Block Development Officer of the area and met with the water board officials and sought their views as well. HCR team talking to the people of both the villages and government officials while making the programme made everyone realize the root cause of the problem was the oversight of the water board. So, even before the programme was produced, the two villages overcame their differences and met the water board officials together to resolve their problem. By the time the programme went on air, the problem was well on its way to be sorted.

At an individual level, women felt that engagement with HCR has enabled them to acquire new knowledge and leanings and consequentially explore and adopt new norms and practices that tangibly reduced their vulnerabilities. Narratives were replete with examples of areas of learnings and new norms and practices explored by women. These included management of natural resources, agricultural practices, disaster preparedness, health remedies and lifestyle choices. Programs encouraged women and their families to reflect and contemplate about prevailing traditional beliefs, new knowledge and practices advocated; others experiences and insights and their relevance to their present context and challenges. The multiple perspectives that HCR programs provided and the debate and dialog triggered among community members together helped build consensus and encourage individuals and families to discard traditional practice and adopt newer ones.

Women's narratives also elaborated upon the problems of unemployment in the region and the role HCR played in negotiating livelihood challenges. HCR programs appraised listeners about emerging employment prospects in the region such as the various government schemes and programs available for skill development and livelihood security; cottage and home based industry options for substantiating family incomes etc. Understanding present and future trends and options enabled women and their families to explore alternatives and seek appropriate solutions to their livelihood challenges. Moreover, with agriculture being the predominant livelihood activity, HCR programs focused on problems faced by the farmers and strategies for enhancing farm incomes. With increasing feminization of agriculture in the region, HCR programs especially focusing on women farmers were a valuable support that was accredited in several narratives. At a collective level, women highlighted HCR's energizing effect on women's groups and community based collectives like Mahila Mangal Dals (Women's collectives) in villages. Showcasing the experiences and actions of local collectives and initiatives through their programs as well as women's interaction with stakeholders in HCR organized activities had an inspirational effect on local women and led them to examine and vitalize their local collectives. Consequently, community based organizations and women's collectives expanded their activities around the issues of climate change, keeping the village commons clean, protecting forests against forest fires and norms for natural resource use and exploitation of resources etc. HCR induced vibrancy in local collectives built solidarity and helped women overcome their perceptions of powerlessness.

The story of Jugadgaon's fifty-year-old Munni Devi not only puts forth her perspectives on HCR's role in helping her overcoming her livelihood struggles but also underscores the aspect of collective adaptations.

I am an ordinary woman who relies on farming and animal husbandry for income. I also work under the state's employment guarantee scheme as the income from traditional sources is not enough for survival. Like rest of the village women, I was confined to my own tasks, unaware of any income supplementing schemes. It is only by listening to HCR's programmes I got to know about them and signed myself up for the employment guarantee scheme. Our village and farmlands being amidst the forests, often fall prey to the forest fires during summers. We were tired of the fires happening and were clueless on how to resolve this issue at our own level. We communicated this issue to the HCR team and during one of their narrowcasting sessions, they brought a programme on the issue of forest fires. Among the various solutions suggested, the one that appealed the most to us was to use collective action as an approach to stop forest fires. Dialoguing more about this in our listener group meetings we ideated on how the women's collective of our village can be mobilized for controlling forest fires. Once there was a fire in the nearby forest, all the women of the village went to stop the fire and prevented the entire forest from burning down. Now we remain alert and collectively handle forest fires on our own.

Women's narratives highlight the cross linkages between gender issues and climate change adaptation efforts in communities. Participatory media like community radio can create mediating mechanisms for reducing gender imbalances in decision making processes in communities regarding environmental issues, eventually lessening vulnerabilities women face in their lives. Participatory communication is not only a means for providing voice to marginalized women's groups but can be a valuable instrument for strengthening local institutions, negotiating power structures and overcoming the powerlessness women experience.

CONCLUSION

Women's empowerment and their abilities to negotiate and adapt to the climate change challenge are intrinsically linked. This chapter explored the role that community media platforms like community radio can play in enabling women to articulate their concerns and negotiate the issues of climate change challenge in their daily lives. If one were to closely look at the term "empowerment" then Batliwala (1994) understands empowerment as how much influence people have over external actions that matter to their welfare, whereas Kabeer's (2001) definition of empowerment focuses on the expansion of people's ability to make strategic life choices in a context where this ability was previously denied. Elaborating on the understanding of empowerment, Stromquist (1993) views empowerment as an idea that expects women understanding their conditions of subordination and the causes of such conditions at micro and macro levels. In other words it involves understanding their self and the need to make choices that go against the cultural norms and practices of their communities.

Drawing on aforementioned definitions, it is important to view the concept of agency in this context as one where women are significant actors in the process of change, which is central to the process of empowerment.

It wouldn't be amiss to state at this juncture that technologies possess great potential to improve the lives of people, however the potential of community radio as a technological medium in the development process can only be realized when the ownership of both the message and the medium—the content and the process reside with the communities (Pavarala and Malik 2007). Communication for empowerment requires community media to act as a *rhizome* (Deleuze and Guattari 1987). Just as a rhizome has no beginning or end, it is always in the middle, between things, in the same way, community media through its innovative activities must function as an instrument giving voice to a group of people related to a specific issue. Acting as a catalyst, it must rearticulate impartiality and neutrality and be a common point for grouping people and organizations active in different types of struggles (Carpentier, Lie, and Servaes 2003).

The hallmark of a good community media initiative is to strive to keep the balance of a rhizome. HCR in its participatory programming, multiplicity of activities, flexibility in functioning and commitment to the struggles of local communities has become a catalytic conduit for voicing and dialoguing concerns of local communities. It has evolved into a *rhizomatic* organization, displaying versatility and maturity. Its multipronged participatory processes have mainstreamed women's voices in the climate change debate and triggered individual and collective changes for women's agency and empowerment for climate change adaptation and mitigation in communities.

NOTE

Draft versions of different sections of this chapter were presented at the ICA 2013 and IAMCR 2013.

REFERENCES

Acunzo, Mario, and Maria Protz. "Collaborative change: A communication framework for climate change adaptation and food security." 2010. http://www.fao.org/docrep/012/i1533e/i1533e00.pdf.

Adger, W. Neil, Saleemul Huq, Katrina Brown, Declan Conway, and Mike Hulme. "Adaptation to climate change in the developing world." *Progress in Development Studies* 3, no. 3 (2003): 179–195.

Agrawal, Arun, and Nicolas Perrin. "Climate adaptation, local institutions and rural livelihoods." In *Adapting to climate change: Thresholds, values, governance,* 350–367. Cambridge: Cambridge University Press, 2009.

Bala, Lakhendra. *Community Radio a Tool of Participatory Communication for Development.* Saarbrücken, Germany: Scholars Press 2013.

Batliwala, Srilatha. "The meaning of women's empowerment: New concepts from action." In Population policies reconsidered: Health, empowerment, and rights, edited by Gita Sen, Adrienne Germain, Lincoln C. Chen, 127–138. Boston: Harvard Center for Population and Development Studies, 1994.

Berkes, Fikret, Carl Folke, and Johan Colding, eds. *Linking social and ecological systems: Management practices and social mechanisms for building resilience.* Cambridge: Cambridge University Press, 2000.

Braidotti, Rosi. "Women, the Environment and Sustainable Development: Emergence of the Theme and Different Views." In *Women, the environment and sustainable development: Towards a theoretical synthesis,* edited by Rosi Braidotti, Ewa Charkiewicz, Sabine Hausler, and Saskia Wieringa, 77–106. London: Zed Books 1994.

Buckley, Steve. "Radio's new horizons Democracy and popular communication in the digital age." *International Journal of Cultural Studies* 3, no. 2 (2000): 180–187.

Carpentier, Nico, Rico Lie, and Jan Servaes. "Community Media: Muting the democratic media discourse?" *Continuum: Journal of Media and Cultural Studies* 17, no. 1 (2003): 51–68.

Collins, Jane. "Women and the environment: social reproduction and sustainable development." *Women and International Development Annual* 2 (1991): 33-58.

Dankelman, Irene, and Joan Davidson. *Women and the environment in the Third World: Alliance for the future.* London: Routledge, 2013.

Dart, Jessica, and Rick Davies. "A dialogical, story-based evaluation tool: The most significant change technique." *American Journal of Evaluation* 24, no. 2 (2003): 137–155.

Davies, Rick, and Jessica Dart. "The Most Significant Change (MSC) technique: A guide to its use." 2005. http://www.clearhorizon.com.au/wp-content/uploads/2008/12/dd-2005-msc_user_guide.pdf.

Deleuze, Gilles, and Felix Guattari. "A Thousand plateaus." 1987. http://danm.ucsc.edu/~dustin/library/deleuzeguattarirhizome.pdf.

Ensor, Jonathan, and Rachel Berger. *Understanding climate change adaptation: Lessons from community-based approaches.* Bourton on Dunsmore, UK: Practical Action Publishing, 2009.

Fahn, J. "Climate change: 'How to report the story of the century. Science and Development Network.'" Scidev, March 16 2009. http://www.scidev.org/en/practical-guides/climate-change-how-to-report-the-story-of-the-cent.html.

Figueroa, Maria Elena, D. Lawrence Kincaid, Manju Rani, and Gary Lewis. "Communication for social change: An integrated model for measuring the process and its outcomes." Working paper, 2002. http://www.communicationforsocialchange.org/pdf/socialchange.pdf.

Fraser, Colin, and Sonia Restrepo-Estrada. *Communicating for development: Human change for survival*. London: IB Tauris, 1998.

Gauthier, J. "Popularize, produce, disseminate! Reference sheets for field researchers." Sheet 12: Radio. Ottawa: IDRC, 2005.

Godfrey, A., E. Pauker, and L. Nwoke. "Is this climate change? Formative research on knowledge and perception of climate change amongst policy makers, opinion formers and mass audiences in Nigeria." London: BBC World Service Trust, 2008.

Hamelink, Cees J. "Social development, information and knowledge: whatever happened to communication?" *Development* 45, no. 4 (2002): 5–9.

Harvey, Blane. "Climate airwaves: Community radio, action research and advocacy for climate justice in Ghana." *International Journal of Communication* 5 (2011): 24.

Howden, S. Mark, Jean-François Soussana, Francesco N. Tubiello, Netra Chhetri, Michael Dunlop, and Holger Meinke. "Adapting agriculture to climate change." *Proceedings of the National Academy of Sciences* 104, no. 50 (2007): 19691–19696.

Jennings, Steve, and John Magrath. "What happened to the seasons?" https://www.oxfam.org.au/wp-content/uploads/2012/02/oaus-whathappenedtoseasons-0110.pdf.

Jones, Lindsey. "Overcoming social barriers to adaptation." Overseas Development Institute, Background Note, July 2010. http://www.odi.org/sites/odi.org.uk/files/odi-assets/publications-opinion-files/6048.pdf.

Kabeer, Naila. "Conflicts over credit: Re-evaluating the empowerment potential of loans to women in rural Bangladesh." *World development* 29, no. 1 (2001): 63–84.

Kollmair, M. "Challenges and Opportunities for Women in the Changing Himalayas." *Gender Perspectives in Mountain Development* 57 (2010): 2–4.

Linggard, Trine, and Mette Moberg. "Women and sustainable development: A report from Women's Forum in Bergen." http://repositorio.cepal.org/bitstream/handle/11362/5886/S9800083_en.pdf;jsessionid=97113ACAD6F079259D843D1AC5FF1E18?sequence=1.

Masters, Lesley, and Lyndsey Duff, eds. *Overcoming barriers to climate change adaptation implementation in Southern Africa*. Johannesburg: African Books Collective, 2011.

Mastny, Lisa. "Melting of earth's ice cover reaches new high." Worldwatch News Brief, March 6, 2000. http://www.worldwatch.org/melting-earths-ice-cover-reaches-new-high.

McClintock, Charles. "Using narrative methods to link program evaluation and organization development." *Evaluation Exchange* 9, no. 4 (2003).

Monyozo, Linje. "Communicating with Radio: What do we know? Findings from selected rural radio effectiveness evaluations." African Farm Radio Research Initiative, Farm Radio International, Ottawa, Canada, 2008. http://www.wsscc.org/sites/default/files/publications/fri_communicating_with_radio_2008.pdf.

Nellemann, C., et al. "Women at the frontline of climate change: gender risks and hopes: a rapid response assessment." United Nations Environment Programme, 2011. http://www.unep.org/pdf/rra_gender_screen.pdf.

Ochieng, B. O. *Effective communication of science and climate change information to policy makers.* Nairobi: IDRC, 2009.

Pavarala, Vinod, and Kanchan K. Malik. *Other voices: The struggle for community radio in India.* New Delhi: Sage, 2007.

Rai, Sandeep Chamling. "An overview of glaciers, glacier retreat, and subsequent impacts in Nepal, India and China." 2005, himalayaglaciersreport2005.pdf.

Rico, María Nieves. "Gender, the Environment and the Sustainability of Development." 1998, http://repositorio.cepal.org/bitstream/handle/11362/5886/S9800083_en.pdf;jsessionid=97113ACAD6F079259D843D1AC5FF1E18?sequence=1.

Saeed, Saima. "Negotiating power: Community media, democracy, and the public sphere." *Development in Practice* 19, nos. 4–5 (2009): 466–478.

Shiva, Vandana. "Violence of the Green Revolution." 1989, http://www.trabal.org/courses/pdf/greenrev.pdf.

Shiva, Vandana, and Maria Mies. *Ecofeminism.* Atlantic Highlands, NJ: Zed Books. 1993.

Singh, R.K. "Annual Progress Report-2009." All India Coordinated Research Project on Agrometeorology-ICAR, G.B. Pant University of Agriculture and Technology, Hill Campus, Ranichauri, Tehri Garhwal, Uttarakhand, 2009.

Stromquist, Nelly. "The theoretical and practical bases for empowerment." *Women, education, and empowerment* 1993, http://www.unesco.org/education/pdf/283_102.pdf.

Tompkins, Emma L., and W. Neil Adger. "Does adaptive management of natural resources enhance resilience to climate change?" *Ecology and Society* 9, no. 2 (2004): 10.

UNDP. *Human development report 2007/2008: Fighting climate change: human solidarity in a divided world.* New York: Oxford University Press for UNDP, 2007.

UNFPA. "The State of World Population 2001. Women Need Support to Break Vicious Cycle of Environmental Degradation, Poverty, Poor Health and High Fertility." https://www.unfpa.org/swp/2001/presskit/english/womenen.htm.

UN Women Watch. "Fact sheet, women, gender equality and climate change." 2009, http://www.un.org/womenwatch/feature/climate_change/downloads/Women_and_Climate_Change_Factsheet.pdf.

Waisbord, S. "The irony of communication for social change." *MAZI Articles, Communication for Social Change Consortium* (August 2007).

8

Citizen Media and Empowerment

An Analysis of Three Experiences of Media Re-Appropriation Carried Out by Women during the Popular Insurrection in Oaxaca, Mexico

Francisco Sierra Caballero, Alice Poma, and Tommaso Gravante

The city of Oaxaca in Mexico became the setting for a popular uprising during mid 2006 initiated by the local section of the teachers' union (Sección XXII-CNTE). The popular movement developed without parties or social organizations to guide its actions. For over six months ordinary people self-organized to protest against the repressive and nepotistic policies of state governor Ulises Ruiz. This *high anti-authoritative dimension* of the popular movement of Oaxaca adds to the cycle of resistance movements in Latin America that emerged in this new millennium together with civil protests in Argentina in 2001, popular mobilizations in El Alto and Cochabamba in Bolivia, Caracas in April 2002, La Paz in February 2003, to name just a few (Zibechi 2007).[1]

With Oaxaca a historically excluded and marginalized social subject in the Mexican sociopolitical reality emerged as well: *women*. Female teachers, housewives, *chavas*,[2] female students, unemployed women, and so on were not only protagonists of the insurrection, but had a central role in the re-appropriation of the city, in the construction of barricades and in the occupation and creation of dozens of messages and media on radio, TV, and websites.

In this chapter we propose an analysis "from below," which inverts the perspective toward ordinary women who participate in media experiences in order to understand how the experience of media appropriation affects the process of empowerment. The analysis will focus on three experiences that were led by "ordinary" women only, meaning they were not activists nor leaders of any social organization: the creation of two "alternative" digital projects called Revolucionemos Oaxaca and Frida Guerrera,[3] and the occupation by Oaxacan women of radio station 96.9 FM and TV Canal 9 of the state radio and television facilities (CORTV) for almost a month. Through these media experiences, we will explain how the women interviewed have lived a "transformation of consciousness and behavior" (Piven and Cloward 1977) triggering a *process of empowerment,* both individual and collective. In this research we consider empowerment as the process of acquisition of power and not as "power over someone," but as "power of," as an emancipating potentiality (Dallago 2006).[4] Empowerment, identified by Wood (2001) as an emotional benefit of protest, is one of the results of mobilizations, which leads to social change (Drury and Riescher 1999, 2000, and 2005; Krauss 1993; Servaes 2013). Incorporating concepts of the critical theory of communication (Sierra 2000, 2010), and reflections on protest and emancipation in Latin America (AA.VV. 2011; Casanova 2008; De Sousa 2008; Holloway 2011; Zibechi 2007;) we will highlight the *emancipating capacity of media and communicative experiences,* which proved to be a laboratory for social change in the region.

This chapter is divided into two parts: in the first one we present the context, cases of study and methodology used. We pay special attention to an explanation of the focus "from below" that characterizes our research. Second, we present an analysis centered on the cultural change that these women have lived through their media experience, that is to say, the process of re-elaboration and redefinition of values, beliefs and identities that lead people to raise awareness of aspects of reality which up to that moment they had not considered, to change their perception of reality, and, finally, to act in consequence. Among the different dimensions emerging from this process of emancipation, and the cultural change lived by the female protagonists, we highlight: (a) *the identification dimension,* that is to say, how the means are transformed into a space of identification and meanings for these women; (b) *the communication dimension,* meaning how the protagonists have elaborated "another" concept of citizen communication; and (c) *the political dimension,* through which we will show the process of empowerment lived by these female protagonists of the media and communicational experiences analyzed. Finally, in order to further approach the complexity of processes of emancipation experiences, we use a *biographical focus* because if culture and identity can bind us, biography makes us unique, and from the perspective of the new collective action and media appropriation the look "from below" demands, consistently, a methodological approximation toward this direction.

WHEN WOMEN SPEAK OUT

The insurgence in Oaxaca is not an isolated event that broke out suddenly on June 14, 2006; instead, it is the outcome of an historic cycle of struggles and resistances that characterize the state of Oaxaca. This insurgence arises from the profound and unresolved social injustices that portray the Oaxacan society in its social and power-driven relations.

Although Oaxaca is rich in natural and cultural resources, it is one of the poorest states in Mexico in economic terms (CONEVAL 2012), with marginalization and social inequality percentages among the highest in the country (CONAPO 2010), with the most affected part of the population being indigenous people and/or belonging to rural communities or peripheral neighborhoods of urban areas. Within this array of *poverty and marginalization*, women suffer a double stigma, both because they are poor and/or indigenous, and because they are women. In this context of inequality (INEGI 2008), women in Mexico suffer discrimination and violence every day, features which are the result of the patriarchal structure that characterizes the political, educational, and economic domestic system. To this contextual frame we can also add the fact that Oaxaca has one of the highest rates of violation of women's human rights in Mexico. In recent years Oaxaca has seen an increase in violence-related crimes and assassinations against women[5] as a result of the intensification of conflicts and repression as part of the low intensity war strategy of the Mexican state. All things considered, when on August 1, 2006, thousands of women decided to take the streets and protest against governor Ulises Ruiz, this represents a huge milestone in the Oaxacan society in terms of questioning and challenging the repressive dynamics of the dominant powers and the hegemonic patriarchal discourse. Initially, women did not occupy an outstanding place in the movement, since as one of the interviewed women said, women at the beginning of the protests "were the ones making coffee, the ones preparing or carrying food, they were the ones cleaning up, they still didn't have the power to decide, to engage in the actions, to be part [in the struggle/movement]" (I9). Moved by their necessity of surmounting that historic social invisibility, even in protest mobilizations, or in other words, "for the participation of women to be noticed" (I9), in the last days of July 2006, after several assemblies, hundreds of women—most of them from poor neighborhoods in the city, many of indigenous origin—self-organized. Without any leaders, parties or social organizations they decided to take the streets and carry out the Marcha de las Cacerolas (The March of the Pots and Pans), which took place in early August that year. The demonstration has a symbolic importance not only for gender reclamation, an element at all new in the

Oaxacan society, but also because from this action emerged the proposal to occupy the facilities of CORTV, property of the state government.

Occupying this TV station, as we will see later, was a unique experience in the life of the women who did it. However, it was also a meaningful stage in the construction of a new social imagery in which for the first time women reverted their traditional roles and took on a prime role in political life. Throughout the twenty days of the occupation of Canal 9, dozens of ordinary women of different social classes and ages were able to manage the state TV and FM radio channel, going on air with the name Radio Cacerolas. The occupied TV and radio station were not only the broadcaster of the demands of the popular movement, but rather they helped to

> call on other women to join the movement. To make women think if the money they had [to make ends meet] was enough, if their children could have access to [a proper] education and a profession, if there were sources of employment; I mean, it was the women themselves who came up with many thoughts, it was our *compañeras* who made other women listen to them and reflect on all this. (I9)

These experiences also helped to empower and strengthen the women who were there occupying the channel, since, as an interviewee expressed, "the mere fact of listening to each other made us stronger."

In addition to Canal 9, the citizenry got involved in different public and commercial radio stations and over twenty websites. Created by ordinary citizens, these websites contributed to breaking the media siege created by official media and drawing international attention to the movement. Moreover, they were fundamental in the organization and construction of the *identity of the popular movement*. For this reason we decided to incorporate them in our analysis, including two projects managed by women which are still online: the portal Revolucionemos Oaxaca and the blog Frida Guerrera. Revolucionemos Oaxaca (http://revolucionemosoaxaca. org). Quoting one of its four female creators,

> because we wanted to kick off with a media project that from our point of view would not have intermediaries, in order to make a more direct communication [than the way it was] about what was happening. We thought it was necessary to create alternative spaces [to debate] issues that didn't exist in commercial media. (I5)

Frida Guerrera (http://fridaguerrera.blogspot.mx/) appears as an individual initiative by an ordinary woman without any previous experience in communication. She aimed to "denounce the serious violations of human rights occurring in Oaxaca, giving voice to the voiceless" (I4).

The blog became a reference point for alternative information in Oaxaca, showing along the years a constant and high professionalization of its female creator. In 2010 the blog was awarded the Carlos Montemayor National Prize for journalistic work in defense of the *triqui* people of San Juan Copala in Oaxaca.

APPROACH FROM BELOW
AND SUBJECT-CENTERED METHODOLOGY

The approach from below suggests paying attention to the people that fight and that, as stated by Jorge Regalado, "had always been there but we did not have the eyes to see them nor ears to hear them" (Regalado 2012: 170). From this perspective, the center of the analysis is not the movement itself as a social actor any longer, but the subjects that fight, struggle and transform the media reality, thus being able to discern the emancipating capacity of the protest and, in this case, the *appropriation* of the media in the protest. For a better understanding of the media experiences of which these women were the protagonists, we found it appropriate to invert the traditional viewpoint of social State-centered movements, into a *people-centered perspective*. Focusing on the subjects means recognizing the capacity of action-reflection and of production of knowledge on the part of the people involved in the struggles and resistances (Freire 1970, 1976). In other words, the protagonists are the authors of their own experience and the interpreters of their own political practice, and all the social reality is the result of these social subjects producing and acting. Finally, among the subjects who fight emerges a category of *los de abajo* [people from below], "this wide conglomerate that includes everyone, and especially women, who suffer oppression, humiliation, exploitation, violence, marginalization" (Zibechi 2008: 6).

As noted in James Scott's research (1985, 1987, 1990) on power, hegemony, resistance and subordination, every subordinate group materially and ideologically resists the relation of dominance through its daily practice, developing as well a *culture of dissent*. Centering the attention toward the subordinate subjects allows comprehending such patterns of resistance that encourages ordinary people to develop emancipating social practices, to build new imageries and ideas and to transform radically the relations of power in their most essentially democratic sense. According to this view, emancipation is a "permanent process of self-education that does not admit recipes nor models; it is a process always unfinished that one has to experience on his/her own" (Zibechi 2007: 33). Paraphrasing, emancipation is a self-learning process that occurs over time and that people re-elaborate individually, thanks to the interaction with others. Each person is then the only author of their own emancipation, built on everyday relations and for which experiences of struggle are favorable contexts. The potential of the approach from below, which makes us invert the look toward the subjects usually ignored by power and the academy, resides in its capacity to revalue the daily nature for the comprehension of social change, as asserted by Holloway (2010: 12):

> Social change is not produced by activists . . ., it is rather the outcome of the barely visible transformation of the daily activities of millions of people. [For this reason] we must look beyond activism, and then, to the millions and millions of refusals and other-doings, the millions and millions of cracks that constitute the material base of possible radical change.

According to this idea, the research (2010–2013)[6] was set out methodologically starting from in-depth interviews, drawing upon the technique of episodic interviews (Flick 2000, 2004). Such method, which consists of exploring the processes to be analyzed through narrations by the subjects as episodes of their experience, allows recognizing and analyzing "the narrative-episodic knowledge with the use of narrations, while the semantic knowledge becomes accessible by means of concrete deliberate questions" (Flick 2004: 118). In our research, it has proven to be a helpful tool since it "facilitates the presentation of experiences in a general, and comparative manner, and at the same time it ensures those situations and episodes are told in their specificity" (Flick 2004: 119). Furthermore, we conducted several interviews with the same women over different years with the main objective of determining that empowerment is a continuous process.

The exclusive use of qualitative research techniques, and in particular interviewing ordinary people is "more useful to rebuild the scattered processes of social construction of the surrounding world, or the way in which abstract ideologies translate into concrete practices" (Della Porta 2010: 69). In this sense, we share what Zibechi proposes when asserting that "the peoples, their cultures and worldviews cannot be understood through quantitative and structural studies only" (2008: 6), and that qualitative methods are to be used provided "the voice, even the look, the feeling, the subjectivity of the subjects under analysis can be expressed" through them (Regalado 2012: 172).

The experience lived in protests is not limited to a personal and individual dimension, instead, it comprises a broader dimension, *the collective one*. For this reason we have considered necessary to address the reflections on the process of empowerment lived by each person in the discussion and collective elaboration by carrying out two focus groups that, as evidenced by Della Porta, "allow us to recreate—almost as in an experiment—conditions similar to those considered as belonging to paths of opinion formation, particularly in social movements" (Della Porta 2014: 15). The first focus group was carried out with the female protagonists of all the media experiences; while the second, due to the relevance of the occupation of Canal 9, was conducted only with the women who participated in storming the facilities. Eventually, in order to draw upon a series of data as large as possible, and taking into account the importance we have given to the biographical approach in the analysis of the cultural change lived by the protagonists, we have considered proper to conduct a series of *life stories* of the women involved. The study of such life stories allowed us to contextualize and organize the data in a time-span longer than the conflict itself, and understand how people build and rebuild their identities with relation to the events, the territory, their biography, etc. Finally, looking at the interviewed subjects not as variables, but as a whole within its ecological, social and historical context, and through their narrations, we have been able to comprehend the social reality as a process and a construction of the female protagonists and present those elements of the change lived by the women interviewed.

Next, we present the analysis of the identification dimension of the process of appropriation, which explores how these women transformed the media into a space of identification and social re-significance.[7]

THE MEDIA AS A SPACE OF IDENTIFICATION AND MEANING

One of the first aspects emerging from the analysis of the interviews and focus groups, which also influences the process of empowerment, is the relation created between the medium and the women; said relation is also nourished by other aspects such as identification, interaction, projection, personalization, territoriality, and privacy. That is to say, when the female protagonists appropriated the medium of communication, they not only developed with it a utilitarian relation whose aim may be to, for example, break the media siege of the mainstream media, as was the case of digital media; but also and simultaneously, these women characterized the medium with their own experiences, their *propia impronta* (Pol Urrútia 1996, 2002). Therefore, these female protagonists through the media practice have projected their personality, or created a new one, they have interacted with each other and with the rest of the world. Thus, through these processes the protagonists provide the media space with an individual meaning.

The process of identification takes place in different ways. One of the first elements of the dialectic process through which people and the medium are linked is the election of the name of the radio, TV or domain of the webpages, blogs, and so on. In the choice of the name, what is reflected are the wishes and motivations that took these people to engage in their struggle. Regarding the website Revolucionemos Oaxaca, as an interviewee told us, the choice of the website's name "meant a change; an indepth change, as if we wanted to put forward something different" (I6). In the project of the digital portal, wishes and the imagery of the female protagonists are projected, in fact, for the women of Revolucionemos Oaxaca, the portal had to mean, both "a revolution in the usual way to make communication" (I5) and reflect "the change we had lived" (I5). This process is even more evident in the experience of the woman who launched the online blog Frida Guerrera, whose name allowed the protagonist to redesign her identity and transform the alias Frida Guerrera into a real subject with its own personality.

This *process of identification and signification* was not exclusive to the protagonists; it was also the result of a collective process of identification, as a female interviewee recalls: "From the moment I started to work on the blog people began to create Frida Guerrera. It was like a need for people to believe there was a figure fighting for them" (I4).

The result of this identification process experienced individually by the protagonists also implies the creation of a sense of belonging linked to the construction of a community and its collective imagery. This was clearly in the case of the women who occupied the facilities of CORTV. In the twenty days of civil occupation, Canal 9's 96.9 FM was transformed into Radio Cacerola, as a remembrance of the Marcha de las Cacerolas on August 1. The Cacerolas, through a process of collective identification, were transformed, from a symbol of a submissive woman confined in its passive role to be a housewife, into tools through which women expressed their wrath and indignation, as well as their noisy participation as an active political subject. Through this process of identification, the occupied radio and television became a new public space intertwined with the daily life of these women from where they could share their problems, including the "women to whom money was not enough, those who suffered domestic or work violence, etc." (I16). The result of this process is the realization of aspects of the reality that they, until that moment, had not considered, such as gender violence, as one of these women living this experience admits:

> Taking *Canal 9* has been very enriching. I had never thought we could be part of a collective and [I could] learn so many things. Now you know what violence against women is and we might be living it without having noticed. (I10)
>
>   On the one hand, the event of *Canal 9* allows elaborating and sharing the personal experience in a collective manner, generating a shared reality; and

on the other hand, the problems (such as everyday violence that each of these women suffered daily) are re-interpreted as a collective problem. In other words, the personal becomes political. Therefore, the occupation and operation of *Canal 9* open up to these women an entire world and a series of problems that had always been present in their lives but which until that moment they themselves had lived as personal events; conversely, sharing in the radio or television programs said problems led to the emergence of collective awakening, or in the words of one interviewee: "the fact of sharing that [on the radio and TV] made the other *compañeras* open their eyes too." (I9)

To sum up, the relation between the media analyzed and the female protagonists is the result of the affective, cognitive and interactive processes they have lived, which displayed the significance of the traits of a *new subjectivity*, willing to dialog and debate, to deliberation and collective decision, with a higher capacity of autonomy and empowerment.

In the following section we analyze another dimension of the change experienced by these women which undoubtedly blends with the dimension previously described: the communicational dimension. Therefore, we present how "another" communication should be, a communication arising from the necessities of the citizenry.

ANOTHER COMMUNICATION
EMERGING FROM A FEMALE PERSPECTIVE

In the analysis of the change lived by the women interviewed in the communicational dimension, a first aspect we wish to highlight is becoming aware of the importance of communicative processes in the society and the power of the mainstream media. Eloquent are the words of an interviewee: "We realized the power the mainstream media have. They tell us about that power and the alienated people of the commercial radio and TV suffer, but we had never lived it before, nor felt it as we do now after taking *Canal 9*" (I9).

While making the radio and television programs or writing the journal articles for their websites the women interviewed started to reflect on the relation between power and communication and the need to have *citizen media*, that is to say, they were an audience that lived the media reality passively and fatalistically and became a critical subject. This process emerged as well in the two focus groups conducted, where the discussion aimed to the potentiality of drawing upon citizen media, which and that can represent people social reality and their needs, as this woman states during a group discussion: "We lack media that are the voice of the people, the commercial media aren't. They use people for their own purposes. (G2 [14]). In the collective deliberations, the asymmetrical relation between the mainstream media and their audience is inverted with regard to reality. For these women, the citizen media should be open to all the community and give the possibility of discussing about matters that affect the community directly. According to this viewpoint, the media should have the capacity to reflect the needs of citizens as well as create or strengthen a sense of community. It is from these reflections that "another" communication stands out, which is not characterized by giving information "only about claiming. Because you can't always be claiming things, it's also necessary to analyze the reality, or why the claims exist, where they come from" (G1 [I4]). That is, a citizen communication must be a necessary tool for developing reflections and analyses within each community of reference. In our collective workshop, the women presented the idea that, in order to establish a dialogic communication between the citizen media and its community, the media must overcome the practice of narrating the events and aim to practice *collective reflection*. In other words, to realize "another" communication, it is necessary to start breaking with the binary logic of problems-solutions of the mainstream media.

The necessity of developing positive proposals out of the possibilities that are available within a community is a common pattern in the interviews, but it is worth noting that for the interviewees it is necessary that the reflection starts *from the people* rather than the intellectuals, politicians or scholars. As recurrently seen in numerous occasions, it is "the perfectly ordinary people" that justify and nourish the media, and it is with these same people it can be possible to build another type of communication, as this interviewee asserts: "A form to make communication is to be in contact with people that want to make something different and that want to reach other people, but also with people that can be immersed in processes of communication that you have developed" (I5). The "other communication" is conceived as a common good, a good for all the collectivity and, therefore, it is not subject to constraints in its use and access. Above all, this "new" communication model is characterized by the rupture of the dominant patriarchal and manly narrations and views that identify women as an object. These authoritative and vertical narrations are replaced by images that symbolize the daily practice of women, as was the case at TV Canal 9, where images on television displayed women, "all of them just sitting down, without poses, with their apron, tired, where you could see their fatigue, they looked tense, they looked somehow happy too, some of them were crying, other were really combative with their fist up high" (I11).

These images represent an entirely repressed world, in need of revealing itself, and they show not only another form of making communication, but also another social *doing*.

CHANGES IN THE POLITICAL DIMENSION

Becoming aware of the potentialities media have is only one dimension in the process of empowerment lived by the protagonists. The very same fact that the analyzed media experiences are inserted in an extremely violent social conflict, such as the insurrection of Oaxaca,[8] sheds light on the narrow link between the appropriation of the media and the experience of the protest. This leads to the fact that the process of empowerment lived by the interviewees does not emerge from a single event as may be the consequences of occupying Canal 9 or managing the webpages; instead, it has to do with a process that is intertwined indivisibly with aspects that relate directly to the experiences of protest and the biography of each subject.

One of the first changes emerging from the interviews is the *total distrust* toward institutions, the State and all the political class, bearing in mind the economic powers gravitating around them, as an interviewee recalls: "We trusted neither the government nor the business sector" (I10).

The consequence of this negative perception of institutional politics is the construction of an *antagonistic identity* between the citizens and the politicians, identified as those responsible for the violent repression and accused of not attending to the demands of society. Both from the analysis of the texts published in websites and the videos by the occupied *Canal 9*, and the individual and collective interviews, emerges a division of the world between "us" (the women, the people, the movement, etc.) and "them" (the politicians, the bankers, the businessmen, etc.). Between these two antagonistic identities, "us" vs "them," there is no convergence, there is no room for dialogue, commitment or forgiveness, as expressed by an interviewee some years after the events: "They made themselves call the 'nice reputable people,' and they said we were the 'disrespectable people.' With those people a huge gap opened and it's still there . . . So it's something we don't forgive. There's no forgiveness or oblivion, that's how it is" (I9).

The division between "them" and "us" definitely leads to a *deconstruction of the institutional spaces* imposed by the political power, causing the emergence of new everyday practices[9] that give birth to new spaces, and also media spaces, from which life will be deployed, produced and reproduced, creating alliances with other experiences or social strata, etc. It is in these new spaces that subordinate groups develop another form of doing politics, of managing the public sphere and of establishing their own legitimacy, which is radically different from the legality and legitimacy of the hegemonic power (Thompson 1975). These practices surpass the institutional practices, they go "farther than elections" (I15), and farther than the act of delegating, thus feeding a process of empowerment that can be observed, for example, in claiming the null need of leaders, as a woman who participated in the occupation of Canal 9 recalls: "We are not in favor of having a leader. We are all capable of proposing, capable of deciding, capable of doing something. What do we need a person to become a leader or ruler for? No, for us all we have to do is working collectively" (I9).

The political practice that arises from below lies on consensus and its target is the common good of the community. For these women doing politics means establishing "a network of relations among people, building something as a whole" (I5), founded on the everyday needs of people. Therefore, the media experiences these women have lived, inserted in the experience of protests, leads to what Piven and Cloward (1977) call a *transformation of consciousness and behavior*, turning those who participate in these experiences and struggles into political subjects that question the values and codes of representation of the dominant system.

The concept emerging from the words—"capable of doing"—of the interviewees retakes us to the concept of empowerment that, as we have anticipated in the introduction, is interpreted as an individual and collective concept of acquisition of power, not as "power over someone" but "power of," as a potentiality (Dallago 2006). And that is expressed by means of a condition in which the protagonists perceive their experiences as learning and doing politics, as an interviewee asserts: "I think 2006 bound women and we have become more participative, more combative, and more sympathetic, and we still are preparing ourselves politically. We continue working to support other women as well" (G2 [(I18]).

The process of empowerment is an individual and collective process that has significant repercussions in society. The experience of the women interviewed during our research displays the close interdependence that exists between the individual change each of them have lived and how said change is reflected in their community. To comprehend the social change it is undoubtedly necessary to analyze the change in the political dimension within the individual aspect as well, since individuals "are not mere bearers of structure" (Jasper 1997: 65); instead, they re-elaborate, build, create and change the reality surrounding them. Thus, in order to understand this capacity of change, it is necessary to pay attention to the subject and his/her biography.

Analyzing the biographical dimension of the process of empowerment related to the media and communication experience has signified comprehending not only why these women have decided to appropriate media, but also comprehending the process that has led them to create their own media, as well as the elements that value their experience in the struggle, how they interpret their reality, and so on. From the *biographical approach*, one of the first aspects we have analyzed has been the learning derived from the participation in the media. To some women, especially the younger ones, their experience made them "awake," "empathize" with those who fight, and become more critical, as a female youth from Revolucionemos Oaxaca mentions: "Now, I experience injustice more than before, and that doesn't happen only in large social movements, it happens with people in general, in everyday life" (I6).

On the whole, all the women agreed that the most important learning was being able to recognize themselves as a collective political subject capable of leaving the marginalization to which Oaxacan society had confined them, in the words of a woman speaking about her life story: "This gave me a very hard experience too. I realized that if we, the women together, could take *Canal 9*, we needed to be united to go on" (H9).

Even though this new political subjectivity needs a transformation of individual consciousness, it is collective and nourished by the affective bonds developed throughout the protest. These bonds, apart from strengthening the creation of a collective identity, which in our cases reveals itself as a "we, the women," sisterly unite the women that shared the media and struggle-driven experience, as observed in this extract: "We feel we can't abandon each other. We can't give up on one another" (H11).

These new and strong bonds between people are unexpected results of the protest and can give life to new political and social projects as is the case of some of the women who occupied Canal 9. After this experience they brought the collective Mujer Nueva (New Woman) to life, with the purpose of continuing the joint construction of new spaces of emancipation, working in the poorest areas of the city and carrying out workshops where they intend to provide other women with the experience and the emotional, legal and practical tools, among others, to be capable of breaking with the daily violence they encounter.

Another aspect of the process of empowerment that rises from the personal biography of the women interviewed is the emergence and/or strengthening of self-esteem. Only through the life stories could we appreciate the importance of the media experience of each woman and thus acknowledge the profound changes they had lived, as a woman who occupied Canal 9 states:

> I didn't speak before. I'm very shy. Now I'm not that shy because of everything I have learned. I used to be a very quiet person. I went through family violence and I feel that made me very shy. Now I realize I changed completely . . . I learned to speak out, instead of shutting up. If I have something to say I let it out and I didn't use to do that; although I had many things to say I wouldn't say a thing because I didn't dare speak or have a word. And I suffered because of that, it was frustrating, it made my self-esteem go down even more. (H9)

The fact that it is these women themselves who evidence the importance of their experience, reveals the *process of action-reflection* they experience (Freire 1970, 1976), which in turn is depicted in bolstering their own
self-esteem. This process is manifested also in what Michel De Certeau
(1984) calls a one thousand ways to do/undo the everyday, that is to say,
the process of action-reflection allows these women to reinterpret their
own everyday through other values. Finally, having analyzed the biographical dimension of these ordinary women that all in all were invisible
in the Oaxacan society, "reveals a larger world of power and resistance,
which to some extent ends up directly challenging the social relations of
power" (Krauss 1993: 248).

CONCLUSIONS

Through the analysis of the experiences of women who occupied a public
television channel and created two web portals with respect to the insurgence in Oaxaca, we have been able to show how subjects empower themselves thanks to these experiences, being able to highlight the emancipating capacity of the media experiences. The process of empowerment lived
by these women, which has surpassed the personal dimension and has
transformed into a collective experience, makes the media experiences a
real laboratory where new identities are created, new social relations are
experienced, thus leading the women involved to create new projects for
social change, as is the case of the collective Mujer Nueva.

The analysis of the process of emancipation lived in the identification
dimension reveals how these women, generally "invisibilized" and without a space for social and political representation of their own, provided
the media with an individual and/or collective meaning. The analysis of
the two focus groups has proven the relation between the individual and
collective dimensions of empowerment, as well as the importance of having alternative and citizen media. To the women interviewed, "another"
citizen communication takes place from the rupture of the dominant
narrations and visions and of the patriarchal practice, which must be
substituted (narrations, visions, etc.) by images that symbolize the daily
practice of women, as put into practice in the TV channel occupied.

The change in the political dimension represents one of the most relevant transformations produced in the women interviewed throughout
their media experiences in the movement of Oaxaca. This process gave
life to a re-elaboration of the concept of doing politics, contributing in
such a way to the transformation of the female protagonists into active
subjects. To these women, life management practices are interpreted as
another form of doing politics, that is to say, as another way of managing

what is public, featured by consensual decisions, horizontal relations and where power is distributed over the whole community.

The biographical approach has proven valuable when analyzing the change that these female protagonists have experienced, since it allows highlighting the importance of the subject in social change, thanks above all to the integration of data that have arisen from the life stories. The analysis has allowed detecting that, regardless of the learning they have lived, all the interviewees: (a) experienced a strengthening of the feeling of self-esteem, (b) contributed to building a female collective identity in which they identify themselves, and (c) participated in the development of new social projects in order to maintain the conquered spaces through media experiences.

Last of all, the approach from below and focused on the subject has allowed us to comprehend how, to these women, the experience of having made alternative media has led to a process of empowerment letting them break with the submissive role assigned by the Oaxacan society. At the same time, we have been able to understand the close relationship between personal change and social change for, as Raúl Zibechi (2007) asserted, when people change themselves, they change the world, and these women are unquestionably contributing to building a new world.

NOTES

1. For an analysis regarding the ways of collective action and the new culture emerging from the protests, see the books by Raúl Zibechi in English, translated and edited by AK Press: *Dispersing Power. Social Movements as Anti-State Forces* (2010); *Territories in Resistance: A Cartography of Latin American Social Movements* (2012).

2. A colloquial word for girls.

3. *Let's Revolutionize Oaxaca* and *Warrior Frida*.

4. Among the many definitions of empowerment that can be found in the literature, we have decided to refer to empowerment as "a socio-psychological condition of confidence in one's abilities to challenge the existing relations of domination" (Druri and Reicher 2005: 35).

5. See the reports of the Observatorio Nacional Ciudadano del Feminicidio (2010 and 2012) and those of the Consorcio para el Diálogo Parlamentario y la Equidad Oaxaca (2011 and 2013).

6. The cases presented in this chapter form part of a wider research that has encompassed the study of all the alternative media arisen during the insurrection of Oaxaca. Part of the research has been funded by the Bilateral Program of Mexico's Ministry of Foreign Affairs (files GRATOM73120812 and POMALI79122913) and by the Mobility Program of the Ibero-American Association of Postgraduate Universities.

7. In order to ensure the interviewees anonymity, at the end of this chapter the reader will find a table of reference concerning the fieldwork conducted and an explanation of the codes utilized throughout this paper.

8. The violent repression on the part of the state during the protests resulted in 23 casualties, 600 arrests "without an arrest warrant," and the forced disappearance of 200 citizens (CCIODH 2007).

9. Some examples provided by the women interviewed refer to the development of alternative markets called *tianguis culturales* to share goods that are cultural rather than material, such as videos, music, and books. Other examples include carrying out workshops on female sexuality, the menstrual cycle, self-defense, and so on.

REFERENCES

AA.VV. (2011). *Pensar las autonomías. Alternativas de emancipación al capital y el Estado*. Mexico: Sísifo Ediciones/Bajo Tierra.

CCIODH (Comisión Civil Internacional de Observación por los Derechos Humanos). (2007). *Informe sobre los hechos en Oaxaca. V Visita: del 16 de diciembre de 2006 al 20 de enero 2007*. Mexico: CCIODH.

CONAPO (Consejo Nacional de Población). (2010). *Índice de marginación por entidad federativa y municipio 2010*. Mexico: CONAPO.

CONEVAL (Consejo Nacional de Evaluación de la Política de Desarrollo Social). (2012). *Los mapas de la pobreza en México*. Mexico: CONEVAL.

Consorcio para el Dialogo Parlamentario y la Equidad Oaxaca. (2011). *Violencia contra las Mujeres. Una herida abierta en Oaxaca. 371 feminicidios ¿Dónde está la justicia? 2004–2011. Recuento ciudadano*. Oaxaca: Consorcio para el Dialogo Parlamentario y la Equidad Oaxaca A.C.

Consorcio para el Dialogo Parlamentario y la Equidad Oaxaca. (2013). *Informe ciudadano ¡JUSTICIA YA! Feminicidio y violencia contra las mujeres en Oaxaca a dos años del gobierno de la alternancia 2011–2012*. Oaxaca: Consorcio para el Dialogo Parlamentario y la Equidad Oaxaca A.C.

Dallago, Laura. (2006). *Che cos'é l'empowerment*. Rome: Carocci Editore.

De Certeau, Michel. (1984). *The Practice of Everyday Life*. Berkeley: University of California Press.

De Sousa Santos, Boaventura. (2008). "Reinventando la emancipación social." In *Pensar el Estado y la sociedad: desafíos actuales*, 15–35. La Paz: CLACSO.

Della Porta, Donatella (2010). *L'intervista qualitativa*. Bari: Editori Laterza.

Della Porta, Donatella (ed.). (2014). *Methodological Practices in Social Movement Research*. Oxford: Oxford University Press.

Drury, John, and Reicher, Steve. (1999). "The Intergroup Dynamics of Collective Empowerment: Substantiating the Social Identity Model of Crowd Behavior." *Group Processes Intergroup Relations* 2: 381–402.

Drury, John, and Reicher, Steve. (2000). "Collective Action and Psychological Change: The Emergence of New Social Identities." *British Journal of Social Psychology* 39: 579–604.

Drury, John, and Reicher, Steve. (2005). "Explaining Enduring Empowerment: A Comparative Study of Collective Action and Psychological Outcomes." *European Journal of Social Psychology* 35: 35–58.

Flick, Uwe. (2000). "Episodic Interviewing." In *Qualitative Researching with Text, Image and Sound: A Practical Handbook,* edited by M. Bauer and G. Gaskell, 75–92. London: Sage.

Flick, Uwe. (2004). *Introducción a la investigación cualitativa.* Madrid: Ediciones Morada/Fundación Paideia Galiza.

Freire, Paulo. (1970). *Pedagogy of the Oppressed.* New York: Herder and Herder.

Freire, Paulo. (1976). *Education, the Practice of Freedom.* London: Writers and Readers Publishing Cooperative.

González Casanova, Pablo. (2008). "La construcción de alternativas." *Cuadernos del Pensamiento Crítico Latinoamericano,* 6. Buenos Aires: CLACSO.

Holloway, John. (2010). *Crack Capitalism.* London: Pluto Press.

INEGI (Instituto Nacional de Estadística y Geografía). (2008). *Prontuario de información geográfica municipal de los Estados Unidos Mexicanos: Oaxaca de Juárez, Oaxaca 2008.* Mexico: INEGI.

Jasper, James M. (1997). *The Art Moral of Protest: Culture, Biography, and Creativity in Social Movements.* Chicago: University of Chicago Press.

Krauss, Celine. (1993). "Women and Toxic Waste Protests: Race, Class and Gender as Resources of Resistance." *Qualitative Sociology* 16 (3): 247–262.

Observatorio Nacional Ciudadano del Feminicidio. (2010). *Una mirada al feminicidio en México. Informe 2010.* http://observatoriofeminicidiomexico.com/publicaciones.html.

Observatorio Nacional Ciudadano del Feminicidio. (2012). *Una mirada al feminicidio en México. Informe 2012.* http://observatoriofeminicidiomexico.com/publicaciones.html.

Piven, Frances F,. and Cloward, Richard. (1977). *Poor People's Movements: Why They Succeed, How They Fail.* New York: Pantheon Books.

Pol Urrútia, Enric. (1996). "La apropiación del espacio. Cognición, representación y apropiación del espacio." *Collecció Monografies Psico-Socio-Ambientals* 9: 45n62.

Pol Urrútia, Enric. (2002). "El modelo dual de la apropiación del espacio." In *Psicología y Medio Ambiente. Aspectos psicosociales, educativos y metodológicos,* edited by R. Mira, J.M. Sabucedo, and J. Romay, 123–132. A Coruña: Asociación Galega de Estudios e Investigación Psicosocial.

Regalado, Jorge. (2012). "Notas deshilvanadas sobre otra epistemología." In *Hacer política para un porvenir más allá del capitalismo,* edited by J. Regalado et al., 167–181. Mexico: Grietas Editores.

Scott, James. (1985). *Weapons of the Weak: Everyday Forms of Peasant Resistance.* New Haven: Yale University Press.

Scott, James. (1987). "Resistance without Protest and without Organization: Peasant Opposition to the Islamic Zakat and the Christian Tithe." *Comparative Studies in Society and History* 29 (3): 417–452.

Scott, James. (1990). *Domination and the Arts of Resistance: Hidden Transcripts.* New Haven: Yale University Press.

Servaes, Jan (ed.). (2013). *Sustainability, Participation and Culture in Communication. Theory and Praxis.* Chicago: University of Chicago Press.

Sierra, Francisco. (2010). "Cultura latina y Sociedad de la Información. Pensar lo procomún." In *Cultura latina y revolución digital. Matrices para pensar el espacio iberoamericano de comunicación*, edited by F. Sierra, C. Del Valle, and J. Moreno, 69–93. Barcelona: Gedisa.

Thompson, Edward P. (1975). *Whigs and Hunters. The Origin of the Black Act*. London: Allen Lane.

Wood, Elisabeth J. (2001). "The Emotional Benefits of Insurgency in El Salvador." In *Passionate Politics: Emotions in Social Movements*, edited by J. Goodwin, J.M. Jasper, and F. Polletta, 267–281. Chicago: University of Chicago Press.

Zibechi, Raul. (2007). *Autonomías y emancipaciones. América Latina en movimiento*. Lima: Fondo Editorial de la Facultad de Ciencias Sociales/UNMSM.

Zibechi, Raul. (2008). *Territorios en resistencia. Cartografía política de las periferias urbanas latinoamericanas*. Buenos Aires: Lavaca editora.

IV

REPRESENTATIONS OF RACE, SEXUALITY, AND GENDER IN THE MEDIA

9

Harassed, Marginalized, and Childless

Gender Inequality in the Australian News Media. A Feminist Analysis

Louise North

One of the most significant changes to shape the Australian news media in the past thirty-five to forty years has been the influx of women into the once male bastion of its newsrooms. Today, just over a third of the journalistic workforce is female and some inroads are being made into key decision making areas (Byerly 2011). The "body count," however, has been the focus of what little academic research there is about female journalists in this country, leaving the *lived* experiences of women with barely a word—let alone a critical analysis. This absence not only points to a general acceptance or privileging of hegemonic masculine newsroom culture—a caldron that allows inequality to flourish, as this chapter will show—but also provides some indication of the low status of feminist media scholarship within the discipline of journalism.

Assessing the status of women in the Australian news media has been a by-product of global studies about journalistic culture (Hanusch 2008), or surveys that map broader changes in the journalistic workforce (Brand and Pearson 2001; Hanusch 2013; Henningham 1993; Schultz 1994). Women journalists, however, have not been silent about ongoing discrimination. Some female journalists in Australia have written about the "blokey" or masculine environments in which they work, or have worked, and how this has affected their careers (see Haussegger 2005;

Mann 2013; Spicer 2014; Trioli 1996; Wilkinson 2013), and media historians like Sharyn Pearce (1998) have documented the lives and challenges of some female journalists during the nineteenth and twentieth centuries.

In 1996 a groundbreaking survey conducted by the industry union, the Media, Entertainment and Arts Alliance, mapped the extent of systemic gender bias and discrimination in the industry (MEAA/IFJ 1996) and provided an important baseline for the industry and for further research. Yet, the union has never replicated the survey, nor has it informed any serious policy/code direction[1] and academics have rarely referred to it. The gendered nature of news production and newsroom culture has largely been ignored by journalism academics—with my monograph *The Gendered Newsroom* (2009) and associated publications (North 2004, 2007, 2009a, 2009b, 2012, 2014a, 2014b) but a small beginning. It is not an academic landscape that I had anticipated after a decade of publishing in this field.

In stark contrast, the more recent and dramatic shifts in the consumption and production of news brought about by digital technology has created nothing short of a seismic wave of concern within industry and the academy. The Australian Press Council, the self-regulatory body of print and online media, began investigations into industry changes brought about by convergence and new technology with a major report in 2006 (APC 2006). It replicated the report in 2007 (Herman 2007), and 2008 (Ryan, Ewart, and Posetti 2008). In the same year, the MEAA published another report, *Life in the Clickstream: The Future of Journalism* (Este et al. 2008) and again in 2010 (Este, Warren, and Murphy 2010). Journalists, too, have published many treatises (including Beecher 2007; Hywood 2011) on the complex issues facing the industry (including the need for sustainable business models) in the twenty-first century. There have been industry conferences on the "future of journalism" (beginning in 2008 with the MEAA organizing "summits" at three east coast cities with new media luminaries like U.S.-based Jay Rosen invited to speak) and there has, of course, been myriad opinion columns (Cordell 2008) in mainstream media. Academics have duly responded to the changes with an outpouring of important research (see, for example, Bruns 2012; Lumby 2002; Martin and Dwyer 2012; O'Donnell, McKnight, and Este 2012; Papandrea 2013; Rowe 2011; Tiffin 2009; Young 2010). In these "future of journalism" debates, female journalists and male journalists are understood and condensed as a *genderless*, homogenous whole. None of the industry reports, or academic work listed here discuss or even acknowledge the ramifications of an ongoing discriminatory culture that has been previously exposed by the 1996 MEAA report. This reluctance to provide a critical analysis of the experiences of female journalists, and how that differs from the experiences of male journalists, is surprising given that the MEAA report, and sections of various global surveys (Byerly 2011;

Gallagher 1995; Henningham 1993; Romano 2010) have raised concerns about women's status in Australian newsrooms since at least 1993. There is also a database collated by the Australian Government via the Workplace Gender Equality Agency that has provided statistical evidence of gender inequity in workforce composition since the early 2000s (WGEA 2014). A simple review of that data from media companies indicates that women journalists in Australia struggle with similar numerical gender inequity as their female peers around the globe. In other parts of the world, feminist media and journalism scholars from England, the United States, India, the Netherlands, Canada, West Indies, Sweden, Korea, New Zealand, and Lebanon have provided a thorough and ongoing assessment of the issues that concern women in journalism (see Byerly 2004; Chambers, Steiner and Fleming 2004; Cho and Davenport 2007; de Bruin 2000, 2004; Djerf-Pierre and Lofgren Nilsson 2004; Edstrom 2011; Joseph 2000; Lavie and Lehman-Wilzig 2005; Melki and Mallat 2014; Merlin-Higgins 2004; Robinson 2005; Ross 2004, 2010; Strong 2011; van Zoonen 1998). While the international literature grows, an Australian focus on the gendered production of news remains limited in comparison to the other major industry change—the ongoing (genderless) debates about technology, convergence and sustainable business models.

The most recent large-scale global survey of female journalists shows that women constitute just over a third of news journalists (34.4%) in Australia (Byerly 2011: 217)[2], compared with 36.1 percent globally. While female journalists have closed the gap with their male colleagues in the lower ranked reporting roles during the past four decades (Byerly 2011) and there is some evidence to suggest that woman are closer to parity with men in regional and rural media organizations compared with metropolitan outlets (North 2009: 116), men still overwhelmingly dominate senior decision-making positions in news organizations in Australia. The 1996 MEAA/IFJ survey ($n = 368$), was the first to survey female journalists about issues specific to them and provided evidence of broad ranging gender discrimination. It found that the most significant issues for female journalists were inequity in promotional opportunities, sexual harassment, and various aspects of childcare and workplace flexibility (MEAA/IFJ 1996: 14). Other concerns included horizontal segregation where women perceived that they were more often allocated soft news stories compared to their male colleagues and that these were not highly valued roles in news organizations. Women were also under-represented in their organizations at every level (MEAA/IFJ 1996: 14). Those findings reinforced other international research.

The question must then be asked: *Is this systemic, ongoing numerical and occupational inequity worthy of more consideration in Australia?* There are of course many industries that are male dominated where women struggle to reach equality on many fronts. There has already been rich analyses of Australian women in accountancy, architecture, science, medicine and law, to name a few (Carey 2002; Cooper 2010; Hanna 2002; Pringle 1998; Thornton 1996). The media, however, is a powerful force that shapes and influences how society understands itself and the events which take place within it. Even in this web 2.0 era where "news" is ubiquitous and constant and produced by an array of professional and citizen content-makers, the majority of news is still derived and consumed via the mainstream media. Thus, its focal mediating function disperses news in a variety of ways, on a variety of platforms reaching consumers and telling them what news is and therefore what is important. If that news is decided upon mostly by men, then consumers are being provided with a mostly male view of the world, privileging what is important and interesting to men. While a majority of men decide what is news, the views of women consumers and female journalists remain marginalized, relegating women to second-class citizens.

To ascertain the changes and the challenges that remain for female journalists the author, in 2012, undertook the largest survey of female journalists in Australia ($n = 577$). Using the 1996 MEAA study as a framework, the survey canvassed journalists from all media platforms, states, and territories and included respondents from all levels of seniority. In sum, it revealed that little has changed. The majority of respondents said that they had experienced sexual harassment by a male colleague (most within the past five years), and struggle to be promoted—hampered by the fact that reviews of work and promotional opportunities are often decided upon by one senior (usually male) manager. The survey responses also indicate that journalism is incompatible to women who care for children with about three-quarters of respondents having no children under fifteen. This is in line with other nations—(see, for example, Melki and Farah 2014: 75, in relation to media in Lebanon)—and a concern raised as early as 1994 by leading feminist media researcher Liesbet van Zoonen (1994). Respondents noted being typically excluded from many hard news rounds, especially sports reporting and business, which arguably stymies women's promotion opportunities (North 2012a, 2012b).

The aim of this chapter is to, first, provide a comparative analysis of the status of women working in the Australian news media with countries of similar media standing around the globe. It will then draw on quantitative and qualitative data from the author's 2012 survey of female journalists in Australia to analyze the key aspects of gender discrimination that remain stubbornly engrained. These include sexual harassment, gendered story allocations, childcare issues, promotional opportunities and pay inequity.

THE STATUS OF FEMALE JOURNALISTS IN AUSTRALIA

During the late 1970s and 1980s there was an influx of women into the reporting ranks of media organizations in most western countries coupled
with the rise of the second wave feminist movement and, in Australia,
the implementation of equal opportunities polices. Australia's Sex Discrimination Act 1984 notes that its aim is to promote equality between
men and women and "eliminate discrimination on the basis of sex" and
"eliminate sexual harassment" in the workplace (AHRC n.d)—an ongoing issue that I will return to in more detail later in the chapter. Since the
early 1990s when academic surveys started to "count" male and female
journalists, women have remained primarily clustered in the lower editorial ranks. Research suggests that women's participation in journalism
has been relatively static since the early 1990s. John Henningham's semi-
nal study in 1992 (and still the largest ever undertaken in Australia) found
that 33 percent of Australian journalists were female (1993); also in 1992
Schultz (1994) established that 30 percent of the journalists she surveyed
were women; in 1995 Gallagher (1995) noted that at the publicly funded
Australian Broadcasting Corporation women comprised 38.5 percent of
reporters and producers/directors; in 2000 Brand and Pearson (2001)
found 39 percent of journalists they surveyed were women; and in 2008
Hanusch (2008: 101) noted that 40 percent of his survey participants
were female. This slow, but steady rise, looked promising until Carolyn
Byerly's (2011) team of global researchers in 2009 and 2010 undertook the
most comprehensive large-scale project to ascertain the status of women
in the news media. Byerly's Australian researchers secured data directly
from six major media groups (covering 2,000 editorial and administra-
tive staff)[3] finding that 34.4 percent of Australian journalists are female
(219). In the past few years, however, two Australian research projects
broadly assessing the Australian journalistic workforce, have suggested
that women now comprise the majority of newsworkers in Australia (see
Hanusch 2013; Josephi and Richards 2012). Neither Josephi and Richards
nor Hanusch make reference to Byerly's report in those publications. Josephi and Richards (2012) surveyed 117 journalists and found 56 percent
to be female, while Hanusch (2013) surveyed 605 journalists and found
55 percent of the respondents to be female. Hanusch noted that his data
provided "reliable evidence to suggest that woman are in fact in a majority in Australian journalism" (2013: 34), although he later acknowledged
Byerly's research and refined his position to suggest that gender inequity
may depend on which media sectors women are employed in (Hanusch
2015). The fact that there is no known or verified list of the number of
journalists in Australia continues to make workforce analysis difficult,

although Hanusch (2013: 32), drawing from data provided by the Bureau of Statistics has estimated that the number is about 10,600.

There is a rise in the number of women in editorial decision-making roles globally and within Australia, albeit coming off a relatively low base and limited by a lack of previous research. In 1995, Margaret Gallagher established that just 3 percent of media organizations worldwide were headed by women, rising to 12 percent when the figures included the top levels of management (external governing boards, and management committees including boards of directors) (Gallagher 1995: 47). Six years later Bettina Peters found that even though women represented more than a third of working journalists around the world, the percentage of women editors, heads of departments or media owners was a minuscule 0.6 percent (Peters 2001: 4). Prior to Byerly's 2011 global study, there was only anecdotal and small survey evidence of gender inequity in decision-making roles in the Australian news media (see Haussegger 2005; MEAA/IFJ 1996). Data provided by media companies to the Federal Government's Workplace Gender Equity Agency provided some information but until recently the variable categorizations of "journalists" made it difficult to distinguish who undertook editorial or management roles. There was a clear gender bias evident in the statistics provided, but drawing reliable conclusions about the gender of those in rank and file and decision-making roles was almost impossible. Nevertheless, the agency (formerly titled the Equal Opportunity for Women in the Workplace Agency) reported a large drop in the percentage of women directors of media companies from 8.3 percent in 2004 to just 4.9 percent in 2010 (Jackson 2011). The most recent report shows that little progress has been made with the figure back to 2004 levels at 8.1 percent (EOWA 2012: 29) In senior editorial and management jobs in Australian newsrooms, the majority of positions are occupied by men (Byerly 2011; Hanusch 2013). In the companies surveyed by Byerly (2011: 219), women make up 20 percent of those in governance (boards of directors), and 10 percent in top-level management (publishers, chief executive officers). The numbers of women in senior management (22%) and middle management[4] (29%) are also low compared to countries with similar media systems like the United States, United Kingdom, and Canada. Hanusch's survey (2013: 34) established that 7.4 percent of female journalists could be classed as senior managers while 21.6 percent of men were in this category, indicating that less than a third (30%) of women are senior managers. In the dominant newspaper sector, just three women hold the position of editor at the nation's twenty-one metropolitan newspaper titles. Two edit a weekend or Saturday edition-only where soft news proliferates, while the other edits the less prestigious, small circulation *Gold Coast Bulletin*.[5]

AUSTRALIA, UNITED KINGDOM, UNITED STATES, AND CANADA: A COMPARATIVE ANALYSIS

To provide some geographical context to the general data situating women in the Australian news media, three countries with similar media systems—the United States, United Kingdom and Canada—will be more closely considered. Australian newspaper and broadcast media closely reflect the American and Canadian model with newspapers dominated by metropolitan rather than national publications (Tiffin 2006), and broadcast media similarly styled (Forde and Burrows 2004). In terms of format and reporting styles, however, Australian newspapers follow the British model. The Australian news media is extremely concentrated, especially in the print sector where the Australian arm of the multi-national conglomerate News Corporation, and Fairfax Media Limited together own about 88 percent of the mastheads (Dwyer 2013). News Corp also owns the Pay-TV channel *Fox News*, while holding substantial interests in Britain and the United States, including the *Times of London*, the *Wall Street Journal*, and the *New York Post*.

While there are similarities in media systems, there are significant differences between the status of women in the Australian news media in all job categories compared with women in the UK, U.S. and Canadian news organizations (see Figure 9.1). At every level Australia lags behind: In the UK, women constitute 36.5 percent of those in governance roles (boards of directors) and 30.2 percent in top level management (publishers, CEOs). Women average 38.7 percent of all journalists,[6] which includes roles like news directors, executive editors, senior editors, correspondents, producers, anchors, directors, writers, and sub-editors, among others (Byerly 2011: 359). Similarly, in the United States women occupy 35.3 percent of governance roles, 23.3 percent of top level management, and average 45.2 percent of journalists (Byerly 2011: 201). In Canada women make up 26.3 percent of those in governance roles, 39.4 percent in top level management and average 51.4 percent in journalistic roles (Byerly 2011: 160). As previously noted, in Australia women constitute 20 percent of those in governance and 10 percent in top-level management and 34.4 percent of journalists. In all countries women are overrepresented in just one category—"sales, finance and administration." In Australia 66 percent of workers in that category are female, while in the UK 59.5 percent are women, in the United States 73.4 percent are women, and in Canada 61.7 percent are women. The chapter now moves on to an analysis of the experiences of female journalists in the Australian news media.

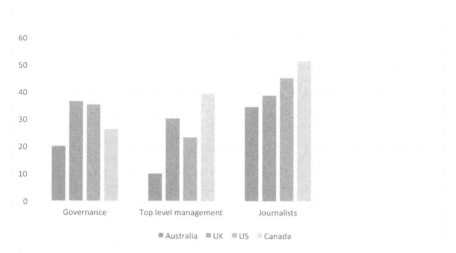

Figure 9.1.   Percentage of female journalists by occupational role. Byerly C.M. *Global Report on the Status of Women in the News Media* (International Women's Media Foundation).

AN OCCUPATIONAL CRISIS: THE CULTURE
OF SEXUAL HARASSMENT IN NEWSROOMS

An increased incidence of sexual harassment was one of the most staggering findings in the 2012 survey. In contrast to the media-driven "post-feminist" era of perceived empowerment and agency for women, sexual harassment *remains* a major issue for all female workers. In Australia almost 1 in 4 women (22%) in the general workforce experience some form of sexual harassment (AHRC 2008: v), while more than 1 in 2 (57.3%) female journalists experience it (North 2012: 62). In the television news sector a staggering 68 percent of women experience harassment (North 2016). Australia's Sex Discrimination Act 1984 defines sexual harassment as "any unwanted or unwelcome sexual behaviour, which makes a person feel offended, humiliated or intimidated" (AHRC nd.) Yet, despite being unlawful for more than twenty-five years, sexual harassment remains an ongoing problem which is experienced by more female journalists than ever before, and at more than double the rate of the general female workforce. Consequently, it is not an understatement to suggest that the ongoing and increased prevalence of sexual harassment in Australian newsrooms is at a crisis point. Contrary to popular belief, sexual harassment is *not* an issue of the past. Of the 57.3 percent of respondents ($n = 304$) in the 2012 survey who said that they had experienced harassment, more than half noted that it had occurred in the last five years and took the form of "objectionable remarks/behaviour," or "inappropriate physical contact." In 98 percent of instances, the harassment was perpetrated by a male colleague. These trends are reflected in the global data. A recent survey conducted by the International Women's Media Foundation found that almost half of the female journalists surveyed had experienced sexual harassment (48 percent of the 683 respondents). Respondents in the global report said the harassment was overwhelmingly perpetrated by male colleagues (Barton and Storm 2013: 22).

To move beyond the statistics, it is important to ask what are the personal and professional ramifications for those who experience sexual harassment? The two Australian reports indicate that harassment undermines the victims' confidence and affects their work, while respondents to the global survey note that there are emotional and/or psychological effects (Barton and Storm 2013: 27). Ross's British study of female journalists notes a similar response, where constant low-level harassment gave women "an underlying sense of inadequacy" (2004: 147). Despite these consequences, very few victims make a formal complaint (13% in both Australian reports), although a larger proportion (32.7%) in the global report. This is not to blame the victims, but rather to raise the point that most don't report incidences of sexual harassment because they see it as a *futile exercise* with little benefit in doing so, fear victimization (Barton and Storm 2013: 25; MEAA/IFJ 1996), or think they can best handle the situation themselves. Many of the 2012 survey respondents downplayed the harassment, noting that it wasn't "serious" enough and that they didn't want to appear "overly sensitive" or "were scared of repercussions."

There has been a lot of objectionable behaviour within the newsrooms—but no one ever complains because nothing is ever done. (Rural/regional newspaper designer/graphic artist, aged 30–34)

Our newsroom feels like a boys club, with the deputy editor, editor and general manager all very matey and sending each other pics of bikini girls etc. Makes it difficult to complain about one of them when you feel they will tell you you're being overly sensitive. (Regional/rural newspaper chief of staff, aged 25–29)

It goes on all the time, and is generally perpetrated by senior managers. Complaining would be futile, not to mention daunting and possibly damaging to my relationships with those managers. (Metropolitan public TV producer, aged 30–34)

He was my COS [chief of staff]. After turning him down, he stopped assigning stories in my direction. I was a junior reporter, and was scared of repercussions if I made a formal complaint. (Metropolitan newspaper editor/online editor, aged 40–44)

From these responses it is evident that women understand harassment as the price they have to pay for daring to step into a male dominated industry. Harassment is about *power*, not sex, so female journalists who are typically en masse in lower status positions compared with their male colleagues have learnt to endure/accept harassment because the reprisals seem too great. Like other surveys of female journalists' experience of sexual harassment including, Ross in the UK (2004) and Opoku-Mensah in Africa (2004), these comments indicate a fear that if a formal complaint is made then it will be the victim, not the perpetrator who will bear the repercussions. Being stigmatized as a complainer, being disadvantaged in important professional relationships with senior managers who hold the key to their career progression, and being seen as *overly sensitive* makes a folly of the masquerade that newsrooms embody a neutral professional ethos (Ross 2004: 147). In these environments women—and their experiences—are understood as "other" to the male norm. With an occupational culture that encourages those who experience harassment to ignore or at best downplay it, it is difficult to envisage where change can come from without a ground swell of support from the union and media managers.

SOFT AND HARD NEWS:
THE "PINK GHETTO" IS ALIVE AND WELL

Female journalists are well aware of the gendered nature of story allocations and the high value ascribed to hard news, which male reporters most often write or broadcast, compared to the lower value, soft news stories which female journalists typically write or broadcast (Ross and Carter 2011: 1149). Horizontal segregation, or as Franks (2013) titles it the "pink ghetto," has stubbornly remained over the past forty years since women started to make significant numerical inroads into newsrooms. While at first glance, the gender of who produces various types of news may seem insignificant to career progress, those who produces hard news are highly valued and therefore have more chance of promotion. Definitions of soft and hard news abound and, aside from feminist assessments, most do not establish a gendered dimension. *Hard news* consists of "factual presentations of events deemed newsworthy" (Tuchman 1973: 113), usually centering on "serious stories about important topics" (Bender et al. 2009: 133) including politics, economics (Lehman-Wilzig and Seletzky 2010: 38; van Zoonen 1998: 36) and public interest matters (Baum 2003), and demands immediate publication. Its corollary, *soft news*, centers on features or human interest stories (van Zoonen 1998: 36), unusual events, (Lehman-Wilzig and Seletzky 2010: 38) and trends, personalities or lifestyle (Brooks et al. 1985). There is no need for soft news to be published immediately because it has little "informational value" and is less prestigious in the news hierarchy. This is not to say that soft news is not prevalent: the increasing tabloidization of the media has seen a proliferation of soft news content. Yet, this has not equated to an elevated status of those stories or the female reporters who typically produce them.

A byline analysis of Australian news content found that male reporters have a stranglehold on hard news stories about politics, government and the economy, while female reporters are most likely to report in soft news in the "science and health" and "social legal" categories (Romano 2010: 9). Romano's research found that 67 percent of stories about politics and government and 73 percent of stories about the economy carried male bylines (Romano 2010: 9), while female reporters' most significant contribution came in the science, health and social legal categories at 41 percent. The MEAA/IFJ report (1996) found that the majority of female journalists surveyed believed that there were story subjects traditionally allocated to women and those areas were considered less important at the respondents' organizations (MEAA/IFJ 1996: 35). Those areas included women's issues and fashion, health, the arts, entertainment and education. In the 2012 survey little has changed in this area. A total of 60 percent of respondents agreed that there were news areas that are traditionally allocated to male reporters (most noting sport and business). Survey respondents wrote that the types of rounds allocated to women typically included health and fashion, followed by soft/feature-type stories, family/childcare, social affairs, education, lifestyle and the arts. While an accurate comparison between the 1996 and 2012 survey is not possible because of how rounds were grouped in the 1996 survey, it appears that more women are working across hard news categories. For example in 2012, 33 percent of respondents said they worked predominantly in the politics round and 18 percent in the business/finance round in the multi-choice question. This compares to 11 percent working in the broad category of "commerce, business, economics, politics, the press gallery, foreign affairs, industrial relations and technology" in 1996. Nevertheless, the low value that news organizations ascribe to soft news, and the reporters who write it are evidenced in responses from women in the 2012 survey.

> The day I see men vying to do social issues will be the day equality has landed. (Metropolitan newspaper sub editor, aged 40–44)
>   At the Herald Sun in the last few years I was there, very experienced female reporters were allocated social and family rounds—even women with no children and no interest in the area. Some of these reporters had come to the Herald Sun from other states as promotions for their hard-hitting journalism and then were given the softest rounds. The Herald Sun editor has quite archaic attitudes to working women. He seems to think they're taking

jobs away from men and working for pin money. (Online news reporter, aged 45–49)

All our "soft" areas, food and wine, arts, literature, entertainment are run by women, none of whom are included in the daily news conferences. (Metropolitan newspaper section/online editor, aged 50–55)

The penultimate and final comments above from two experienced journalists are revealing for their insights into the low value that news organizations, and reporters, place on soft news and those who edit those areas. Even though one respondent notes that women have senior roles in editing soft news sections, in reality their perceived authority is diffused by not being allowed access to the daily news conference where story content is debated and decided upon. The daily news conference is male and soft news is a take-it-or-leave-it secondary consideration. With many female journalists placed in that category, it is not surprising that so few have the will to challenge the normative journalistic culture, and its gendered presumptions about who should write soft and hard news.

YOUNG AND CHILDLESS: THE MOTHERHOOD "PROBLEM" IN JOURNALISM

The preponderance of female journalists in the Australian news media who are childless is an indicator that the industry remains inflexible and incompatible with motherhood. The 1996 MEAA/IFJ survey found that 75 percent of respondents did not have children under fifteen, and in 2012 that remains about the same (73%). This is the case even though three-quarters of the respondents in the current survey were aged between twenty-five and forty-nine—the age bracket where women are most likely to care for children. Respondents noted that workplace arrangements are inflexible and do not accommodate women with childcare responsibilities, and also there was a lack of on-site childcare facilities which meant that women found it difficult to work overtime or shiftwork, even if they are prepared to do so. Byerly's (2011) research amplifies the problem finding that just a third of media organizations in Australia offer childcare assistance. The motherhood "problem" is not new or specific to journalism, but has been an ongoing area of gender inequality that media researchers around the globe have identified since the late 1970s (Byerly and Warren 1996; Lafky 1991; Ross 2001; Melki and Mallat 2014; North 2009; Organ et al. 1979).

Female journalists understand, and many seem to accept, that the repercussion of such lack of support for those with children is that career progression is curtailed or ceases altogether. More than half of the respondents in the 2012 survey agreed that promotional opportunities are affected by childcare responsibilities. The major themes to arise from the question "Can you indicate why women's promotional opportunities are affected by their childcare responsibilities?" were a normalization of a *male-centric view* of the job of a journalist, and a lack of onsite care facilities that severely restricts women's ability to work as much as they would like, which caused inequity with their male colleagues in terms of promotion. The most unsettling element in this data is that women tend to see childcare through a neo-liberal lens—as their *individual* problem that they have to personally manage so as to become a valuable, disembodied, autonomous worker. The survey participants' comments rarely note that it is a structural inequality that hampers women from having equal opportunity to promotion. This perspective is perhaps not surprising considering the normalizing process that is activated by women's incorporation into a largely male profession where routines that have been engrained by this domination means that "male perspectives are constructed as unproblematic, uncontested and, most importantly, apparently value free" (Ross 2001: 533).

Deadlines are deadlines. They are inflexible. Women self-select away from advancement rather than over commit. (Metropolitan newspaper reporter, aged 40–44)

I don't think it's a deliberate thing. It's just that women have to divide their time, don't want to or can't work full-time, and that counts them out of a lot of senior positions. (Metropolitan newspaper reporter, aged 35–39)

It is unfortunate women's promotional opportunities are affected by their child or children, but I do understand and accept why; simply put a person can't be in two places at once, even if they want to be. It seems more women than men take on the primary carer role while still trying to be the peak performance journo she used to be. It can't work, and I think news managers sense that. (Commercial TV reporter, aged 40–44)

The structure of some roles require particular time commitment and/or overtime that many women are keen to do, but can't support through lack of adequate childcare. We currently support multiple part-time arrangements in our workplace, but part-time or job-share is difficult for some positions—it disadvantages other staff. (Metropolitan radio chief of staff, aged 40–44)

Childcare responsibilities are often cited by female journalists, in this survey, and male journalists in others, as the main reason why women do not attain, or attempt to seek, key decision-making positions in news organizations (North 2009; Torkkloa and Ruoho 2011). It is, however, not as simple as accepting a single essentialist framework to understand women's disadvantage in promotional opportunities. Having childcare responsibilities alone does not explain why women's careers in journalism do not progress as well as men's.

"I ASK. THEY REFUSE":
GENDER INEQUITY IN PAY AND PROMOTION

It is generally accepted that female journalists earn less money than their male colleagues in most countries, although accessing reliable salary data from media companies continues to prove difficult (Byerly 2011: 28). In the early 1990s Gallagher (1995: 55) found that Australian women journalists earned on average 74 percent of male journalists' average earnings, and although those figures were based on a relatively small sample, they provided a starting point. In 2003, journalist Sally Jackson reported that there continues to be a glaring gender disparity in average weekly earnings of journalists in all age groups and that it widens with age. The ABS statistics that she provided revealed that the pay gap was least when young journalists entered the industry—women earned 2.5 percent less than men between fifteen and twenty-four years of age. As men and women rose up the ranks the pay gap increased with women aged twenty-five to thirty-four earning 8 percent less, between thirty-five and forty-four—15 percent less, forty-five and fifty-four—21 percent less, and those female journalists aged fifty-five plus earned 20 percent less than their male counterparts (Jackson 2003: 3). The data used by Jackson is for female journalists with no children working full-time and confirms that with or without children, female journalists in Australia are paid less than their male counterparts. Byerly's 2011 data also indicates that men make considerably more than women in all occupational levels (2011: 218), although she does warn that her findings can be read only as a tentative interpretation, due "to the sparse amounts of data provided from the companies surveyed." Nevertheless, what has been collated does add an important link in the story about *gendered pay inequality* in Australian journalism.

What else might stand in the way of women's promotional opportunities? The majority of survey respondents say that promotions are decided by the editor alone with no formal performance review based on objective criteria. Another issue that affects promotion is the large percentage of female journalists (35.5%) employed on individually negotiated contracts as opposed to an industry negotiated and imposed awards. This shift to contracts effectively enforces pay inequity because remuneration becomes hidden and therefore more difficult to address. Moreover, women's pay is affected by a *lack of objective criteria for promotion,* the promotion of "like by like" (i.e., managers advancing those they identify most with), and bias in the allocation of news assignments (i.e., the soft news/hard news binary discussed above) (Jackson 2003). When asked to comment on how they had negotiated their pay rises some 2012 survey respondents comments included:

I ask. They refuse despite adequate criteria for a merit-based pay rise. I have been thwarted five times in 12 years—receiving only miniscule award rises in this time. (Metropolitan newspaper feature writer, aged over 56)

Don't bother as I feel it's personality based rather than performance based. (Metropolitan newspaper sub-editor, aged 50–55)

Negotiating a new contract is generally a terrifying experience. You either hire a manager who takes 20% of your gross salary or take the horrifying option of negotiating a new deal for yourself. A new deal doesn't always mean a pay rise. It has, on occasion, meant a pay cut and/or changes in duties. Every negotiation I have ever participated in has been with one to three men. Every negotiation has involved meetings where duties, conditions and remuneration are agreed upon verbally. In every negotiation I have always had to fight for the verbal undertakings to be honoured in writing. I have been called a pedant. I have had men at various levels of the network demand to know "what I want," answering "what was promised verbally in writing" has sometimes prompted these "managers" to yell at me. There are usually a minimum seven drafts of contracts until the final draft reflects most of what has been promised. By the end of it, you are so beaten down, you just sign the bloody thing. Men I know in the organisation have been taken out to lunch or dinner to renegotiate. This has never happened to me. (Commercial television executive producer, aged 45–49)

All three respondents acknowledge that a merit-based system of promotion does not exist, leaving the path to promotional success based on an "old boys" network of established connections with key (male) decision-makers. For an industry that largely views itself as a profession (Davis 2010), the fact that commercial organizations have failed to implement a functioning merit-based model begs the question of why? The frustrating and demoralising experience outlined by the executive producer, above, indicates that even when agreements are made they have to be continually fought for, undermining her confidence at every level.

CONCLUSION

This chapter has provided an overview of key equity issues for women working in the Australian news media. The data, in the main, paints a picture of a largely marginalized, harassed and childless female workforce that has changed little in the past fifteen or so years. While more women are slowly rising to key editorial decision-making ranks and the variety of rounds they now cover include more of the prestigious hard news areas, the challenges remain immense. Female journalists in Australia are experiencing sexual harassment at crisis levels—more than twice the rate of the general workforce—they are paid less for the same jobs as their male peers, and they are hampered by a lack of suitable options for childcare support and so most are young and single, or childless. *Entrenched horizontal segregation* means women do the bulk of the less valued soft news reporting, which adversely affects their career progression. Statistics by their very nature, however, erase the lived experiences of respondents, so while overarching quantitative research is vital to mapping and locating gender disparity, more qualitative research must be undertaken to fully understand the gendered newsroom and the women journalists who have largely been ignored in Australia by their industry, their union and academic researchers. I was recently reminded of the transformational and/or reflective impact of research that gives women a voice, and why it is vital that it continues. After I completed a radio interview about women in journalism in Australia, a senior female metropolitan newspaper journalist posted a message to me on Facebook (September 27, 2014) to say that what I had talked about:

> Actually made me cry. I don't spend much time these days thinking about how things really are. I think it must be like what happens to a brumby when someone puts a harness on it for the first time. But years later, it's standing calmly at the hitching post, resigned to something that is not the way it should be.

NOTES

1. Although, in 2013 the MEAA endorsed the establishment of a Women in Media networking and mentoring group and says it is also "campaigning for paid superannuation during periods of unpaid parental leave for all media workers. Closing the gender gap in pay, retirement income and career opportunity is also central to what MEAA wants to achieve through this program" (WiM: n.p.).

2. This figure was arrived at by averaging the statistics for workers in four journalistic categories of Byerly's 2011 study: senior management, middle management, senior level and junior level professional staff (219). Other categories like "sales, finance and administration," "technical professional" (i.e., camera and sound staff) and "production and design" (graphics and scene designers) were excluded from the figures as they could not be defined as journalists.

3. This is a rare, and arguably much more accurate, approach to data collection. The majority of Australian surveys collate samples from a snowballing method, or from databases like Margaret Gee's Media Guide (2011).

4. These two occupational levels include roles like news directors and executive editors who decide on news assignments and take part in other tasks associated with shaping the news.

5. At the time of writing (May 2015) Michelle Gunn edited the *Weekend Australian*, Jenni O'Dowd—the Saturday edition of the *Daily Telegraph* in Sydney, and Cath Webber—the *Gold Coast Bulletin*.

6. The percentage for the category "journalist" in the UK, US and Canada was arrived at (as above) by averaging the statistics for workers in the four journalistic categories of Byerly's 2011 study: senior management, middle management, senior level and junior level professional staff, (219).

REFERENCES

Australian Human Rights Commission (AHRC). (n.d.). "Sexual Harassment." .https://www.humanrights.gov.au/our-work/sex-discrimination/guides/ sexual-harassment.

Australian Human Rights Commission. (2008). *Sexual Harassment: Serious Business—Results of the 2008 Sexual Harassment National Telephone Survey.* Sydney: Human Rights and Equal Opportunity Commission. https://www.humanrights.gov.au/sites/default/files/content/sexualharassment/serious_business/SHSB_Report2008.pdf.

Australian Press Council (APC). (2006). *State of the News Print Media in Australia.* Sydney: Australian Press Council.

Barton, Alana, and Hannah Storm. (2014). *Violence and Harassment against Women in the News Media: A Global Picture.* New York: Women's Media Foundation and the International News Safety Institute. http://www.iwmf.org/sexual-harassment/.

Beecher, Eric. (2007). "War of Words: The Future of Journalism." *Monthly*, June. http://www.themonthly.com.au/issue/2007/june/1283826117/eric-beecher/ war-words.

Brand, Jeffrey, and Mark Pearson. (2001). "The Newsroom vs. the Lounge Room: Journalists' and Audiences' Views on News." *Australian Journalism Review* 23(2): 63–89.

Brooks, Brian S., George Kennedy, Daryl R. Moen, and Don Ranly. (1985). *News Reporting and Writing.* New York: St. Martin's Press.

Bruns, Axel. (2012). "Journalists and Twitter: How Australian News Organisations Adapt to a New Medium." *Media International Australia* 44: 97–107.

Byerly, Carolyn. M. (2011). *Global Report on the Status of Women in the News Media.* Washington DC: International Women's Media Foundation.

Byerly, Carolyn. (2004). "Feminist Interventions in Newsrooms." In *Women and Media: International Perspectives,* edited by Karen Ross and Carolyn Byerly, 109–131. Oxford: Blackwell.

Byerly, Carolyn M., and Catherine Warren. (1996). "At the Margins of Centre: Organized Protest in the Newsroom." *Critical Studies in Mass Communication* 13(1): 1–23.

Carey, Jane. (2002). "Departing From Their Sphere? Australian Women in Science, 1880–1960." In *Departures: How Australia Reinvents Itself,* edited by Xavier Pons, 175–183. Melbourne: Melbourne University Press.

Chambers, Deborah, Linda Steiner, and Fleming Carole. (2004). *Women and Journalism*. London: Routledge.

Cho, Sooyoung, and Lucinda D. Davenport. (2007). "Gender Discrimination in Korean Newsrooms." *Asian Journal of Communication* 17(3): 286–300.

Cooper, Kathie. (2010). "Accounting by Women: Fear, Favour and the Path to Professional Recognition for Australian Women Accountants." *Accounting History* 15(3): 309–336.

Cordell, Marni. (2008). "It's Your ABC, Literally." *New Matilda,* November 11. https://newmatilda.com/2008/11/11/its-your-abc-literally.

Davis, Michael. (2010). "Why Journalism Is a Profession." In *Journalism Ethics: A Philosophical Approach*, edited Christopher Myers, 91–102. New York: Oxford University Press.

de Bruin, Marjan. (2004). "Organizational, Professional and Gender Identities: Overlapping, Coinciding and Contradicting Realities in Caribbean Media Practices." In *Gender and Newsroom Cultures: Identities at Work,* edited by Marjan de Bruin and Karen Ross, 1–16. Cresskill, NJ: Hampton Press.

de Bruin Marjan. (2000). "Gender, Organizational and Professional Journalism." *Journalism* 1(2): 217–238.

Djerf-Pierre Monika and Monica Lofgren Nilsson. (2004). "Gender-Typing in the Newsroom: The Feminization of Swedish Television News Production 1958–2000." In *Gender and Newsroom Cultures: Identities at Work,* edited by Marjan de Bruin and Karen Ross, 79–104. Cresskill, NJ: Hampton Press.

Dwyer, Tim. (2013). "Australia's Lamentable Media Diversity Needs a Regulatory Fix." *Conversation,* March 21. http://theconversation.com/australias-lamentable-media-diversity-needs-a-regulatory-fix-12942.

Edstrom, Maria. (2011). "Is There a Nordic Way? A Swedish Perspective on Achievements and Problems with Gender Equality in Newsrooms." *Media Studies* 2(3–4): 64–75.

Este, Jonathan, Christopher Warren, and Flynn Murphy. (2010). *Life in the Clickstream: The Future of Journalism.* Redfern: MEAA.

Este, Jonathan, Christopher Warren, Louise O'Connor, Matt Brown, Ruth Pollard, and Terry O'Connor. (2008). *Life in the Clickstream II: The Future of Journalism.* Redfern: MEAA.

EOWA (Equal Opportunity for Women in the Workplace Agency). (2012). *Australian Census of Women in Leadership.* https://www.wgea.gov.au/sites/default/files/2012_CENSUS%20REPORT.pdf.

Forde, Susan, and Elizabeth Burrows. (2004). "The Faces of News, Now and Then: An Historical Profile of Journalists in Australia and Overseas." In *When Journalism Meets History,* edited by Sybil Nolan, 91–100. Melbourne: RMIT.

Franks, Suzanne. (2013). "Hard Evidence: Is There still a Gender Bias in Journalism?" *Conversation,* November 13. http://theconversation.com/hard-evidence-is-there-still-a-gender-bias-in-journalism-19789.

Gallagher, Margaret. (1995). *An Unfinished Story: Gender Patterns in Media Employment.* Paris: UNESCO.

Gee, Margaret. (2011). *Margaret Gee's Australian Media Guide.* North Melbourne: Crown Content.

Hanna, Bronwyn. (2002). "Australia's Early Women Architects: Milestones and Achievements." *Fabrications* 12(1): 27–57.

Hanusch, Folker. (2015). "Breaking the Glass Ceiling? Some Notes on Gender and Merit in Australian Journalism." In *Pathways to Gender Equality in Australia: The Role of Merit and Quotas*, edited by Diann Rodgers-Healey, 72–87. Minnamurra: Australian Centre for Leadership for Women.

Hanusch, Folker. (2013). "Journalists in Times of Change: Evidence from a New Survey of Australia's Journalistic Workforce." *Australian Journalism Review* 35(1): 29–42.

Hanusch, Folker. (2008). "Mapping Australian Journalism Culture: Results from a Survey of Journalists' Role Perceptions." *Australian Journalism Review* 30(2): 97–109.

Haussegger, Virginia. (2005). *Wonder Woman: The Myth of "Having It All."* Sydney: Allen and Unwin.

Henningham John. (1993). "Characteristics and Attitudes of Australian Journalists." *Electronic Journal of Communication* 3(3/4). http://www.cios.org/EJCPUBLIC/003/3/00337.HTML.

Herman, Jack R. (ed.). (2007). *State of the News Print Media in Australia.* Sydney: Australian Press Council.

Hywood, Greg. (2011). "The Future of Journalism Looks Bright." *Australian*, November 21. http://www.theaustralian.com.au/media/opinion/the-future-of-journalism-looks-bright/story-e6frg99o-1226200523027.

Jackson, Sally. (2011). "Numbers of Women at the Top Shrinking Despite Hard Work." *Australian,* August 29. http://www.theaustralian.com.au/media/numbers-of-women-at-the-top-shrinking-despite-hard-work/story-e6frg996-1226124037418.

Jackson, Sally. (2003). "Equal Work but Women Journalists Get Less Pay Than Their Male Counterparts." *Australian* (features section), May 23, B3.

Joseph, Ammu. (2000). *Women in Journalism: Making News.* New Delhi: Konark Publishers.

Josephi, Beate, and Ian Richards. (2012). "The Australian Journalist in the 21st Century." In *The Global Journalist in the 21st Century*, edited by David Weaver and Lars Willnat, 115–125. New York: Routledge.

Lafky, Sue. (1991). "Women Journalists." In *The American Journalist: A Portrait of US News People and their Work,* edited by David Weaver and G. Cleveland Wilhoit, second edition, 87–103. Newbury Park, CA: Sage.

Lavie, Aliza, and Sam Lehman-Wilzig. (2005). "The Method Is the Message: Explaining Inconsistent Findings in Gender and News Production Research." *Journalism* 1(6): 66–89.

Leaver, Kate. (2014). "If a Woman Is 'Okay' with It, Is It still Sexual Harassment?" *Mamamia,* May 20. http://www.mamamia.com.au/news/fitzy-and-wippa-apology/.

Lehman-Wilzig, Sam N., and Michal Seletzky. (2010). "Hard News, Soft News, 'General' News: The Necessity and Utility of an Intermediate Classification." *Journalism* 11(1): 37–56.

Lumby, Catharine. (2002). "The Future of Journalism." In *The Media and Communications in Australia,* edited by Stuart Cunningham and Graeme Turner. Sydney: Allen and Unwin.

Mann, Effie. (2013). "Lisa Wilkinson and Annabel Crabb Lament Viewer Obsession with Female TV Journalists' Appearance." *Daily Life*, October 28, http://www.dailylife.com.au/news-and-views/lisa-wilkinson-and-annabel-crabb-lament-viewer-obsession-with-female-tv-journalists-appearance-20131028-2wbge.html.

Martin, Fiona and Tim Dwyer. (2012). *Addressing Convergence: Operational, Legal and Ethical Trends in Online and Cross-Media News Production*. Sydney: University of Sydney. http://www.presscouncil.org.au/uploads/52321/ufiles/Addressing_Convergence-Martin-Dwyer.pdf.

MEAA/IFJ (Media, Entertainment and Arts Alliance, and the International Federation of Journalists). (1996). *Women in the Media in Asia: Participation and Portrayal*. Sydney: MEAA.

Melki, Jad, and May Farah. (2014). "Educating Media Professionals with a Gender and Critical Media Literacy Perspective: How to Battle Gender Discrimination and Sexual Harassment in the Media Workplace." http://www.unesco.org/new/fileadmin/MULTIMEDIA/HQ/CI/CI/pdf/publications/gamag_research_agenda_melki_farah.pdf.

Melki, Jad P., and Sarah E. Mallat. (2014). "Block Her Entry, Keep Her Down and Push Her Out: Gender Discrimination and Women Journalists in the Arab World." *Journalism Studies*, doi: 10.1080/1461670X.2014.962919.

Melin-Higgins, Marjan. (2004). "Coping with Journalism: Gendered Newsroom Culture." In *Gender and Newsroom Cultures: Identities at Work*, edited by Marjan de Bruin and Karen Ross, 197–222. Cresskill, NJ: Hampton Press.

North, Louise. (2016). "Behind the Mask: Women in Television News." *Media International Australia*.

North, Louise. (2014a). "The Gender of 'Soft' and 'Hard' News: Female Journalists' Views on Gendered Story Allocations." *Journalism Studies*, doi: 10.1080/1461670X.2014.987551.

North, Louise. (2014b). "Still a 'Blokes Club': The Motherhood Dilemma for Journalism." *Journalism: Theory, Practice and Criticism*, doi: 10.1177/1464884914560306.

North, Louise. (2012a). "'Blokey' Newsrooms still a Battleground for Female Journalists." *Australian Journalism Review* 34(2): 57–70.

North, Louise. (2012b). "The Gendered World of Sports Reporting in the Australian Print Media." *JOMEC Journal of Journalism, Media and Cultural Studies*, 2. http://www.cardiff.ac.uk/jomec/research/journalsandpublications/jomecjournal/2-november2012/index.html.

North, Louise. (2009a). "Blokey Newsroom Culture." *Media International Australia* 132: 5–15.

North, Louise. (2009b). "Gendered Experiences of Industry Change and the Effects of Neoliberalism." *Journalism Studies* 10(4): 506–521.

North, Louise. (2009c). *The Gendered Newsroom: How Journalists Experience the Changing World of Media*. Cresskill, NJ: Hampton Press.

North, Louise. (2007). "'Just a Little Bit of Cheeky Ribaldry'?: Newsroom Discourses of Sexually Harassing Behaviour." *Feminist Media Studies* 7(1): 81–96.

North, Louise. (2004). "Naked Women, Feminism and Newsroom Culture." *Australian Journal of Communication* 31(2): 53–68.

O'Donnell, Penny, David McKnight, and Jonathan Este. (2012). *Journalism at the Speed of Bytes: Australian Newspapers in the 21st Century.* Sydney: MEAA.

Opoku-Mensah, Aida. (2004). "Hanging In There: Women, Gender and Newsroom Cultures Africa." In *Gender and Newsroom Cultures: Identities at Work,* edited by Marjan de Bruin and Karen Ross, 105–117. Cresskill, NJ: Hampton Press.

Organ, Christine L., Charlene J. Brown, and David Weaver. (1979). "Characteristics of Managers of Selected US Daily Newspapers." *Journalism Quarterly* 56(4): 803–809.

Papandrea, Franco. (2013). *The State of the Newspaper Industry in Australia, 2013.* Canberra: University of Canberra. http://www.canberra.edu.au/faculties/arts-design/attachments/pdf/n-and-mrc/State-of-the-Newspaper-Industry-web-publication.pdf.

Pearce, Sharyn. (1998). *Shameless Scribblers: Australian Women's Journalism, 1880–1995.* Rockhampton: Central Queensland University Press..

Peters, Bettina. (2001). *Equality and Quality: Setting Standards for Women in Journalism.* Brussels: International Federation of Journalists.

Pringle, Rosemary. (1998). *Sex and Medicine: Gender, Power and Autonomy in the Medical Profession.* Cambridge: Cambridge University Press.

Robinson Gertrude J. (2005). *Gender, Journalism and Equity: Canadian, US and European Perspectives.* Cresskill, NJ: Hampton Press

Romano, Angela. (2010). *Who Makes the News? The Global Media Monitoring Project 2010, National Report Australia.* http://www.whomakesthenews.org/images/stories/restricted/national/Australia.pdf.

Ross, Karen. (2010). *Gendered Media: Women, Men and Identity Politics.* Lanham, MD: Rowman and Littlefield.

Ross, Karen. (2004). "Sex at Work: Gender Politics and Newsroom Culture." In *Gender and Newsroom Cultures: Identities at Work,* edited by Marjan de Bruin and Karen Ross, 145–162. Cresskill, NJ: Hampton Press.

Ross Karen. (2001). "Women at Work: Journalism as Engendered Practice." *Journalism Studies* 2(4): 531–544.

Rowe, David. (2011). "Obituary for the Newspaper? Tracking the Tabloid." *Journalism* 12(4) 449–466.

Ryan, Inez, Jacqui Ewart, and Julie Posetti (eds.). (2008). *State of the News Print Media in Australia.* Sydney: Australian Press Council.

Schultz, Julianne. (1994). "The Paradox of Professionalism." In *Not Just Another Business: Journalists, Citizens and the Media,* edited by Julianne Schultz, 35–51. Sydney: Pluto Press.

Spicer, Tracey. (2014). "Tracey Spicer: This Is What I Look Like without Make-Up," *Daily Life,* November 16. http://www.dailylife.com.au/dl-beauty/tracey-spicer-this-is-what-i-look-like-without-makeup-20141115-3kfbl.html.

Strong, Catherine. (2011). "Female Journalists in New Zealand Daily Newspapers: From Early Career to Gender Gap in Editorship." PhD diss., Massey University.

Tiffin, Rodney. (2009). "'Australian Journalism.'" *Journalism* 10(3): 384–386.

Tiffin, Rod. (2006). "The Press." In *The Media and Communications in Australia,* edited by Stuart Cunningham and Graeme Turner, second edition, 91–112. Sydney: Allen and Unwin.

Thornton Margaret. (1996). *Dissonance and Distrust: Women in the Legal Profession.* Melbourne: Oxford University Press.

Trioli, Virginia. (1996). *Generation F: Sex, Power and the Young Feminist.* Port Melbourne: Minerva.

Van Zoonen, Liesbet. (1998). "One of the Girls? The Changing Gender of Journalism." In *News, Gender and Power,* edited by Cynthia Carter, Gill Branston, and Stuart Allan, 33–46. London: Routledge.

Van Zoonen. Liesbet. (1994). *Feminist Media Studies.* London and Thousand Oaks, CA: Sage.

Wilkinson, Lisa. (2013). "Lisa Wilkinson Presents Annual Andrew Olle Lecture." *702 ABC Sydney,* October 28. http://www.abc.net.au/local/stories/2013/10/25/3876439.htm.

Women in Media (WiM). (2013). "About Us." http://womeninmedia.net/about-us/.

Workplace Gender Equality Agency (WGEA). (2014). "Public Reports." https://www.wgea.gov.au/public-reports-0.

Young, Sally. (2010). "The Journalism 'Crisis.'" *Journalism Studies* 11(4): 610–624.

10

Cross-National Coverage of Rape and Rape Culture

A Community Structure Approach

John C. Pollock, Lucy Obozintsev, Hannah Salamone, Lauren Longo, and Stephanie Agresti

Rape has become normalized throughout societies across the world, an act that many societies have learned to accept as inevitable. A study provided by the United Nations indicates that women aged fifteen to forty-four are at a greater risk of being raped than from "cancer, car accidents, war and malaria" ("Ending Violence" 2012, para. 5). Although men are also victims of rape, the violation is far more common against women. In order to better reflect state criminal codes, as of January 2012, the U.S. Department of Justice has newly defined rape as "the penetration, no matter how slight, of the vagina or anus with any body part or object, or oral penetration by a sex organ of another person, without the consent of the victim" (U.S. Department of Justice 2012).

The problem may be understood under the broader concept of "rape culture." Marshall University's Department of Women's Health defines rape culture as "an environment in which rape is prevalent and in which sexual violence against women is normalized and excused in the media and popular culture" (Women's Center 2012, para.1). This idea is further normalized through communicative mediums such as television, advertisements, film, and so on, which have participated in accepting the idea of rape.

Public opinion on how the issue should be addressed is dependent on how media frame stories relating to rape and rape culture. To frame a story is to "select some aspects of a perceived reality and make them more salient in a communicating text, causal interpretation, moral evaluation, and/or treatment recommendation" (Entman 1993: 52). For purposes of this study, two umbrella media frames are considered likely; a "government" frame and a "society" frame. A *government frame* implies that it is primarily the responsibility of each country's government to implement stricter laws and harsher consequences for acts of rape. By contrast, the *society frame* calls on the general population and non-governmental organizations to re-evaluate the laws and consequences for acts of rape.

This study will examine cross-national media coverage of rape and rape culture, focusing specifically on newspapers. Newspapers were chosen for myriad reasons, foremost due to the circumstance that well-educated, economic, and political leaders draw a substantial proportion of their news knowledge from newspapers. In addition, newspapers are notorious intermedia agenda setters and content providers for other media, including news transmitted by television, radio, and the internet. It has also been established that newspapers excel at providing community forums for discussion of critical issues. It is therefore important to evaluate how newspapers, in particular, frame current issues among media worldwide.

The analysis of rape and rape culture will be examined through the community structure approach, associating various aspects of societal characteristics/demographics with social and political reporting (Pollock 2007: 23). Prevailing media models suggest that media affect society, but the community structure approach recognizes that characteristics of distinct societies can shape the types of news stories covered in the media, specifically newspapers. A more formal definition states that the *community structure approach* is "a form of quantitative content analysis that focuses on the ways in which key characteristics of communities (such as cities) are related to the content coverage of newspapers in those communities" (Pollock 2007: 23). Since its development in the early twentieth century, the study of the community structure approach has advanced due to the contributions of various communication scholars.

The initial groundwork for the community structure approach was outlined by Robert Park (1922) of the University of Chicago when he addressed how scholars should study media as it is influenced by society. Years later University of Minnesota scholars Philip Tichenor, George Donohue and Clarice Olien (1973, 1980, 1995) furthered Park's original work by developing the "guard dog" hypothesis and structural pluralism. The "guard dog" hypothesis expects that media typically reflect the interests of political and economic elites as opposed to those of the general public (Donohue, Tichenor, and Olien 1995; Pollock 2007: 24). The concept of "structural pluralism" (Tichenor, Donohue, and Olien 1980) proposes "that larger, more diverse, socially pluralistic communities would be associated with greater diversity in media, especially newspaper reporting on critical issues" (Pollock 2007: 1). However, the Tichenor, Donohue, and Olien studies focused almost entirely on cities and counties in Minnesota, excluding other states and nations.

Scholars who studied with Tichenor, Donohue and Olien made further contributions to the community structure approach by conducting studies in one or two cities (Hindman 1999; McLeod and Hertog 1992;). In their studies, McLeod and Hertog (1992, 1999) found that media often reflect the size of protest groups. Hindman (1999) discovered that in the new information era, mass media function better as proponents of social change and can more closely depict audience choices. Demers and Viswanath (1999) suggest that newspapers can either be agents of social control or social change. Pollock and colleagues (2007, 2013b, 2015) have made three special contributions to the community structure approach in recent articles and books by: (a) expanding geographic and demographic diversity by conducting the first nationwide, multi-city studies; (b) combining standard content analysis measures of article "direction" or tone with additional measures of editorial "prominence" to fashion a sensitive, composite "Media Vector" for each newspaper's reporting on a particular issue; and (c) confirming that, contrary to the guard-dog hypothesis expectation that media favor elites, newspapers are frequently capable of mirroring the interests of the most "vulnerable" population segments.

Recent studies that build upon the community structure approach strengthen its validity. "Shaping the Agenda of Local Daily Newspapers: A Methodology Merging the Agenda Setting and Community Structure Perspectives" analyzed the effects society has on agenda setting. It asserts that "both local influence arising from the nature of the local community and national influence arising from professional journalistic standards of what is newsworthy are at play in the determination of a local daily newspaper's news agenda" (McCombs and Funk 2011: 13). Reviews of recent community structure contributions can be found in work by Nah and Armstrong (2011), Yamamoto (2013), and an annotated bibliography by Pollock (2013a).

Making use of the community structure approach enhances research on the association between societal characteristics/demographics of specific countries and variations in newspaper coverage of rape and rape culture. Media coverage of rape and rape culture may be affected by many different variables, but in this exploration two main research questions will be investigated:

RQ1: How much variation is there in cross-national coverage of rape and rape culture?

RQ2: How closely linked is variation in cross-national coverage of rape and rape culture with the social/demographic characteristics of different nations?

Several hypotheses reflecting conventional wisdom may be considered when examining cross-national media coverage of rape and rape culture. For example, this study hypothesizes that the higher the GDP in a country, the greater the media emphasis on government responsibility for rape and rape culture. Nations with higher GDP per capita and more privileged citizens are more likely to report favorably on human rights issues. Citizens who reside in privileged nations are "buffered from financial and occupational uncertainty" and thus tend to be more receptive to moral claims on human rights issues (Pollock 2007: 53). Thus, issues that are viewed as "imperiling either privileged groups or a relatively stable, secure way of life," such as rape and rape culture, will be associated with reporting emphasizing government responsibility for rape and rape culture in order to address public concerns (Pollock 2007: 53). By contrast, this study also expects that the higher the infant mortality rate in a nation, the less media support for government responsibility to reduce rape and rape culture. It is reasonable to assume that a nation with low health standards would be less likely to manifest media support for government efforts to address human rights claims. Therefore, nations with higher GDP per capita—and higher health standards—will be more likely to display media demands for government responsibility for the prevention of rape and perpetuation of rape culture, while nations with higher levels of "vulnerability," including high infant mortality rates, will likely manifest media coverage less likely to support government activities to reduce rape and rape culture.

LITERATURE REVIEW

The global examination of rape and rape culture has been discussed substantially in various academic disciplines such as sociology and women and gender studies. Despite its popularity in other academic fields, the field of communication studies has yet to focus substantially on media coverage of rape and rape culture.

An initial search performed through Communication and Mass Media Complete and ComAbstracts databases showed limited results detailing the relationship between mass media and rape culture. Key terms searched ranged from "rape" to "gender violence." The lack of research on rape culture in the field of communication studies is more apparent when the words "rape" AND "culture" are used. Searching the terms "rape" AND "media" resulted in a total of 215 articles. Although several articles relating to rape culture were published in 2013, far less research has been done in the field of communication studies in comparison to other fields.

One article examined the case of Kim Duthie, a seventeen-year old Australian teenager who "came to public attention when she posted naked pictures of two prominent St. Kilda Australian Football League (AFL) players on Facebook . . . to be seeking revenge on the players' teammate for getting her pregnant" (Waterhouse-Watson and Brown 2011: 4). The article claimed that this event reinforced the "pervasive myth that women are prone to lie about rape and sexual abuse" (Waterhouse-Watson and Brown 2011: 4). Despite using additional case studies about sexual assault in Australia, this study failed to address the effect mass media has had on rape culture.

The sole article found in ComAbstracts using the search terms "rape" AND "culture" built upon a previous study which suggested that "college campuses foster a rape culture in which date rape (most commonly, rape of women) is an accepted part of campus activity" (Burnett, Mattern, Herakova, Kahl, Tofola, and Bornsen 2009: 465). This study examined the responses of students who were asked about "rape as they experienced it or knew about it on campus" (Burnett et al. 2009: 465). The study neglected to introduce the role that mass media, specifically newspapers, have in shaping rape culture within this particular community.

Unlike the field of communication studies, sociology has provided far more scholarship on the topic of rape culture. For instance, the database Sociological Abstracts yielded 540 results using the search term "rape" AND "media." One study selected 35 different societies to examine how societal norms in those societies influence rape culture. The study found that, cross-nationally, rape is "regulated rather than prohibited" (Rozee 1993: 499). When the terms "rape" AND "culture" were entered together into this database, 758 results were obtained. When the terms "rape," "culture," AND "media" were searched together—which yielded 97 possible results—in the Sociological Abstracts database, a relevant article entitled, "The Teaching of Corporate Culture: Sexual Symbolism in Mass Media" appeared. This article suggested that symbolic and subliminal techniques are used by the corporate sector to shape public attitudes and behaviors (Milano and Whitehead 1990). This article asserted that the power of persuasion of the corporate sector is often underestimated or ignored due to the nature of its "non-threatening cultural format" to consumers, and that corporate-style sexual imagery can be linked to critical social problems like rape (Milano and Whitehead 1990, para. 3). Thus, this article suggested that media, especially corporate media, have a relationship with rape and rape culture (and its perception) due to how rape is portrayed.

Like sociology, the field of women and gender studies provides ample information on rape and rape culture. The database GenderWatch produced 5,909 results when searching "rape" AND culture. One particularly strong study asserted that the portrayal of rape in popular media has allowed it to become normalized. Sexual violence in ads and sexualizing rape scenes in movies and television have enhanced rape culture in today's society (Pearson 2000).

The field of communication studies has produced very little research regarding rape and rape culture and its relationship with media. By contrast, fields such as sociology and women and gender studies have given this serious social issue far more attention. This paper attempts to address the imbalance of information in the field of communication studies by investigating links between national demographics and cross-national media coverage of rape and rape culture.

HYPOTHESES

Violated Buffer Hypothesis

The violated buffer hypothesis suggests that "the greater the proportion of privileged citizens in a (community), the more unfavorable newspaper reporting is likely to be on issues framed as 'ominous,' hazardous to physical safety or a secure, predictable way of life" (Pollock 2007: 53). This hypothesis stems from the buffer hypothesis, which examines news stories in a similar light. The buffer hypothesis suggests that communities with higher levels of privilege tend to have more favorable media coverage of human rights claims (Pollock 2007). Privilege in both contexts refers to cross-national characteristics such as GDP, GDP per capita, literacy rates and life expectancy rates in particular countries. Examining these variables of privilege in conjunction with newspaper reporting of rape and rape culture will be useful.

The violated buffer hypothesis is supported by numerous U.S. and cross-national studies. One U.S. study comparing multi-city coverage found that "the higher proportion of privilege (especially income or education) in a (community), the less positive the expected media coverage of biological threats or threats to a cherished way of life" (Pollock 2007: 113). The negative depiction of tobacco is especially important in communities of privilege because tobacco is a major threat to children of both non-privileged and privileged groups (Pollock 2007: 102–114).

Another U.S. study supporting the violated buffer hypothesis focused on newspaper coverage of women in combat. Conducted by Pollock, Mink, Puma, Shuhala, and Ostrander (2001), this study found that women in combat were seen as threats to the conventional idea that women should be protected from danger. Similarly, a U.S. study concerning Magic Johnson's HIV announcement found that coverage of Johnson's announcement was less favorable in more privileged communities (Pollock 2007: 211–229).

In cross-national coverage, the role of privilege is significant when exploring critical health communication issues and is often associated with favorable coverage of NGO or government responsibility to address them. "International Coverage of United Nations' Efforts to Combat AIDS: A Structural Approach" (2005) found that the higher the level of privilege in a country (e.g., GDP or GDP per capita) the more favorable the coverage of UN efforts to fight AIDS (Gratale et al. 2005). A similar study concluded that the higher level of privilege in a country, the more favorable the coverage of Non-Governmental Organizations' efforts to fight AIDS (Eisenberg, Kester, Caputo, Sierra and Pollock 2006). In another cross-national study, the higher the GDP per capita, the more media emphasis on government responsibility for human trafficking (Alexandre et al. 2014).

Some other studies, by contrast, find measures of privilege associated with greater media emphasis on "society" (rather than government) efforts to address critical human rights issues. The higher the literacy rate and the higher the percent satisfied with their water services in cross-national reporting, the *less* media emphasis on government responsibility for water handling (Wissel et al. 2014). Similarly, the higher the GDP percapita, percent satisfied with water services, or male or female life expectancy at birth, the *less* media emphasis on government responsibility for child labor (Kohn and Pollock 2014).

In some instances, individuals in privileged communities may experience a "buffer" that protects them from physical, emotional or economic problems more commonly faced by less privileged communities. The aforementioned studies illustrate how some issues can become threats to an existing way of life cherished by privileged groups, violating these "buffers." Rape and the culture surrounding it can violate anyone, anywhere. Furthermore, it is reasonable to assume that a larger proportion of privileged citizens would sympathize with those suffering the consequences of rape and rape culture. Most previous studies support links between privilege and support for NGO or government action to address human rights issues. It is further assumed that living in a political system viewed as "less corrupt" is also a form of privilege. Therefore:

H₁: *The higher a nation's GDP, the more coverage emphasizes government responsibility to end rape* (CIA Factbook 2012).

H$_2$: *The higher a nation's GDP per capita, the more coverage emphasizes government responsibility to end rape* (CIA Factbook 2012).

H$_3$: *The higher the nation's literacy rate, the more coverage emphasizes government responsibility to end rape* (CIA Factbook 2012).

H$_4$: *The higher a nation's male life expectancy at birth, the more coverage emphasizes government responsibility to end rape* (CIA Factbook 2012).

H$_{5a}$: *The higher a nation's female life expectancy at birth, the more coverage emphasizes government responsibility to end rape* (CIA Factbook 2012).

H$_{5b}$: *The higher the percent satisfied with access to water services, the more coverage emphasizes government responsibility to end rape* (CIA Factbook 2012).

H$_{6a}$: *The higher a nation's "happiness" score, the more coverage emphasizes government responsibility to end rape* (World Happiness Report 2012).

H$_{6b}$: *The higher a nation's score on a "Corruption Perception Index" (or the less corrupt a government is viewed), the more coverage emphasizes government responsibility to end rape* (Transparency International 2012).

Health care access. A strong indicator of privilege in any community is access to health care. A country that places a high level of concern for the health of its citizens may produce more coverage emphasizing government responsibility for rape and rape culture. With increased access to health care, it is safe to assume that a country would expect media favoring government action to reduce the prevalence or incidence of rape. Therefore:

H$_7$: *The greater the number of physicians per 100,000 people in a country, the more coverage emphasizes government action to end rape* (United Nations Statistics 2011).

H$_8$: *The greater the number of hospital beds per 100,000 in a country, the more coverage emphasizes government responsibility to end rape* (United Nations Statistics 2011).

The Vulnerability Hypothesis

The vulnerability hypothesis expects that a (community) with a higher percentage of people below the poverty level will likely manifest media coverage directed toward the "vulnerable group's concerns" (Pollock 2007: 137). The community structure approach, unlike a market perspective, "expects media coverage to display some resonance with a wide range of publics" and further research has confirmed the notion that newspapers "can reflect the interests of vulnerable populations" (Pollock 2007: 137). Although vulnerable groups are not typically associated with "maximum newspaper readership," the media still mirror their interests and concerns in communities of interest (Pollock 2007: 137). The vulnerability hypothesis directly opposes the Olien, Donohue, and Tichenor "guard dog" hypothesis, which claims that media seldom advance human rights claims, but rather serve to reinforce the interests of social and economic elites (Donohue, Tichenor, and Olien 1995).

Various community structure studies confirm that communities with high levels of poverty tend to provide more sympathetic coverage of human rights issues, such as rape and rape culture. An association was found between higher levels of poverty and favorable US coverage of legislation concerning a Patients' Bill of Rights (Pollock 2007: 146–156). U.S. communities with higher proportions below the poverty line are also associated with less favorable coverage of capital punishment (Pollock 2007: 138–146). Another U.S. study confirmed the vulnerability hypothesis, finding more favorable U.S. media coverage of the *Roe v. Wade* Supreme Court decision that legalized abortion in cities with higher percentages below the poverty line (Pollock and Robinson 1977; Pollock, Robinson and Murray 1978).

Among cross-national studies, the higher the percent of women or men who know condom use prevents the transmission of HIV, the more media emphasis on government responsibility for HIV/AIDS (Etheridge et al. 2014). Anomalously, the higher the number of cases of cholera/100,000 in a country, the less media emphasis on government responsibility for HIV/AIDS (Etheridge et al. 2014). Yet the higher the percent undernourished, the more media emphasis on government responsibility for HIV/AIDS (Etheridge et al. 2014). Consistently, the higher the percent of children under five with diarrheal disease, the higher the percent without improved water services, and the higher the infant mortality rate, the more media emphasis on government responsibility for water handling (Wissel et al. 2014). Similarly, the higher the infant mortality rate and the higher the percent of population under 14 in a country, the more media emphasis on government responsibility for child labor (Kohn and Pollock 2014). In parallel with most other community structure studies, poverty level, percentage of population without access to improved water sources, percent of agricultural land (signifying dependence on agriculture), and fertility rate are all significantly associated with cross-national media support for genetically modified organisms, which offer more disease-resistant crops (Peitz et al. 2015).

Evidently, communities with higher proportions of vulnerable populations, whether that vulnerability takes the form of economic or health vulnerability, are often associated with more favorable coverage of their concerns. Since vulnerable groups are hardly immune from rape, and may be even more susceptible to rape because they tend to live in areas with higher crime rates, they have a vested interest in coverage of the issue. Given their susceptibility to the issue, it would be reasonable to assume that vulnerable groups would support government involvement in ending rape and rape culture. Therefore:

H_9: *The higher a nation's infant mortality rate, the more coverage emphasizes government responsibility to end rape* (United Nations Statistics Division 2011).

H_{10}: *The higher a nation's poverty level, the more coverage emphasizes government responsibility to end rape* (United Nations Statistics Division 2011).

H_{11}: *The higher a nation's fertility rate, the more coverage emphasizes government responsibility to end rape* (United Nations Statistics Division 2011).

H_{12}: *The higher the percent without improved water services, the more coverage emphasizes government responsibility to end rape* (Human Development 2010).

H_{13}: *The higher the percentage of HIV infected orphans, the more coverage emphasizes government responsibility to end rape* (CIA World Factbook 2012).

H_{14}: *The greater number of cases of cholera per 100 in a nation, the more coverage emphasizes government responsibility to end rape* (CIA World Factbook 2012).

H_{15}: *The higher a nation's Gini inequality index, the more coverage emphasizes government responsibility to end rape* (CIA World Factbook 2012).

H_{16}: *The higher the percent of a nation's population under 14, the more coverage emphasizes government responsibility to end rape* (United Nations Statistics Division 2010).

H_{17}: *The greater percentage of those undernourished, the more coverage emphasizes government responsibility to end rape* (United Nations Statistics Division 2006).

H_{18}: *The higher a nation's AIDs prevalence rate, the more coverage emphasizes government responsibility to end rape* (United Nations Statistics Division 2006).

The Stakeholder Hypothesis

The stakeholder hypothesis expects that the amount of variation in media viewpoints is dependent on the size of a city's stakeholder groups. It has been determined in U.S. studies that the larger the city, the greater the variety of political and social viewpoints covered in the media (Tichenor, Donohue, and Olien 1973, 1980). Additionally, the greater the size of stakeholder groups within a city, the more favorable the coverage of such stakeholders' concerns (McLeod and Hertog 1992, 1999; Pollock 2007: 172).

Female Empowerment

Coverage of rape and rape culture often focuses on rape's relevance to women. One may assume that the higher the number of empowered females in a city, the more women will take it upon themselves and their peers to work to end rape and to abolish the acceptance of rape culture.

Evidence for the association of female empowerment with government responsibility for addressing social issues is mixed. The International Water and Sanitation Centre found that when women participate in the running of a project, the project is more effective and sustainable than when it is designed and run without women (Task Force on Gender and Water 2006: 2). One cross-national study found that the higher the percent females in the workforce, the more media emphasis on government responsibility for HIV / AIDS (Etheridge et al. 2014). Other studies, however, yielded different results. One exploration found that the higher the female literacy rate, female school life expectancy or percent satisfied with female freedom of choice in a country, the less media emphasis on government responsibility for water handling (Wissel et al. 2014). Another cross-national examination concluded that the higher the female school life expectancy, the less media emphasis on government responsibility for child labor (Kohn and Pollock 2014). With these recent studies in mind, it is reasonable to articulate the following hypotheses:

H_{19}: *The higher a nation's female literacy rate, the less coverage emphasizes government responsibility to end rape* (CIA World Factbook 2012).

H_{20}: *The greater female school life expectancy, the less coverage emphasizes government responsibility to end rape* (CIA World Factbook 2012).

H_{21}: *The higher a nation's percentage of women in the work force, the less coverage emphasizes government responsibility to end rape* (United Nations Statistics Division 2010).

H_{22}: *The higher a nation's percentage of females who are satisfied with their freedom of choice, the less coverage emphasizes government responsibility to end rape* (Human Development Report 2010).

Resources and Infrastructure

Energy production and consumption is of great concern in countries everywhere, ensuring that groups producing or consuming large quantities of various energy resources are extremely important stakeholders. A cross-national study found that the higher the rate of coal production worldwide, the greater the newspaper support for government intervention in Libya (English et al. 2012). Another study found that the greater the level of oil and natural gas production, as well as natural gas consumption in a nation, the greater the media support for government responsibility to address climate change (Pollock, Reda et al. 2010).

By contrast, on social issues such as child labor, Muslim immigration, and aid to refugees, higher energy production or consumption are often linked to less media emphasis on government action. For example, the higher the industrial production growth rate, the less media emphasis on government responsibility for child labor (Kohn and Pollock 2014). Similarly, the greater the number of terawatt hours of electricity production in a country, the less favorable the coverage of Muslim immigration (Wright et al. 2008). Consistently, the higher the rate of electricity consumption in a country, the less the media support for disaster/earthquake relief in Haiti (Mankowski, Tronolone and Miller 2012). On balance, mindful of the findings regarding cross-national coverage of social and human rights issues, it is reasonable to assume that groups producing and consuming more energy resources will be less supportive of government action to end rape and rape culture:

H_{23}: *The higher a nation's natural gas consumption, the less coverage emphasizes government responsibility to end rape* (CIA World Factbook 2011).

H_{24}: *The higher a nation's natural gas production, the less coverage emphasizes government responsibility to end rape.* (CIA World Factbook 2012).

H_{25}: *The higher a nation's oil consumption, the less coverage emphasizes government responsibility to end rape.* (CIA World Factbook 2012).

H_{26}: *The higher a nation's oil production, the less coverage emphasizes government responsibility to end rape.* (CIA World Factbook 2012).

H_{27}: *The higher a nation's electricity consumption, the less coverage emphasizes government responsibility to end rape.* (CIA World Factbook 2012).

H_{28}: *The higher a nation's electricity production, the less coverage emphasizes government responsibility to end rape.* (CIA World Factbook 2012).

H_{29}: *The higher a nation's coal consumption, the less coverage emphasizes government responsibility to end rape.* (CIA World Factbook 2012).

H_{30}: *The higher a nation's coal production, the less coverage emphasizes government responsibility to end rape.* (CIA World Factbook 2012).

H_{31}: *The higher a nation's industrial production growth rate, the less coverage emphasizes government responsibility to end rape.* (CIA World Factbook 2012).

METHODOLOGY

In order to investigate coverage of rape and rape culture cross-nationally, 21 leading newspapers from 21 countries were chosen according to reputation or availability on leading databases. The following publications were selected: *Accra Mail, China Daily, Daily Nation,* the *Daily News,* the *Herald,* the *Japan Times, La Nación,* the *Namibian,* the *New Strait Times,* the *New Times, New Vision,* the *New York Times,* the *Sydney Morning Herald,* the *Star, This Day,* the *Times,* the *Times of India,* the *Times of Zambia,* the *Toronto Star, Turkish Daily News,* and *El Universal.* Articles from a specific time frame within Newsbank and All Africa databases were selected, each having a minimum of 250 words, yielding 308 articles total.

The sample data were selected from a span of about five years, dating from June 5, 2008 to September 27, 2013 (two weeks after four men in India were sentenced to death by hanging after a gang-rape conviction). The starting date represents two weeks prior to the day that the UN Security Council unanimously adopted Resolution 1820, which was officially implemented on June 30, 2009. This Resolution called for all member states to take effective steps towards preventing sexual violence in order to maintain international peace and security.

Article Prominence

Article prominence is measured by placement, headline word count, article word count and number of graphics or pictures. Article placement is determined based upon an article's location in a newspaper, such as the first page, inside section, etc. Considering these criteria, an article is given two scores. The first score illustrates prominence, reflecting the editorial decision as to how important the article in question is. An article can obtain a score ranging from three to sixteen points, a higher score indicating more prominence. The distribution of a prominence score may be seen in Table 10.1 below.

Article Direction

Once the prominence score is determined, an evaluation of the article's direction is analyzed by its content and tone. The articles collected were

Table 10.1. Media Vector Calculation-Prominence

Dimensions	4	3	2	1
Placement	Front Page, First Section	Front Page, Inside Section	Inside Page, First Section	Other
Heading Size (# of words)	10+	8–9	6–7	5 or fewer
Article Length (# of words)	1,000+	750–999	500–749	250–499
Photos/Graphics	2 or more	1		

categorized under one of three frames indicating the direction of the article: government responsibility, societal responsibility, or balanced/neutral responsibility.

Government Responsibility

Articles emphasizing government support for ending rape-related crime, raising awareness about rape and rape culture, or justifiably convicting an assailant were coded as "government responsibility." One example of holding government responsible for reducing the prevalence of rape and rape culture was an article that detailed how Kenya's first lady Lucy Kibaki was enraged at the national teachers' union's inaction in disciplining "rogue members involved in rape" (Shiundu 2010, para.1). The writer claimed that it was the responsibility of the Teachers Service Commission (a government agency that employs teachers) to discipline teachers who engaged in such heinous crimes. Additionally, the writer mentioned that the First Lady believed that the rise in rape cases was due to "inadequate laws to address sexual offences," therefore, suggesting that the government should do more to prevent such crimes (Shiundu 2010, para. 9). This article was coded as "government responsibility" because it critiqued a governmental agency's handling of rape-related crimes.

Societal Responsibility

Articles interpreted as society being primarily responsible for ending rape-related crimes were coded as "societal responsibility." Such articles named non-governmental activity, non-governmental organizations (NGOs) or cultural influences as responsible for ending rape-related crime and rape culture. One article addressed preventing physical and sexual violence against women by describing the efforts of a particular conference held in Ankara that aimed to "raise public awareness and attract men's attention to the issue of violence against women" ("Men asked to" 2008, para.2). This article suggested that society and its members were responsible for reducing violence.

Balanced/neutral

Articles that did not define either government or society as responsible for ending rape crime or held either group equally responsible were coded as "balanced/neutral." For example, one article detailing the ten-year sentence given to someone for raping a thirteen-year-old girl did not call upon either the government or society for action. The writer simply reported the facts of the case and did not hold the government or society responsible ("Official gets 10-year" 2009, para. 1).

Of the 308 articles coded, 174 of them were read separately by two coders, resulting in a Scott's Pi coefficient of inter-coder reliability of .732.

Media Vector Calculation

Once a total of twenty-one newspapers from as many countries were analyzed, the Janis-Fadner Coefficient of Imbalance was utilized in order to calculate a "Media Vector." The Media Vector, which resembles vectors used in physics to combine direction and magnitude in order to measure impact, combines two different coding methods in order to measure article "projection" onto audiences (Pollock 2007: 49). The first method focuses on "the amount of attention or 'prominence' an article receives" (Pollock 2007: 48). The second coding method focuses on "direction" or "perspective" based on the article's content and the specific issues being studied (Pollock 2007: 48–49). The combined scores for the Media Vector range from +1.00 to -1.00 points. Media Vector scores that fell between +1.00 and 0 indicated government responsibility. Scores that ranged from 0 and -1.00 were deemed societal responsibility, shown in Table 10.2.

Procedure

In order to examine the relationship between Media Vectors and national characteristics, Pearson correlations and regression analysis were used. Pearson correlations determined which national characteristics

Table 10.2. Media Vector Formula*

g = sum of the prominence scores coded "government responsibility"

s = sum of the prominence scores coded "societal responsibility"

n = sum of the prominence scores coded "balanced/neutral"

$r = g + s + n$

If $g > s$ (the sum of the government prominence scores is greater than the sum of the societal prominence scores), the following formula is used:

Government Media Vector:

$$GMV = \frac{(g^2 - gs)}{r^2} \text{ (Answer lies between 0 and +1.00)}$$

If $g < s$ (the sum of the societal prominence scores is greater than the sum of the government scores), the following formula is used:

Societal Media Vector:

$$SMV = \frac{(gs - s^2)}{r^2} \text{ (Answer lies between 0 and –1.00)}$$

* Media Vector copyright John C. Pollock, 2000–2015.

were strongly linked to Media Vectors. Regression analysis revealed the relative strength of each independent variable or the significance of each national characteristic. These two statistical procedures established connections between national characteristics and newspaper coverage of rape and rape culture.

RESULTS AND SCALE CONSTRUCTION

This study examined cross-international newspaper coverage of rape and rape culture by comparing Media Vectors from 21 nations during the period of June 19, 2008 to September 27, 2013. The *Daily Nation* had the highest Media Vector at .3056, while South Africa's the *Star* had the lowest Media Vector at –.382, a range of .6643. A majority of twelve of the twenty-one Media Vectors, or about 57.1 percent, ranging from –.0204 to –.3587, emphasized societal responsibility to end rape. Only nine, or 42.9 percent of the nations, yielded Media Vectors emphasizing government responsibility to take action against rape and rape culture, ranging from .0053 to .3056.

Strikingly, African nations comprised a majority of nations displaying coverage emphasizing societal action, with Zambia (–.0293), Zimbabwe (–.0444), Uganda (–.0848), Egypt (–.0907), Namibia (–.097), Rwanda (–.1109), and South Africa (–.3587) displaying negative Media Vectors. Table 10.3 displays the complete list of twenty-one Media Vectors.

Pearson correlations connected differences in national characteristics to variations in coverage. The degree of association between national Media Vectors and characteristics were matched in order to yield results specific to the global issue of rape and rape culture. The complete list of Pearson correlations is found in Table 10.4.

The Vulnerability Hypothesis Significant but Disconfirmed; Linked not to "Government" but to "Societal" Responsibility for Rape (HIV Infected Orphans, AIDS Prevalence)

The vulnerability hypothesis originally predicted that the higher the proportions of vulnerable populations in a nation, the greater the media emphasis on government responsibility to end rape. Characteristics representing vulnerability, including the percentages of HIV infected orphans ($r = -.423$, $p = .018$) and AIDS prevalence ($r = -.335$, $p = .051$), were indeed found significant yet negatively correlated with government responsibility for addressing rape. Both of these characteristics surprisingly deemphasized government responsibility to end rape and rectify rape culture.

Table 10.3.   Media Vector by Nation

Nation	Newspaper	Media Vector
Kenya	*Daily Nation*	.3056
India	*Times of India*	.2804
Japan	*Japan Times*	.2247
United Kingdom	*Times*	.1714
Argentina	*La Nación*	.1115
Nigeria	*This Day*	.0876
Ghana	*Accra Mail*	.053
Malaysia	*New Strait Times*	.0105
United States	*New York Times*	.0053
Mexico	*El Universal*	−.0204
Zambia	*Times of Zambia*	−.0293
China	*China Daily*	−.0431
Zimbabwe	*Herald*	−.0444
Uganda	*New Vision*	−.0848
Egypt	*Daily News*	−.0907
Namibia	*Namibian*	−.097
Canada	*Toronto Star*	−.1102
Rwanda	*New Times*	−.1109
Australia	*Sydney Morning Herald*	−.1311
Turkey	*Turkish Daily News*	−.2836
South Africa	*Star*	−.3587

Coverage emphasizing either more of less government responsibility for rape and rape culture were not significantly associated with other indicators of vulnerability such as the Gini inequality index ($r = -.304$, $p = .070$), population below fourteen ($r = -.003$, $p = .495$), or percent satisfied with water services ($r = -.064$, $p = .373$). The findings suggest that media coverage emphasizing government responsibility to end rape and rape culture is not at all associated with those who would be most affected by rape and rape culture (i.e., "vulnerable" groups). Indeed the opposite is found, suggesting that the problem of rape be left to "society." Perhaps this pattern can be attributed partially to the circumstance that many vulnerable groups are not typically associated with "maximum newspaper readership" (Pollock 2007: 137).

The Violated Buffer Hypothesis: Confirmed (Happiness Score)

The violated buffer hypothesis claims that "the greater the proportion of privileged citizens in a city, the more unfavorable newspaper reporting is likely to be on issues framed as 'ominous,' hazardous to physical safety or a secure, predictable way of life" (Pollock 2007: 53). In concert with

Table 10.4. Pearson Correlation Results

National Characteristic	Pearson Correlation	Significance
% HIV infected orphans	−.423	.018*
Happiness score	.365	.037*
AIDS prevalence	−.335	.051*
Female condom use	−.315	.062
Gini inequality index score	−.304	.070
Female expectancy at birth	.264	.101
Female school life expectancy	.232	.132
Male life expectancy at birth	.221	.144
Length nation's road network	.217	.149
% of nation's population without access to improved water services	.178	.197
% of females in the workforce	−.177	.199
Hospital beds/100,000	−.153	.232
Female literacy rate	−.147	.242
Literacy rate	−.138	.255
AIDS incidence rates	−.120	.284
% of population covered by a mobile phone network	−.103	.313
% children <5 with diarrheal disease	.095	.326
Corruption perception Index (high score = less corrupt)	−.088	.353
% of females who are satisfied with their freedom of choice	−.082	.348
% men who know condom use prevents HIV	.080	.352
Physicians/100,000	−.079	.353
Infant mortality rate	.077	.358
Poverty level	.074	.363
% of citizens who are satisfied with their freedom of choice	−.068	.373
Journalists imprisoned in a nation	−.065	.379
% satisfied with water services	−.064	.380
% undernourished	.063	.382
Fertility rate	.051	.404
Stock of direct foreign investment at home	.046	.413
Nation's industrial production growth rate	.044	.417
Coal consumption	−.043	.418
Cases of cholera/100,000	.038	.429
Broadband subscriptions/1,000 in a nation	−.038	.429
% of women who know condom use prevents HIV	.023	.457
Freedom of the press report score	−.008	.484
% population <14	−.003	.495
GDP per capita	.003	.495
Prevalence of condom use among males	−.002	.495
Daily newspapers/1,000	−.001	.498

** Significant at .01 level; * Significant at .05 level.

the violated buffer hypothesis, the buffer hypothesis suggests that communities with a higher level of privilege tend to correlate with favorable newspaper coverage of human rights claims, in this case government responsibility for rape and rape culture (Pollock 2007).

In this study the "happiness score," a characteristic of privilege and thus associated with the violated buffer hypothesis, was found significant. Each country's "happiness score" was collected from what has become an annual global survey published by the Sustainable Development Solutions Network: A Global Initiative for the United Nations, co-led by Jeffrey Sachs, director of the Earth Institute at Columbia University. Happiness score ($r = .365$, $p = .037$) had a significant correlation with a greater emphasis on government responsibility to end rape. As expected, the happiness score had significant correlations with GDP per capita ($r = .351$, $p = .043$), literacy rate ($r = .429$, $p = .016$), male life expectancy at birth ($r = .721$, $p = .000$), female life expectancy at birth ($r = .727$, $p = .000$), and percentage of a nation's citizens satisfied with water services ($r = .519$, $p = .004$). These variables aid in justifying the expectation that the more privileged a country, the more likely citizens are to be "happy" and rely on the government to promote happiness. In this case, "happiness" may be associated with ending the social scourge of rape and unhealthy rape culture.

Regression Analysis: Privilege and Vulnerability

A regression analysis linking significant variables with the Media Vector scores revealed that only one variable was significant: "Percent of orphans infected with HIV" accounted for 17.9% of the variance. Percent of orphans infected with HIV was linked with coverage supporting less "government" responsibility and more "social" responsibility regarding rape and rape culture. Accordingly, media can be shown to reflect in some way the interests of the most vulnerable population segments. Table 10.5 displays the regression analysis.

Table 10.5.   Regression Analysis of National Characteristics

Model	R (Equation)	R Squared (Cumulative)	R Squared Change	F Change	Significance of F Change
Percent of orphans infected with HIV	.423	.179	.179	5.018	.035

CONCLUSION AND FURTHER RESEARCH

Significant findings categorized under the vulnerability and violated buffer hypotheses sections indicated that two of the three national characteristics support coverage emphasizing societal eradication of rape and rape culture (HIV infected orphans and AIDS prevalence). Overall, most media sampled worldwide declare society to be the responsible party for ending rape in their respective nations. These findings suggest that citizens of vulnerable populations possibly do not trust their domestic governments to handle societal issues and tend to look for assistance elsewhere.

Along with gathering quantifiable data through confirming and disconfirming hypotheses, article coders directly examined where each country's selected newspaper laid primary responsibility for the eradication of rape. Based on Media Vector scores, a strong majority of countries placed responsibility on society to end rape and amend rape culture. For example, India's overall Media Vector score of .2904 emphasized government responsibility in ending the rape crisis. Yet closer examination of articles gathered from the *Times of India* showed that the country's leading paper has taken dramatic year to year shifts in its stance, as illustrated by Media Vector scores.

For example, articles published from 2008 to 2011 emphasized government intervention in rape cases with an extremely high Media Vector score of .3977. When compared to articles published from 2012, the year the infamous New Delhi gang rape occurred, to 2013, however, the scores changed dramatically. Articles published between these recent years yielded a Media Vector score of .0947, which also emphasized government responsibility to end rape but was significantly lower than the previous score. This shift on the reporting of rape and rape culture may highlight awareness in Indian media and perhaps citizens regarding problems with traditional patriarchal values. Disaggregating overall Media Vector scores into two time periods reveals that India and other countries may be in a transitory phase of establishing where responsibility lies regarding the effort to end rape and rape culture.

Given the lack of substantial numbers of publications within communication studies databases on the issue of rape and rape culture, several recommendations for further media research can be offered. Our findings suggest that most countries do not trust their domestic governments to eradicate rape, especially in countries with high proportions of "vulnerable" populations. A comprehensive study could be conducted to compare media coverage on rape and rape culture between developing and developed countries. If developed countries skew towards government responsibility while developing countries mostly skew societally, our suggested interpretation of results would be reconfirmed. These data could be extremely useful for rape-related non-governmental organizations, which could choose to use this information to either target populations who are relying on them, or work on partnering with governments in an effort to build a stronger domestic trust.

REFERENCES

Alexandre, K., Sha, C., Pollock, J.C., Baier, K., and Johnson, J. (2014). Cross-national coverage of human trafficking: A community structure approach. *Atlantic Journal of Communication, 22* (3/4), 160–174.

Burnett, A., Mattern, J., Herakova, L., Kahl, D., Tofola Jr., C., and Bornsen, S. (2009). Communicating/muting date rape: A co-cultural theoretical analysis of communication factors related to rape culture on a college campus. *Journal of Applied Communications Research, 37*, 465–485.

Central Intelligence Agency. (2012). The World Factbook. https://www.cia.gov/library/publications/the-world- factbook/.

Demers, D., and Viswanath, K. (Eds.). (1999). *Mass media, social control, and social change: A macrosocial perspective*. Ames: Iowa State University Press.

Donohue, G.A., Tichenor, P.J., and Olien C. (1995). A guard dog perspective on the role of media. *Journal of Communication, 45*, 115–132.

Eisenberg, D., Kester, A., Caputo, L., Sierra, J., and Pollock, J.C. (2006, November). *Cross-national coverage of NGO's efforts to fight AIDS: A community structure approach*. Paper presented at the annual conference of the National Communication Association, San Antonio.

Ending violence against women and girls. (2012). United Nations. http://www.un.org/en/globalissues/briefingpapers/endviol/index.shtml.

English, C., O'Conner, B., Smith, K., and Pollock, J.C. (2012, November). *Cross-national newspaper coverage of revolution in Libya: A community structure approach*. Paper presented at the annual conference of the National Communication Association, Orlando, FL.

Entman, R. M. (1993). Framing: Toward clarification a fractured paradigm. *Journal of Communication, 43*(4), 52.

Etheridge, J., Zinck, K., Pollock, J.C., Santiago, C., Halicki, K., and Badalamenti, A. (2014). Cross-national coverage of HIV/AIDS: A community structure approach. *Atlantic Journal of Communication, 22* (3/4), 175–192.

Franiuk, R., Seefelt, J. L., and Vandello, J. A. (2008). Prevalence of rape myths in headlines and their effects on attitudes toward rape. *Sex Roles, 58* (11–12), 790–801.

Gratale, S., Hagert, J., Dey, L., Pollock, J., D'Angelo, P., Braddock, P., D'Amelio, A., Kupcha, J., and Montgomery, A. (2005, May). *International coverage of United Nations' efforts to combat AIDS: A structural approach*. Paper presented at the annual conference of the International Communication Association, New York City.

Heath, L., Gordon, M.T., and LeBailly, R. (1981). What newspapers tell us (and don't tell us) about rape. *Newspaper Research Journal, 2* (4), 48–55.

Hindman, D.B. (1999). Social control, social change and local mass media. In D. Demers and K. Viswanath (Eds.), *Mass media, social control, and social change: A macrosocial perspective,* 99–116. Ames: Iowa State University Press.

Human Development Reports. (2010). *2009/2010 human development report.* http://hdrstats.undp.org/indicators/58.html.

Kohn, J.G., and Pollock, J.C. (2014, July). Cross-national coverage of child labor: A community structure approach. *Atlantic Journal of Communication, 22* (3/4), 211–228.

Mankowski, E., Tronolone, R., and Miller, M. (2012, November). *Cross-national coverage of disaster relief in Haiti: A community structure approach.* Paper presented at the annual conference of the National Communication Association, Orlando, FL.

McCombs, M., and Funk, M. (2011). Shaping the agenda of local daily newspapers: A methodology merging the agenda setting and community structure perspectives. *Mass Communication and Society, 14, 1*–15.

McLeod, D.M., and Hertog, J.K. (1992). The manufacture of public opinion by reporters: Informal cues for public perceptions of protest groups. *Discourse and Society, 3,* 259–275.

McLeod, D.M., and Hertog, J.K. (1999). Social control, social change and the mass media's role in the regulation of protest groups. In D. Demers and K. Viswanath (Eds.), *Mass media, social control, and social change: A macrosocial perspective,* 305–331. Ames: Iowa State University Press.

Men asked to raise voices against domestic violence. (2008, November 16). *Turkish Daily News.* http://infoweb.newsbank.com/

Milano, F., and Whitehead, W. (1990). *The teaching of corporate culture: Sexual symbolism in the mass media.* http://search.proquest.com/socabs/docview/61713462/abstract/1408DCB917759DD4EC2/14?accountid=10216.

Mink, M., Puma, J., and Pollock, J., et. al (2001, November). *Nationwide newspaper coverage of women in combat: A community structure approach.* Paper presented at the annual conference of the National Communication Association, Atlanta.

Nah, S., and Armstrong, C. (2011). Structural pluralism in journalism and media studies: A concept explication and theory construction. *Mass Communication and Society, 14* (6), 857–878.

Norris, P. (2000). *A virtuous circle: Political communications in postindustrial societies.* Cambridge, UK: Cambridge University Press.

Official gets 10-year sentence for rape of 13-year-old girl. (2009, October 4). *China Daily.* http://infoweb.newsbank.com/.

Olien, C.N., Donohue, G.A., and Tichenor, P.J. (1995). Conflict, consensus, and public opinion. In T.L. Glaser and C.T. Salmon Eeds.), *Public opinion and the communication of consent,* 301–322. New York: Guilford Press.

Organisation for Economic Co-operation and Development. (2011). *Statistics from A to Z.* http://www.oecd.org/statistics/

Park, R. (1922). *The immigrant press and its control.* New York: Harcourt.

Pearson, A. (2000, August). Rape culture: Media and message. *Off Our Backs, 30,* 13. http://search.proquest.com/docview/197128320?accountid=10216.

Peitz, K., Pollock, J.C., Watson, E., Esposito, C., Nichilo, P., and Etheridge, J. (2015). *Cross-national coverage of Genetically-Modified Organisms: A community structure approach.* Paper presented at the biannual DC Health Communication Conference, April, Washington, DC.

Pollock, J.C. (2007). *Tilted mirrors: Media alignment with political and social change: A community structure approach.* Cresskill, NJ: Hampton Press.

Pollock, J.C. (2008). Community structure model. In W. Donsbach (Ed.). *International encyclopedia of communication,* 870–873. London and New York: Blackwell.

Pollock, J.C. (2013a). Community structure research. In P. Moy (Ed.), *Oxford Bibliographies Online.* New York: Oxford University Press.

Pollock, J.C. (Ed.). (2013b). *Media and social inequality: Innovations in community structure research.* New York: Routledge.

Pollock, J.C. (Ed.). (2015). *Journalism and human rights: How demographics drive media coverage.* New York: Routledge

Pollock, J.C., Maltese-Nehrbass, M., Corbin, P., and Fascanella, P.B. (2010, October). Nationwide newspaper coverage of genetically-modified food in the United States: A community structure approach. *Ecos de la Comunicación, 3* (3), 51–75.

Pollock, J.C., Reda, E., Bosland, A., Hindi, M., and Zhu, D. (2010, June). *Cross-national coverage of climate change: A community structure approach.* Paper presented at the annual conference of the International Communication Association, Singapore.

Pollock, J. C., and Robinson, J. L. (1977). Reporting rights conflicts. *Society, 13* (1), 44–47.

Pollock, J. C., Robinson, J. L., and Murray, M. C. (1978). Media agendas and human rights: The Supreme Court decision on abortion. *Journalism Quarterly, 5 3*(3), 545–548, 561.

Rozee, P. D. (1993). Forbidden or forgiven? Rape in cross-cultural perspective. *Psychology of Women Quarterly, 17* (4), 499–514. http://search.proquest.com/docview/61366509?accountid=10216.

Shiundu, A. (2010, February 7). AAGM: First lady angered by rape in schools. *Nation.* http://infoweb.newsbank.com/.

Task Force on Gender and Water. (2006). *Gender, water and sanitation: A policy brief.* www.unwater.org/downloads/unwpolbrief230606.pdf.

Tichenor, P.J., Donohue, G., and Olien, C. (1973). Mass communication research: Evolution of a structural model. *Journalism Quarterly, 50,* 419–425.

Tichenor, P.J., Donohue, G., and Olien, C. (1980). *Community conflict and the press.* Beverly Hills, CA: Sage.

Transparency International. (2012). Corruption perceptions index 2012. http://cpi.transparency.org/cpi2012/results/.

United Nations Population Division. (2010). *UNSD statistical databases.* http://www.un.org/esa/population/.

United Nations Statistics Division. (2006). *UNSD statistical databases.* http://unstats.un.org/unsd/databases.htm.

United Nations Statistics Division. (2011). *UNSD statistical databases.* http://unstats.un.org/unsd/databases.htm.

U.S. Department of Justice. (2012, January 6). Attorney general Eric Holder announces revisions to the uniform crime report's definition of rape. http://www.justice.gov/opa/pr/2012/January/12-ag-018.html.

Waterhouse-Watson, D., and Brown, A. (2011). Women in the "grey zone"? Ambiguity, complicity and rape culture. *M/C Journal, 14*(5), 4. http://ezproxy.tcnj.edu:2063/login.aspx?direct=true&db=ufh&AN=66984484&site=ehost-live.

Wissel, D., Ward, K., Pollock, J. C., Hipper, A., Klein, L., and Gratale, S. (2014). Cross-national coverage of water handling: A community structure approach. *Atlantic Journal of Communication, 22* (3/4), 193–210.

Women's Center. (2012). What is the "rape culture"? http://www.marshall.edu/wpmu/wcenter/sexual-assault/rape-culture/.

Wright, J.B., Giovenco, D., DiMarco, G., Dato, A. Homes, A.C., and Pollock, J.C. (2008). *International newspaper coverage of Muslim immigration since September 11, 2001: A community structure approach.* Paper presented at the annual conference of the National Communication Association, San Diego, CA.

World happiness report. (2012). http://worldhappiness.report/.

Yamamoto, M., and Ran, W. (2013, December). Drug abuse violations in communities: community newspapers as a macro-level source of social control. *Journalism and Mass Communication Quarterly, 90*, 629–651.

11

Multiculturalism as a Disempowering Paradigm

The Canadian Case

Fay Patel

Canada's multicultural policy has been a bone of contention in Canadian newspapers ever since its inception in 1971 with arguments dichotomized between the policy's positive embrace of multicultures as an empowering medium versus its negative impact as a weak nation building model (Karim 2008). Over the decades, in spite of the contention among the public, Canada and her multiculturalism policy continues to be an influencing factor among immigrants who perceive Canada as a haven from oppressive regimes. Bloemraad (2011) maintains that, according to the Multiculturalism Policy Index, "Canada and Australia rank highest as having adopted the broadest range of multicultural policies." One of the most attractive aspects of Canadian immigration to date is her multicultural policy. Canada's multicultural policy remains one of the most attractive aspects of Canadian immigration.

Multiculturalism inspires notions of respect, dignity and a humane approach to building the strength of Canada's citizenry. Nonetheless, it obscures the socio-economic inequities that are present in Canadian society where immigrant populations are dispersed across the vast land under guise of their right to celebrate their "differences." The reality of the Canadian immigrant experience becomes clear when immigrant populations seek employment in their regional homes, send their children to school and when they begin to live the Canadian multicultural dream and strive to be accepted, embraced and accommodated as part of the Canadian cultural mosaic. Gomarasca (2013) contends that "multiculturalism, with few exceptions, tends to conceive different cultures as cognitive islands." When Canadian immigrants find, shortly after arrival, that they are marginalized in various public and political spaces on the basis of employment experience and qualifications, cultural practice, race, and language, it is at that point that the Canadian multicultural dream begins to fade rapidly. Other ongoing tensions arise when immigrants are expected to integrate, assimilate and acculturate in order to be "truly Canadian" while at the same time they are encouraged to celebrate their "difference."

Karim (2002) contends that the notion of multiculturalism upholds the legitimacy of a variety of cultures in the country, and argues that this is a contested view as noted in media reports. His studies have alluded to the presence of inequities in socio-cultural engagement among immigrant populations and Canadians and to the constant struggle among immigrants to remain relevant in the Canadian economic and political spheres. Both Karim and Bloemraad acknowledge that the views expressed in the media and in research studies highlight a mixed response from the Canadian public (including immigrants and other Canadians). Bloemraad (2011) argues that although multiculturalism is regarded as a recognition and accommodation of minority cultures, critics also view it as an approach that "reifies differences, undermines a cohesive collective identity, and hinders common political projects." She contends that "empirical research on these questions is mixed" and "evidence on the socioeconomic consequences of multiculturalism is mixed." Karim and Bloemraad highlight the range of perspectives and research studies on the subject of multiculturalism, in general, and Canada's multicultural model, in particular.

It is apparent from a review of literature (Bloemraad 2011; Hoyos 2014; Hyman, Meinhard, and Shields 2011; Joshee, Reva, and Sinfield 2010; Karim 2002) that the momentum of the research and the public media debate on Canada's multicultural policy and the associated socio-economic inequities have become more complex and more urgent in recent years. Currency of such debate is evident in the ongoing political debate and media coverage of the Citizenship Act Bill C -24 which will inevitably create "two classes of citizens" and promote a "second-class citizenship" model: one for Canadian born citizens and the other for foreign born Canadian citizens. Bill C-24 is expected to counter current global terrorism in which perpetrators of terrorism who are dual citizenship holders are assumed to have "divided loyalties" and "lack of tangible attachment to Canada" (Adam et al. 2014). An area of importance in the current debate on citizenship is the perspective of immigrant populations who have chosen Canada in addition to their naturalized homelands. From that perspective, as citizens and residents of the Canadian democracy, immigrants also have a right to choose if they want to be included in the Canadian mosaic.

The Multiculturalism Policies (MCP) Index (2015), a Queens University Canada project, monitors the evolution of multiculturalism policies in twenty-one Western democracies. Along with Canada, included in the list of the twenty-one Western democracies are Australia, New Zealand, the United States of America, the United Kingdom, Finland, Japan, Greece, and Germany. The Index study found that among other outcomes, "despite the perception of a backlash and retreat from immigrant multiculturalism, the evidence suggests that multiculturalism policies have persisted, and in many cases, continue to expand." The study found that there was little or no support for the claim that MCPs have negative effects on social solidarity, social capital, or immigrant integration or that MCPs are having positive effects. However, in the author's view, based on her lived experience, the MCP is experienced as a disempowering paradigm, from an immigrant minority perspective. As noted by Boylorn (2008), "lived experience allows a researcher to use a single life to learn about society and about how individual experiences are communicated." The author argues that multiculturalism in the Canadian case is a disempowering paradigm in spite of marketing it as a positive nation building policy to potential immigrants.

To disempower someone is to provide minimal or no opportunity for their own development and that of their societies, remove their confidence, privilege, authority and right to act on their innate and acquired knowledge, and to disable them by not providing the support they require to flourish as significant contributors of knowledge to their local and regional communities. It is devaluing their contribution, dismissing their perspective, disrespecting their indigenous knowledge and disregarding their human capital. Schmidtke (2007) asserts that successful multicultural integration of immigrants is dependent on providing them with opportunities to engage in public debate and in policy-making.

Immigrant knowledge is undervalued and disregarded in the same way that *indigenous knowledge* has been discarded in international development by the Western nations over centuries in favor of Western philosophical and scientific thought. Gilbert (2003) and Servaes (1999) question the usefulness of the Western concept of "development" that carries assumptions of Western superiority and devaluation of other cultural belief systems. Immigrants are confined to their demarcated spaces in public and professional forums much like the Apartheid regime that segregated people on the basis of race in South Africa. The socio-economic and political inequities (Hoyos 2014; Joshee, Reva, and Sinfield 2010) of Canadian multiculturalism, and its disabling impact, are presented from the perspective of immigrant experience in Canadian society and evidence drawn drawn from studies on multiculturalism, immigrant experience, migration, integration, and marginalization.

On arrival into Canada, as with entry into any foreign land, immigrants are faced with new challenges and choices that include adaptation to a new lifestyle, language, and culture. More importantly, as an urgency they need to find a source of income based on their experience, qualifications and skills. Immigrants undergo various stages of culture shock. When the "honeymoon" stage is over, immigrants find that Canada's multicultural policy and practice along with her efforts to integrate newcomers is bewildering and overwhelming. On the one hand, they feel that their cultural norms and practices are accepted, recognized and accommodated whereas on the other hand they remain isolated from the mainstream socio-economic and political environment. Immigrant engagement with local society is largely through English language and cultural festival programs. This creates opportunities for them to celebrate their national traditions and "cultural wealth" (Patel, Li, and Sooknanan 2011) and to also volunteer in community events as they slowly blend into their local environment. Unlike Folson's racially profiled description of only "non-white" people as immigrants, in this chapter immigrant refers to all people who are from Europe, United Kingdom, United States of America, Asia, Africa and Latin America.

In 1988, the Canadian Multicultural Act was passed to ensure that Canadian immigrants took their respective colorful places in the Canadian mosaic. The Canadian Heritage website proudly claims that "this marked a milestone towards urging federal institutions to respect Canada's multicultural character and reflect the cultural, ethnic and racial diversity of Canadian society." More specifically, multiculturalism aimed at "preserving culture, reducing discrimination, enhancing cultural awareness and understanding, and promoting culturally sensitive institutional change at the federal level." However, immigrants' lived experience is different from the abstract notions of multiculturalism as espoused by policy makers and politicians. Boylorn (2008) asserts that lived experience leads to a self-awareness that acknowledges the integrity of an individual life and how separate life experiences can resemble and respond to larger public and social themes, creating a *space for storytelling, interpretation, and meaning-making*.

Oral tradition remains the most effective medium of transmitting history, culture, and messages based on lived experience among diverse groups and nations around the world. This chapter draws from both lived experience as well as from research. Scott-Dixon (2006) maintains that various forms of representation, self-expression, as well as the strategy of speaking from lived experience provide tools for political activism for many marginalized groups. Immigrants in Canada fit the profile of marginalized groups and this is visible in different forms as they make efforts to blend into the Canadian socio-economic sphere. Even within an environment that advocates multiculturalism, immigrants face various forms of disabling and disempowering practices.

Canadian immigration policies and practices have a number of contradictions such as inviting immigrants to celebrate differences in cultural practice, on the one hand, and then, on the other hand, to coerce them, through hidden agendas, into integration and assimilation into the Canadian cultural fabric. Tensions between living the Canadian multicultural dream as culturally diverse groups and blending into the socio-economic sphere become visible when immigrants seek employment. New immigrants are required to have prior "Canadian experience." Until mid to late 2000s, employment-hiring practices in Canada carried a "Canadian experience" requirement for newly arrived immigrants. This employment practice was modified in 2013 by the Ontario Human Rights Commission (OHRC) to remove the requirement, with growing criticism of the OHRC decision.

Furthermore, the points system used by Canadian immigration to assess language, education and skills levels misleads immigrants into believing that their foreign acquired skills and qualifications guarantees them a place in the Canadian economy and creates false hope to lead a contented life. The notion that multiculturalism is equivalent to equity and fairness in the Canadian social, political and economic sphere may also contribute to assumptions that immigrants gain access into the Canadian economy without prejudice. However, the preceding discussion about prior Canadian work experience and the points system along with lived experience perspectives of immigrants reveal that immigrants are disempowered through Canadian multicultural policies and practices because their personal and professional knowledge, skills, and qualifications are devalued in the Canadian workplace after they arrive in Canada. Such practices disempower immigrants and marginalize them, regarding them as "insignificant others" in Canadian society, treating them as less able and denying them their rightful place in Canadian mainstream society which espouses equal opportunities under the guise of multiculturalism. Multiculturalism, therefore, is not a unifying factor among all of Canada's peoples and has not respectfully placed immigrants within mainstream society.

MULTICULTURALISM: WHAT DOES IT MEAN?

Hoyos (2014) asserts that Canadian society is known for its multicultural mosaic, consisting of different social communities who co-exist, regardless of differences in ethnic origin or religious belief. Canada and Canadians are warmly embraced in the global sphere because of their adoption of multiculturalism as a celebration of multicultures. Bloemraad (2011) is of the view that multiculturalism can be categorized as "demographic" from different perspectives: for example, it can refer to the co-existence of existing minority groups categorized according to language, religion and origin or it can refer to a new wave of immigrant within similar categories. She further contends that multiculturalism can also be framed as "political philosophy" referring to ideas that are held by people, institutions and governments and also by political theorists to recognize diversity, and as public policy which encourages the implementation of multiculturalism in various public spaces to accommodate and celebrate diversity. It appears that multiculturalism is synonymous with accommodation and tolerance of diverse cultural practices and norms to which immigrants can subscribe alongside their "integration" into Canadian society. Herein lie various contradictions and tensions. Whereas multiculturalism is seen as a way of celebrating diversity and recognizing the differences in cultural norms and practices, integration refers to the way by which immigrant should become members of their receiving society. According to Li (2003) Canadian government documents from 1993 carry conflicting messages and assert that there is evidence of contradictory approaches which speak of integration as accepting immigrants' differences on one hand, but insisting upon immigrants complying with the normative values and national standard of Canada on the other.

The Canadian Heritage website describes Canadian multiculturalism as "fundamental to our belief that all citizens are equal. Multiculturalism ensures that all citizens can keep their identities, can take pride in their ancestry and have a sense of belonging." Gilbert claims that national identity in non-Western cultures is bound by *common descent* (on the basis of common ancestry and genealogy) and not by a *common economy* which seems to be the key focus for nation building among immigrants in Canada. However, multiculturalism does not encourage a "sense of belonging" because immigrants do not share *common descent* and so they experience conflict in establishing a "sense of belonging" (Gilbert 2003).

Immigrants assume that Canada's multicultural policy will act as a protective barrier against all harm in the personal and public spheres of Canadian life. This is an assumption of the Canadian Heritage Foundation as stated on the Canadian Heritage website "the Canadian experience has shown that multiculturalism encourages racial and ethnic harmony and cross-cultural understanding, and discourages ghettoization, hatred, discrimination and violence." However, in reality, multicultural policies and practices do not offer protection from hate crimes, from prejudice and discrimination, and from the harsh, unkind reminder in the tone and body language of fellow Canadians that immigrants are different. In fact, multicultural policy and practice may accentuate acts of hatred, violence, and discrimination. In the author's lived experience, the reality of the underlying currents of hate and discrimination became evident a couple of months after obtaining her residency, when in response to her sharing of perspectives in the local Windsor, Ontario newspaper, she received clearly articulated messages that "Patel . . . [and another immigrant academic] should go back where they came from." No resident or immigrant should ever have to hear this retort in any of the world's twenty-one democracies (MCP Index) that hold multiculturalism as their assurance of a safe and welcoming land.

Hoyos (2014) notes that "critics argue that multiculturalism promotes ghettoization and balkanization, and encourages segregation and discrimination. It leads its members into a sole awareness of its own kind, highlighting ethnic, religious and cultural differences." Nevertheless, "Canada is portrayed as a multicultural showcase, a society to be envied for its diversity management," according to Wallis and Kwok (2008). The question one has to ask is why Canada continues to be marketed as a *multicultural showcase*?

Canadian policy on multiculturalism is fraught with many shortcomings, which tend to disable and disempower immigrants in their new work and life environment. Multicultural policy operates along the lines of the *deficit model of communication*, which places the burden of responsibility for success and failure primarily on the recipient of the communication, in this case, on the immigrant. The deficit model of communication refers to an emphasis on inadequacies and deficiencies in the recipient of the communicated message, which is more frequently applied (as noted in lived experience) to immigrants of color. Li (2003) maintains that "immigration critics often compare the difficulty of integrating recent immigrants to the ease" of integrating early settlers who were mainly Caucasian. Li asserts that the subtext is clear, that earlier immigrants were Europeans; today's immigrants are mostly Asians and Africans so recent immigrants from Asia and Africa are less likely to embrace Canada's identity. It appears that, with reference to multiculturalism in Canada and her immigrants, the deficit communication model places responsibility on the immigrant to make every effort to acculturate and to fit into the Canadian cultural mosaic.

The deficit model, with respect to immigrants, communicates negative messages and suggests that the immigrant is inadequate in several ways, which include lack of proficiency in the language of the host country, and has insufficient skills and qualifications for the Canadian workplace. Folson (2008) explains that the "common notion of immigrant is a non-white person who is professionally challenged and speaks with an accent." In the context of this chapter, reference to immigrants includes those of Caucasian descent. Canadian immigrants are viewed as "inadequately trained" even though they had undergone a rigid point system assessment during the immigration visa application process. The race, gender, and culture of immigrants in Canada may determine their opportunities and limitations in a personal and professional basis.

RACE, GENDER, AND CULTURE IN AN ORGANIZATIONAL FRAMEWORK

Exploring the issues of race, gender, and culture in a Canadian organizational context through the eyes of an immigrant reveals that prejudice and discrimination are present in spite of the promise of the multicultural dream and illusions of social equity. Furthermore, it appears that the national multicultural policy does not remove the racial, gendered, and cultural barriers to success in the Canadian workplace for immigrants. Race, gender, and culture are critical factors that affect an immigrant's right to live a contented and fulfilled life in the host society. Unless immigrants have a decent paying job, they cannot have access to food and shelter and hence, how can they be content? Working as taxi-drivers and part-time teachers will not provide adequate financial resources to sustain a contented family life.

Multicultural policy and practice do not eradicate barriers of race, gender, and culture in an immigrant's personal and professional life. It may, in fact, perpetuate a deeper level of prejudice on the basis of race, gender, and culture which become defining factors for suitable employment, service to local communities, and especially in regard to access to education, employment, health, and social services. This means that local Canadians and government service officials will continue to profile immigrants in a stereotypical way to see if they fit into the "government assistance program" or qualify for "handouts" for immigrants and if they can participate in the programs for multicultural groups.

Of course, an immigrant's entry into the workforce is further hampered because organizations are not adequately prepared for recruiting immigrants who have different levels of skills, unfamiliar accents, inadequate or no Canadian experience, and are not Caucasian. She may or may not be a likely candidate for a position in an organization because the organization: has not diversified to integrate designated minority groups; does not have any higher level positions available for women; and is still an "all white" organization. So how has this changed from the historically embedded goal to create a white only nation-state?

Evidence from the growing literature, raging debates in the media and immigrant life stories suggests that immigrants to Canada have been misled into believing that Canada is a culturally and racially friendly nation that espouses multiculturalism as a respectful recognition of diverse cultures. Li (2003) claims that Canada "promotes conformity as a desirable outcome for immigrants and for Canada, despite the rhetorical commitment to diversity and multiculturalism" and that "immigration discourse has a tendency to reify specific cultural and racial differences and to represent them as threats to Canada's core values."

MISLEADING IMMIGRANTS

The media portrays Canada as a land of opportunity and wealth where her population enjoys a good life. Poverty, hardship, and homelessness in Canada are never mentioned. Wallis and Kwok (2008) claim that the media is controlled by a privileged few and that it carries multiple messages of Canada being a good country to live in and that her people live a content life. They believe that the media contributes to "the illusion of a content population in Canada." This is further endorsed by global agencies such as the United Nations which ranks Canada "as one of the best countries in which to live" (Wallis and Kwok 2008). In the late 1960s, Canada's immigration system introduced the points system as a strategy to move away from the pre-1960s objective of keeping Canada's population "white only" (Wallis and Kwok 2008: 12). The points system was designed in principle to focus on language proficiency, education, and skills levels in order to establish broader cultural diversity. However, the points system misleads and misinforms immigrants about their likelihood to find employment in Canada, after arrival in Canada. Bloemraad (2011) asserts that "labor market policies, educational institutions, and welfare state structures likely influence economic integration much more than policies of multiculturalism." However, both lived immigrant experience and research contest such a view when one considers how many immigrants have to resort to other means of economic integration for survival because they have not had opportunities to be fully integrated into the Canadian economy through labor policies, retraining in new career paths in local educational institutions, and not qualifying for welfare programs.

The lived reality for the immigrant is different because the high points score assessed during the immigration paper process has no relevance after they receive their landed immigrant and permanent residency visas and long after they have made the long, arduous journey to Canada. The points system score is never again reviewed by an immigration official, employment agency, and by the Ministry of Labour; nor is it aligned and matched to a job category to meet the gaps in the Canadian workforce. Once landed, the immigrant faces another long, frustrating process of contacting employment agencies to verify qualifications and experience through countless applications to provincial and national assessment agencies and/or to licensing boards. The outcome is often a realization that the new immigrant does not fit into a Canadian organizational framework because of inadequacies in skills, qualifications and language proficiency or perhaps the Canadian job market has reached saturation point. Immigration Watch Canada has alluded to the fact that the immigration high intake has resulted in "negative economic consequences for a minimum of 1.5 million Canadians who are looking for work; increased demand for housing; and that pursuit of diversity has led to the perception that Canada is being recolonized." The new immigrant is then directed to agencies which facilitate retraining and up skilling in a new career path to fit into the Canadian workplace.

RETRAINING PROGRAMS AND THE NEGATIVE MESSAGES

With regard to the retraining of immigrants, government agencies such as Citizen and Immigration Canada (CIC) and Social Sciences and Humanities Research Council (SSHRC) offered a wide range of grants over the last decade to retrain immigrants. For example, in Windsor, Ontario a number of agencies received a substantial government grant in 2008 to assist new immigrants with enhanced language skills and job placement preparation. Agencies advertised for suitable trainers to work with new immigrants to upgrade their skills. This was evident in a review of the large number of training and teaching jobs advertised by agencies on the government service website jobbank.gov.ca in the months of July, August, and September 2008, for example. Among the agencies advertising such jobs were the following: the Multicultural Council, the YMCA, the New Canadian Centre for Excellence, and Windsor Women Working with Immigrant Women. The University of Windsor, which offered workshops funded by SSHRC to provide legal and business information for new immigrants wanting to start a business, not only received grants to help train immigrants on business matters but also to research access to health and social services among new immigrants (grant received from Centre of Excellence for Research on Immigration and Settlement). One might question why immigrants who have already met rigid immigration skills assessment requirements and acceptable scores on the Immigration Canada points system have to be retrained shortly after their arrival in Canada?

Other questions related to structural dysfunction and misalignment of immigrant job skills and qualifications to job needs in Canada are pertinent here. Do the different government departments (Immigration and Citizenship and Labor) work together when they review immigrant applications? Do existing and new labor policies and practices ensure that new immigrants (already approved by Canadian Immigration) are smoothly transitioned into the workplace? Do the government departments of labor and of immigration adequately prepare and train small and large corporations, government and non-government employment agencies to recruit immigrants on a fair and equitable basis? Immigrant lived experience and the literature suggest that there is a *dysfunctional relationship* between the department of Immigration and Citizenship and the Ministry of Labour. It is, perhaps, for this reason that recruitment agencies and independent employers in small and large corporations have turned away immigrants because of lack of "Canadian experience." How can immigrants have Canadian workplace experience if they have not been employed in the Canadian workforce since their arrival? It took decades to introduce equity for immigrant recruitment in the Ontario Human Rights Commission in 2013 to remove the discriminatory recruitment requirement of "prior Canadian experience" for immigrants. Immigration Canada Watch (IWC) contested the Ontario Human Rights Commission (OHRC) decision to regard the employment criteria of "prior Canadian experience" as a degree of discrimination against Canadian workers. ICW regards the decision by the OHRC as a decision that is "amateurish" and "a result of careless and ill-informed research" (Ontario Human Rights Commission).

Other issues that arise in regard to the surplus funds available for retraining immigrants include: is this a political strategy or budget excess. As noted earlier, funds are available for retraining immigrants under guise of "government assistance programs" handouts. Nevertheless, the key question remains: why do immigrants need retraining when they come with professional qualifications which the immigration department has already recognized as suitable for employment during the interview and processing of the permanent resident visa stage? The critical review of multiculturalism as a disempowering paradigm has led to the uncovering of barriers and key anomalies in immigrant processing, new immigrant job recruitment and retraining processes. Recommendations to remove the barriers to full settlement rights for immigrants in Canada are presented in the next section.

RECOMMENDATIONS

In order to empower immigrants and recognize their significant contributions to the Canadian economy, the government is urged to revisit and reassess immigration policies, recruitment practices and the multicultural policies. Realignment of government policies and practices is critical in ensuring that immigrants are relocated to the mainstream. A reframing of Canadian government policy and practice will require reshaping communication and nation building protocols in order to find mutually acceptable strategies that are genuinely inclusive, equitable and respectful of diversity of knowledge, experience and perspectives.

Recommendations for policy redevelopment and seeking innovative solutions are noted below.

- A careful examination of the immigration selection process points system should be undertaken to ascertain its alignment with labor law requirements and recruitment processes
- Channels of communication should be transparent and clear between immigration officials, labor law practitioners and recruitment agencies to effectively align new immigrant talents, skills and qualifications to job needs so that immigrants move directly from immigrant visa status into employment when they arrive as permanent residents.
- Key stakeholders (in the domestic workforce) in large and small corporations including the human resources teams should undergo retraining of recruitment policy and practice, development of their intercultural communication skills, and various anti-discrimination training programs in conflict resolution and reconciliation; commitment to the Human Rights Codes, diversity, multiculturalism, and equity to prepare them for a culturally diverse workforce.

The recommendations above will place the burden of responsibility on the Canadian government and the Canadian host community (within and across organizations in local, regional and national contexts) to practice equity and inclusivity in welcoming new immigrant communities.

CONCLUDING REMARKS

Banting and Kymlicka (2012) contend that the debate about the success or failure of multiculturalism in an international context is at a discourse level rather than a national policy level. They claim that it is based on "generalizations about the rise and fall of multiculturalism, and its success or failure, without systematic cross-national measurement" and argue that the MCP Index research is a framework to investigate these generalizations. Further, they note that at this stage in the debate multiculturalism may be rejected by countries in favor of "civic integration" as a way to negotiate a more compatible model. In their view, "the Canadian model is best described as multicultural *integration*." Whether the rejection of multiculturalism is at a discourse or policy level is insignificant in the real life experience of the immigrant minority. There should be cognizance of the fact that the lived experience of the immigrant minorities continues to be a struggle to participate in the life of the host society from a socio-economic perspective. Berry explored the notion of multiculturalism as integration within a balanced perspective for "the two underlying values of *diversity* and *equity*" and argues that these may be regarded as acceptable alternative multicultural options among some groups.

Canada is regarded, in marketing and tourist promotional campaigns, as the best country in the world for quality living. However, in order to live up to that expectation, she must be proactive in enacting and sustaining equitable policy and practice among immigrants to ensure that all Canadians experience quality lifestyles. After all, immigrants are tax-paying members who have already overcome much socio-economic and political hardship in their other lives (where they grew up) before arriving on Canadian soil. The conference *Multiculturalism Turns 40* held in 2011 produced a non-exhaustive list of topics that raised critical concerns and challenges in Canada's multicultural history. Among the topics of that conference are the questions posed in this chapter and sentiments shared about various aspects of multiculturalism and ethnic identity, multiculturalism and immigrant integration, multiculturalism and social cohesion, the role of the media and multicultural policy, multiculturalism, equality and social justice (Wong and Guo 2014). Immigrants have earned their rightful place in the Canadian multicultural landscape. As residents and citizens of Canada, they should be treated with respect and dignity. In becoming active and significant contributors to Canada's growing economy, they will also remain a vibrant part of her socio-cultural heartbeat, share her political aspirations to remain the one nation in the world that upholds humanity as her first principle of citizenship.

REFERENCES

Adams, Michael, Macklin, A. and Omidvar, R (2014). "Citizenship Act will create two classes of Canadians." May. 21. http://www.theglobeandmail.com/globe-debate/citizenship-act-will-create-two-classes-of-canadians/article18778296/.

Banting, K. and Kymlicka, W. (2012). "Is there really a backlash against multi-culturalism policies? New evidence from the multiculturalism policy index." GRITIM-UPF Working Paper Series no. 14. www.upf.edu/gritim.

Berry, J.W. (2011). "Integration and multiculturalism: Ways towards social solidarity." *Peer Reviewed Online Journal Papers on Social Representation*, vol. 20, 2.1–2.21. http://www.psych.lse.ac.uk/psr/.

Bloemraad, (2011). " The debate over multiculturalism: Philosophy, politics and policy." September 22. http://www.migrationpolicy.org/article/debate-over-multiculturalism-philosophy-politics-and-policy.

Boylorn, R. M. (2008). "Lived experience." In *The Sage Encyclopedia of Qualitative Research Methods*. http://srmo.sagepub.com/view/sage-encyc-qualitative-re-search-methods/n250.xml.

Christian, Joppke. (2010). *Citizenship and Immigration.* Cambridge: Polity Press.

Dewing, M. (2013). "Canadian multiculturalism 2013 update." *Parliamentary Information and Research Services.* http://www.parl.gc.ca/Content/LOP/ResearchPublications/2009-20-e.pdf.

Folson, R.B. (2008). "Representation of the immigrant." In M.A.Wallis and S. Kwok, eds., *Daily Struggles: The Deepening Racialization and Feminization of Poverty in Canada,* 39–47. Toronto: Canadian Scholar's Press.

Gilbert, J. (2003). "Two worlds, integration, synthesis or conflict? Psychological perspectives on cultural identity." *Conference proceedings of African Studies Association of Australiasia and the Pacific.* http://afaap.org.au/Conferences/2003/Gilbert.PDF .

Gomarasca, Paolo. (2013). "Multiculturalism or hybridisation? Cultural mixing and politics. diversities." UNESCO. www.unesco.org/shs/diversities/vol15/issue2/art6.

Hoyos, K. (2014). "Canadian multiculturalism, same as it ever was?" *Coolabah,* no. 13. http://www.ub.edu/dpfilsa/coolabah134hoyos.pdf.

Hyman, H., Meinhard, A. and Shields, J. (2011). "The role of multiculturalism policy in addressing social inclusion processes in Canada." Centre for Voluntary Sector Studies, Ryerson University Working Paper Series. http://www.ryerson.ca/cvss/working_papers.

Immigration Watch Canada. (2015). "Inadequate jobs for 1.5 million people and high immigration intake." http://www.immigrationwatchcanada.org/.

Information on Apartheid in South Africa. (2008). http://www.beaconforfree-dom.org/about_database/south%20africa.html.

Information on funds for new immigrants. (2008). http://www.cic.gc.ca/english/DEPARTMENT/MEDIA/RELEASES/2008/2008-03-19.asp.

Information on grant distribution. (2008). http://www.cic.gc.ca/english/DE-PARTMENT/MEDIA/backgrounders/2008/2008-03-19.asp.

Information on University of Windsor research grant. (2008). http://www.uwindsor.ca/units/socialjustice/main.nsf/SubCategoryFlyOut/8157B9DCDB29AB4B852572340058DADF.

Joshee, Reva, and Sinfield, I. (2010). "The Canadian multicultural education policy web: Lessons to learn, pitfalls to avoid." http://journals.sfu.ca/mer/index.php/mer/article/view/9.

Karim, K. (2002). "The multiculturalism debate in Canadian newspapers: The harbinger of a political storm." *Journal of Migration and Integration*, vol. 3, nos. 3 and 4 (Summer/Fall): 439–455.

Karim, K. (2008). "Press, public sphere, and pluralism: Multiculturalism debates in Canadian English-language newspapers." *Canadian Ethnic Studies*, vol. 40, no. 1: 57–78. http://muse.jhu.edu/journals/ces/summary/v040/40.1.karim.html.

Li, Peter. (2003). "Deconstructing Canada's discourse of immigration:. Integration." PCER11 Working Paper Series, Working Paper no. WP04-03, August. http://www.ualberta.ca/~pcerii/WorkingPapers/WP04-03.pdf.

Multiculturalism Policy Index. http://www.queensu.ca/mcp/.

Ontario Human Rights Commission Policy on Removing the "Canadian experience" barrier. http://www.ohrc.on.ca/en/policy-removing-%E2%80%9Ccanadian-experience%E2%80%9D-barrier.

Patel, F., Li, M., and Sooknanan, P. (2011). *Intercultural communication: Building a global community*. Pt. 1: *The Canadian Multiculturalism Act—15 years later*. New Delhi: Sage. Review of jobs in Windsor, Ontario. http://www.jobbank.gc.ca/.

Rudmin, F.W. (2003). "Critical history of the acculturation psychology of assimilation, separation, integration and marginalization." *Review of General Psychology*, vol. 7, no. 1: 3–37.

Schmidtke, O. (2007). "(Dis-)empowering immigrants in Canada: Political advocacy of immigrant and minority organisations promoting cultural diversity in the health care sector/" *International Journal of Migration, Health and Social Care*, vol. 3, no. 3: 20–28.

Scott-Dixon, K. (Ed.). (2006). *Trans/forming feminisms: Trans-feminist voices speak out*. Toronto: Sumach Press.

Servaes, Jan. (1999). *Communication for development: One world, multiple cultures*. Cresskill NJ: Hampton Press.

Wallis, M.A., and Kwok, S. (Eds.) (2008). *Daily Struggles: The Deepening Racialization and Feminization of Poverty in Canada*. Toronto: Canadian Scholar's Press.

"What is multiculturalism?" Canadian Heritage. http://www.canadianheritage.gc.ca/progs/multi/what-multi_e.cfm.

Wong, L., and Guo, S. (2014). "Multiculturalism turns 40: Reflections on the Canadian policy." *Canadian Ethnic Studies*, vols. 1–3. http://www.crr.ca/en/programs/25-multiculturalism/24735-multiculturalism-turns-40 reflections-on-the-canadian-policy.

Conclusion

Studying Complex Inequalities

Jan Servaes

A t the end of this journey through two volumes, that focused on the theory and praxis of social inequalities in media and communication, we need to ask ourselves: what are the lessons learned and how can we further improve our understanding of these highly controversial but very substantial and complex issues?

As we stated at the outset, the nature and pattern of inequality in societies is shaped by particular historical contexts, social structures, economic and cultural configurations. The various forms of inequalities—economic, political, cultural, technological, and social—manifest themselves in race, gender, ethnicity, religion, and, in general, the social stratification they create in society. Issues of poverty, gender inequality, class struggle, racial discrimination, economic imbalances, and other social fractures continue to shape the social analysis of participation, exclusion and inclusion in society.

The selected chapters, either from a theoretical or practical perspective, have tried to detail complexity by zooming in on specific media, communication formats, social problems and injustices, audiences or target groups, at different levels of societal analysis. Most contributions scrutinized a specific type of inequality, henceforth more or less following the typology presented by scholars such as Wilkinson and Picket (2009) or

Van Dijk (2012, 2013): technological, immaterial, material, social, and educational. However, some went beyond these traditional categorizations to dig deeper into, what Goran Therborn (2013: 49) calls, the roots, dynamics and interactions of the three kinds of inequality: vital, existential and resource based:

- *Vital inequality*, referring to socially constructed unequal life-chances of human organisms;
- *Existential inequality*, the unequal allocation of personhood, that is of autonomy, dignity, degrees of freedom, and of rights to respect and self-development;
- *Resource inequality*, providing human actors with unequal resources to act.

Therborn observes that conventional studies of inequality are mainly concerned about resource inequalities. However, in his opinion, "the three dimensions interact and intertwine, and should always be suspected of doing so" (Therborn 2013: 51), because they all relate to *four basic mechanisms of (in)equality production*: "Inequalities are produced and sustained socially by systemic arrangements and processes, and by distributive action, individual as well as collective. It is crucial to pay systemic attention to both" (Therborn 2013: 55). These four basic cumulative and interrelated mechanisms of (in)equality production are: distanciation/approximation, exclusion/inclusion, hierarchization/de-hierarchization, and exploitation/redistribution-rehabilitation.

The relative importance of these mechanisms of inequality and equality is at the centre of scholarly as well as political controversies about world development, although the mechanisms are usually only implied in area-specific notions, reflecting the under-theorized field of inequality (Therborn 2013: 67).

STUDYING IN/EQUALITY IN THE "GLOBAL VILLAGE"

Let's take up Therborn's challenge and try to further problematize the "field of in/equality" from a theoretical and methodological perspective.1

While we did position our books in a "global perspective," we need to realize that globalization is *not* a product of the post-war period, or even the twentieth century, as many historians will explain (see, for instance, Hopkins, 2002). Therefore, Held, McGrew, Goldblatt, and Perraton (1999: 414) conclude that "globalization is neither a wholly novel, nor primarily modern, social phenomenon. Its form has changed over time and across the key domains of human interaction, from the political to the ecological.

Moreover . . . globalization as a historical process cannot be characterized by an evolutionary logic or an emergent telos."

In other words, beyond a general awareness and agreement of the *global interconnectedness*, there is substantial disagreement as to how globalization is best conceptualized, how one should think about its causal dynamics, how one should characterize its structural, socio-economic consequences, and which implications it has on state power and governance. This debate has developed three different theses on globalization: a (hyper)globalist perspective, a skeptical or traditionalist perspective, and, a transformationalist perspective.

Cochrane and Pain (2000: 22–23) summarize these theses as follows:

1. *Globalists* see globalization as an inevitable development, which cannot be resisted or significantly influenced by human intervention, particularly through traditional political institutions, such as nation-states.

2. *Traditionalists* argue that the significance of globalization as a new phase has been exaggerated. They believe that most economic and social activities are regional, rather than global, and still see a significant role for nation-states.

3. *Transformationalists* believe that globalization represents a significant shift, but question the inevitability of its impacts. They argue that there is still significant scope for national, local, and other agencies.

Our interpretation of this classification is that the globalist and the traditionalist perspectives are both very extreme in their views. The globalists advocate that the world changes toward a more homogenous global culture and toward all kinds of new global structures. The traditionalists take the other extreme stance and advocate that nothing really revolutionary is happening. In our opinion, the transformationalist perspective is not so much a compromise between the two, as it is a less extreme and more modest interpretation of what is happening. Transformationalists argue that the world does go through changes—in a sense as she has always gone through changes—but they do believe that some of these changes form a conglomerate of changes that does account for something to be interpreted as "new."

Lie (1998, 2003) and Servaes and Lie (2008) made an inventory of such a *conglomerate of changes* in a cultural atmosphere and identified the following components: (1) the interrelated processes of the emergence of interdisciplinarity, (2) the increasing role of the power of culture, (3) the birth of a new form of modernization, (4) the changing role of the nation-state, and, (5) the emerging attempts to address the link between the global and the local. The total conglomerate of changes accounts for something new,

but especially the last issue of linking the global with the local was identified as a central point of change.

But, how can this conglomerate of global changes be linked to in/
equality and political-economic and social change at local levels and from
within local levels?

What these two volumes on social inequalities, media, and communication have shown is the reiteration of the globality of social inequalities.
However, this universalism of inequalities does not imply generic experiences, the contributors have been able to reveal the various contours of
social inequalities from subjective perspectives with specific positionality
from their different local geographical spaces in relation to media and
communication experiences.

GLOBALIZING INEQUALITIES

I want to recall the "old" Latin-American discussion on transnationalization and dependency, which partly inspired the development of my
"multiplicity" paradigm (Servaes 1999). Sunkel and Fuenzalida (1980)
best summarized it in four succinct points:

a. The capitalistic system has evolved in recent decades from an international to a transnational or global system with the transnational
   corporations as the most significant actors.
b. The most striking feature of the actual system is the polarized development of transnationalization on the one hand, and national
   disintegration on the other.
c. Of particular interest is the emphasis on culture which is the main
   stimulator of a new transnational community of people from different nations, but with similar values and ideas, as well as patterns of
   behavior.
d. The ultimate result is the parallel existence of varying sectors within
   the same national borders. In other words, the national societies are
   generating a variety of counter processes that assert national and/or
   subnational values, sometimes reactionary, sometimes progressive.

Thirty-five years later, these points still sound surprisingly fresh. The
"wording" would probably be different in today's jargon, and some
second-level observations may need some further articulation, but—in
general— this could well do as the *outline* for a research framework on
global in/equality in media and communication.

Especially if we add a few more specifics: for instance, the observation
by Giddens (1995: 4–5) that "Globalization does not only concern the

creation of large-scale systems, but also the transformation of the local, and even personal, context of social experience." In addition, Sen's (2004) contribution to the cultural freedom and human development discussion by arguing that *capabilities* help us to construct a normative conception of social justice. The way Homi Bhabha (1994) rethinks questions of identity, social agency and national affiliation, and why globalization must begin at home; linked to Appadurai's (2001: 17) argument that globalization is an interactive process in which "locality" and "globality" interact via the shrinking of space-time in the world system. In other words, globalization as the widening, deepening and speeding up of worldwide interconnectedness in all aspects of contemporary social life.

Jan Pakulski (2004: 14) arrived at a similar argument regarding inequality based on the following propositions:

- Socio-economic inequalities have been increasing within the most rapidly globalizing advanced societies, especially in the Anglo-American democracies that embrace deregulation and economic liberalization.
- The key trend in these societies is toward growing ranks of the affluent and very rich, most of whom are "corporate-rich" and represent "new wealth."
- Socio-political inequalities seem to change in two opposed directions: one trend is toward democratization and a further extension of citizenship, the other is toward the concentration of power in the hands of non-elective elites.
- There has been also a trend toward the increasing American hegemony that encompasses economic, military, diplomatic and cultural dimensions.
- In the socio-cultural sphere, inequalities "narrow down," and this egalitarian trend is clearly linked to declining traditionalism. The established hierarchies of status, in particular gender and ethno-racial hierarchies, are either crumbling or coming under growing critical scrutiny.
- Some aspects of racial divisions persist, but racial discrimination per se has been losing legitimacy and public support, especially among educated and affluent city dwellers.
- Established hierarchies of taste have been undermined by an increasing "polytheism of values," individualism, and rapidly diversifying lifestyles. While sumptuary capacities and lifestyles vary, claims to a unilateral "cultural superiority" are hard to sustain.

Potentially, such a *framework* integrates global dependency thinking, world-system theory, a normative (human) rights perspective, and local, grassroots, interpretative, participatory theory and research on social change.

Perhaps to further contextualize the globalizing tendency of inequality, we need to relook the history of the (post)modern world. This "relook" compels us to engage the trajectory of world development from the era of the rise of the developmental state to the current dominant neo-liberal nature of globalization. Pollin (2003) observes that the transformation of the developmental state that became widespread after World War II and the decolonization period of the 1970s witnessed a series of state interventionist policies to promote economic growth, increase equality, and encourage social cohesion. Undoubtedly, some of these policies were controversial in many instances; an example is the economic interventionist and modernist approach proposed by foreign nations in developing nations with ultimate goal of discouraging drive toward socialism that characterized the Cold War era. The rise of a modern form of capitalism epitomized by neoliberalism has become a predominant economic ideology that governs the world with repercussion on economic viability and social-cultural wellbeing. The aggressive advancement of neoliberalism in the less developed countries by the Washington Consensus of the U.S. government, the International Monetary Fund and the World Bank coupled with the adoption and transmission of this ideology into political platforms of developing nations played a major role in the shaping of the current global economy (Pollin 2003). The unequal benefits that accrue to nations due to neoliberalism create a pattern of winners and losers. The free trade policies and liberalization tendencies open many developing nations to foreign transnational corporations who set up "sweatshops" for the manufacturing of products to be consumed in the developed countries. The poor in these less developed nations are left with no choice but to participate in this process for a meager income as handout to step out of abject poverty. The social and human costs of this system evidenced at a micro level reveal the unequal nature of the current global economic system.

GLOBALIZED IN/EQUALITY AND (CULTURAL) IDENTITIES

What globalization really is and what it means to human beings with regard to (cultural, national, ethnic) identity continues to be a matter of discussion as various cultures manifest different and fragmented identities. The term *cultural identity* refers to two complementary phenomena: on the one hand, an inward sense of association or identification with a specific culture or subculture; on the other hand, an outward tendency within a specific culture to share a sense of what it has in common with other cultures and of what distinguishes it from other cultures (for an elaboration, see Servaes 1999).

If we adopt Anderson's (1983) idea of imagined communities, we have to accept that culture and identity are an evolving process positioning the individual as an active participant in the consumption of global communication. The subconscious references and choices that we make on a daily basis attach meaning to the "messages" we receive, which is related to our concept of self and other. This view emphasizes the exchange of meaning taking place in the local consumption of global messages. In order to understand and study this properly we need to start with Eriksen (1993: 150), from the assumption that identity is locally constructed, and that "people still live in places." Bude and Dürrschmidt (2010) therefore suggest that—contrary to the prevailing overemphasis on mobility and deterritorialization—an existential turn that orients future globalization thinking more toward issues of belonging, choice and commitment, and the rhythmicity of social relations should be considered. To highlight the processual character of this shift of perspective, they draw on the paradigmatic figure of the *homecomer*. She or he embodies the ambivalence between the lure of global options and the need for commitment to lasting bonds. Thus, they do not argue for a post-mortem on globalization theory, but maintain that a deeper understanding of globalization as a "way of being in the world" would require a phenomenologically inclined repositioning of the concept.

STUDYING GLOBALIZED IN/EQUALITY
FROM WITHIN LOCALIZED APPROPRIATION

Thompson (1995) argued that the relation between structured patterns of global communication, on the one hand, and the local conditions under which media products are consumed, on the other hand, can best be understand as the *axis of globalized diffusion and localized appropriation*:

> While communication and information are increasingly diffused on a global scale, these symbolic materials are always received by individuals who are situated in specific spatial-temporal locales. The appropriation of media products is always a localized phenomenon, in the sense that it always involves specific individuals who are situated in particular social-historical contexts, and who draw on the resources available to them in order to make sense of media messages and incorporate them into their lives. And messages are often transformed in the process of appropriation as individuals adapt them to the practical contexts of everyday life. The globalization of communication has not eliminated the localized character of appropriation

but rather has created a new kind of symbolic axis in the modern world. (Thompson 1995: 174).

Not only can globality influence locality, the latter can also induce changes in the global arena and this process could be called globalization from below, local globalization or *grassroots globalization*.

The term *global communication* could then be defined as a flow of ideas, services, cultural products and technology that includes the global diffusion and local consumption of culture, values, social, political and economic concepts. These factors have had an impact, via different communication modes, on a different locality in a different way at a different speed from the past to the present. See, for instance, the interesting analysis of the interplay of religion and culture in Thai HIV Aids campaigns (Malikhao 2012).

The task for a researcher is to examine the processes of "bottom-up" change and to reveal distinctive structures of meaning:

a. the characteristics and dimensions of the socio-cultural reference framework (i.e., the worldview, the ethos/value system, socio-cultural organization, and their symbolic representations);
b. the interaction and interrelation with the environment of power and interests; and
c. the "ideological apparatuses" by which the socio-cultural reference framework is produced and through which it is at the same time disseminated.

A MATRIX TO STUDY IN/EQUALITY IN MEDIA AND COMMUNICATION

Elsewhere, Lie and Servaes (2000) adopted a convergent and integrated approach in studying the complex and intricate relations between globalization, consumption, and identity (see Figure 12.1). Such an approach would allow problems to converge at *key crossings* or nodal points. Researchers then are rid of the burden of studying linear processes in totality, for example production and consumption of global products, and instead are allowed to focus on the nodal points where processes of in/equality intersect.

Several such nodal points can be identified, including production, regulation, representation, consumption, action, and local points of entry into the communications flow. The nodal points approach highlights the richness of globalization as an area of research, however it is also important to note that all these dimensions do rest on certain axial principles.

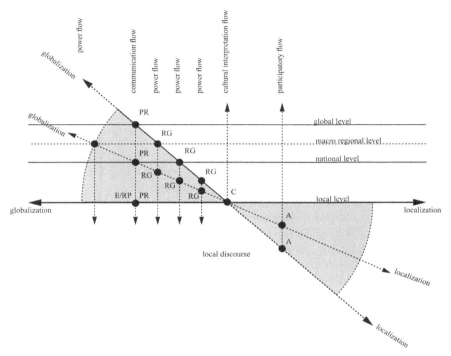

Figure 12.1.   Nodal points of research in a people-centered perspective on globalization/localization. A= Action; C= consumption; E= entry; RG= regulation; RP= representation; PR= production.

Social inequalities, human and environmental *sustainability* have become such central themes in global communication. Considerations and assessments of in/equality or sustainability are necessary to ensure a world worth living in for future generations. Besides political-economic approaches, *we also need socio-cultural approaches* to understand inequality or sustainability better. Moreover, it is essential to recognize that these problems are complex or *wicked,* and do not result in one single solution that is right or wrong, good or bad, or true or false. These are problems in which many stakeholders are involved, all of them framing the problems and issues in a different way.

Lennie and Tacchi (2013) claim that standard indicators (which are widely applied by both academics and policymakers) are unable to capture these complex realities and relationships:

They can be useful ways of measuring change but not of capturing the reasons behind social change. In Communication for Development (C4D), and in particular the Communication for Social Change approach, indicators should be developed through dialogue and negotiation between key participants, so that they are chosen based on local assessments of what participants want to know and why, and they are more realistic and useful. While quantitative indicators are emphasized in mainstream Monitoring and Evaluation (ME) approaches, for C4D they often need to be qualitative to be most effective and appropriate. An alternative systems approach requires indicators that are flexible and encompass complexity, or, the use of alternatives to indicators such as stories of significant change and "verifying assumptions." (Lennie and Tacchi, 2013: 7)

Hence, we wish to introduce *another way* of assessing the impact of inequality in communication by using "sustainability" as the main focus of analysis. The *matrix* for the study of social problems (such as in/equality) in media and communication forms part of an ongoing research project (see Servaes, 2013, 2014; Servaes, Polk, Shi, Reilly, and Yakupitijage, 2012).

For each indicator we raise a set of questions designed to specifically measure the sustainability of a social change development communication project. We defined "sustainability" by analyzing whether the channels are compatible with both the capacity of the actors and the structural and conjunctural factors? If they are, the project will have a higher likelihood of being sustainable in the long run. We asked to what extent was the process participatory and consistent with the cultural values of the community? Was the message developed by local actors in the community and how was it understood? Our research shows, the more local and interactive the participation—in levels, communication approaches, channels, processes, and methods—the more sustainable the project will be, and hence it would contribute to less inequality.

We don't claim that the indicators we present are the only ones available. For sure, other contextual indicators,—such as financial structures, levels of professionalism and / or governance mechanisms—could also be considered and developed further.2

One of the key aspects in this matrix is the issue of participation. Participation is essential not only in understanding inequality in media and communication, but equally in addressing inequities. Participation forces us to confront positionality of power and the marginality of groups in society. As evidenced by the contributions in these two volumes of social inequalities, media and communication, positionality of power and marginality push to the forefront of social inquiry the issue of empowerment. As a result scholars in these two volumes ask critical questions about how the social constructions of history, gender, economy, race, and class define who can (not) shape narratives about people and how such narrative in the media shape lived-experiences.

Table 12.1. Matrix for the Study of Social Problems (Such as In/equality) in Media and Communication

Main Focus:
– In/equality
– Governance
– Health
– Education
– Environment
– Sustainable Development
– Other
Level:
– Global
– International
– Regional
– National
– Local
Factors:
– Structural
– Conjunctural
Beneficiaries:
– General
– Specific
Actors/Stakeholders:
– Decision-makers
– Policymakers
– Practitioners
– Other
Funding:
– International Agencies
– Bilateral agencies
– National authorities
– NGOs/CSOs
– Local organizations
– Other
Media (Channels):
– Interpersonal/Face-to-face
– Group
– Old media: print, TV, radio
– New Media: social, mobile
– ICTs, Internet
– Multi-media
Communication Approach:
– Behavioral change communication (interpersonal communication)
– Mass communication (community media, mass media, and ICTs)
– Advocacy communication (interpersonal and/or mass communication)
– Participatory communication and communication mobilization (interpersonal communication and community media)
– Communication for structural and sustainable social change (interpersonal communication, community mobilization, and mass communication)

(continued)

Table 12.1. *(continued)*

Communication Process:
- One-way
- Top-down, Vertical
- Two-way
- Bottom-up
- Horizontal
- Other

Communication Strategy:
- Extension/Diffusion of Innovations as a development communication approach
- Network development and documentation
- ICTs for Development
- Social Marketing
- Edutainment (EE)
- Health Communication
- Social mobilization
- Information, Education and Communication (IEC)
- Institution building
- Knowledge, attitudes and practices (KAP)
- Development Support Communication (DSC)
- HIV/AIDS community approach
- Community Participation
- Other [open]

Methods for Analysis
- Quantitative
- Qualitative
- Participatory
- Mixed
- Other

Background and Context:
- Structural and conjunctural factors (e.g., history, migration, conflicts)
- Policy and legislation
- Service provision
- Education systems
- Institutional and organizational factors (e.g., bureaucracy, corruption)
- Cultural factors (e.g., religion, norms and values)
- Socio-demographic factors (e.g., ethnicity, class)
- Socio-political factors
- Socio-economic factors
- Physical environment
- Other [open]

Aspects of Social Change:
- 1a. Short Term   1b. Long Term
- 2a. Instrumental   2b. Sustainable

HOMECOMING IN A RHIZOME

If we return to the concept of "homecoming" by Bude and Dürrschmidt (2010) and link it to the concept of "becoming" by Deleuze and Guattari (1987) and the feminist and postcolonial analysis presented by Hourya Bentouhami-Molino (2015), we may being able to position and further define the framework we need for future research. From this perspective *participation* unfolds as a trans-individual force rather than individualized interactivity. Deleuze and Guattari (1987: 216–217) call it the ongoing negotiations between the "molecular" (micro level of politics) and the "molar" (the structural segmentations at a macro-political level): "Molecular escapes and movements would be nothing if they did not return to the molar organizations to reshuffle their segments, their binary distributions of sexes, classes and parties." The importance of a localized perspective therefore resides in their inherent capacity to be more creative and imaginative.

Moving away from personal or collective subjectivity and concomitant representational logics of identification and substitution, we could use the term *rhizome* and "rhizomatic" to describe theory and research that allows for multiple, non-hierarchical entry and exit points in data representation and interpretation. The rhizome presents history and culture as a *fluid cloud* or wide array of attractions and influences with no specific origin or genesis. A rhizome allows incorporating aspects of contingency, fluidity, and elusiveness in the analysis of global inequalities in media and communication (see also Carpenter, Lie, and Servaes 2012).

CONCLUSION

The topics and debates in global communication research may have shifted and broadened. They have shifted in the sense that they are now focusing on issues related to complexity, hybridity of cultures, (post)modernity, multiplicity, multiculturalism, inequality, sustainability, transdisciplinarity, leadership, learning and participation instead of their previous concerns with "modernization," "dependency," "synchronization," and "cultural imperialism." With these "new" discussions, the debates have also shifted from an emphasis on homogeneity toward an *emphasis on differences*. In contrast to mainstream views on globalization, which center on the political economy, the global industry and have a capitalist-centered view of the world, here, the focus is on *situating* the field of globalization in the local, on the link between the global and the local and in how the global is perceived in the local. Therefore, the field is no longer focused on local versus global, national versus international levels of analysis. In the current world state, globalization and localization are seen as interlinked processes and this marks *a radical change in thinking* about social inequalities in media and communication. It could integrate macro- and micro-theory and lead to interesting cross- and transdisciplinary experiments in both theory and praxis.

NOTES

1. This part relies on arguments earlier developed and presented in Servaes (2015).

2. Other interesting methodological frameworks and techniques have been presented in previous chapters; and, for instance, in Pascale (2013) or Pollock (2013).

REFERENCES

Anderson, B. (1983). *Imagined communities: Reflections on the origin and spread of nationalism*. London: Verso.

Appadurai, A. (2001). Grassroots globalization and the research imagination. In A. Appadurai (Ed.), *Globalization*, 1–21. Durham and London: Duke University Press.

Bentouhami-Molino, H. (2015). *Race, cultures, identities. Une approche feminist et postcoloniale*. Paris: Presses Universitaires de France.

Bhabha, H. (1994). *The location of culture*. London: Routledge.

Bude, B., and Jörg Dürrschmidt. (2010). What's wrong with globalization? Contra "flow speak"—towards an existential turn in the theory of globalization. *European Journal of Social Theory* 13: 481–500.

Carpentier N., Lie R., and J. Servaes. (2012). Multitheoretical Approaches to Community Media: Capturing Specificity and Diversity. In Fuller L. (ed.), *The Power of Global Community Media*, 219–236. New York: Palgrave Macmillan.

Cochrane, A., and K. Pain. (2000), A Globalizing Society? In D. Held (ed.). *A Globalizing World? Culture, Economic, Politics*, 5–45 London: Routledge.

Deleuze, G., and F. Guattari. (1987). *A Thousand Plateaux. Capitalism and Schizophrenia*, Minneapolis: University of Minnesota Press.

Eriksen, T.H. (1993). *Ethnicity and Nationalism. Anthropological Perspectives*. London: Pluto Press.

Giddens, A. (1995). *Modernity and self-identity: Self and society in the late modern age*. Cambridge: Polity Press.

Held, D., A. McGrew, D. Goldblatt, and J. Perraton. (1999). *Global transformations. Politics, economics and culture*. Cambridge: Polity Press.

Hopkins, A. G. (ed.) (2002). *Globalization in World History*. London: Pimlico.

Lennie, J., and J. Tacchi. (2013). *Evaluating communication for development. A framework for social change*. London: Routledge Earthscan.

Lie, R. (1998). What's new about cultural globalization? Linking the global from within the local. In J. Servaes and R. Lie (Eds.), *Media and politics in transition: Cultural identity in the age of globalization*, 141–155. Leuven: ACCO.

Lie, R. (2003). *Spaces of Intercultural Communication. An interdisciplinary Introduction to Communication, Culture, and Globalizing/Localizing Identities.* Cresskill, NJ: Hampton Press.

Lie, R., and J. Servaes. (2000). Globalization: Consumption and Identity. Towards researching nodal points. In Wang, G., J. Servaes and A. Goonasekera (Eds)., *The new communications landscape. Demystifying media globalization,* 307–332. London: Routledge.

Malikhao, P. (2012). *Sex in the village. Culture, religion and HIV/AIDS in Thailand.* Penang and ChiangMai: Southbound/Silkworm Books.

Pakulski, J. (2004). *Globalising inequalities. New patterns of social privilege and disadvantage.* Crows Nest, NSW: Allen and Unwin.

Pascale, C-M (ed.). (2013). *Social Inequality and The Politics of Representation.* Los Angeles: Sage.

Pollin, R. (2003). *Contours of descent: U.S. economic fractures and the landscape of global austerity.* New York: Verso.

Pollock, J. (ed.). (2013) *Media and social inequality. Innovations in community structure research.* London: Routledge.

Sen, A. (2004). Cultural liberty and human development. In S. Fukuda-Parr (Ed.), *Human development report: Cultural liberty in today's diverse world.* New York: United Nations Development Programme.

Servaes, J. (1999). *Communication for development: One world, multiple cultures.* Creskill, NJ: Hampton.

Servaes, J. (ed.). (2013). *Sustainability, participation and culture in communication. Theory and praxis.* Chicago: University of Chicago Press.

Servaes, J. (ed.). (2014). *Technological determinism and Social Change. Communication in a Techn-Mad World.* Lanham, MD: Lexington Books.

Servaes, J. (2015). Studying the global from within the local. *Communication Research and Practice* 1 (3), 242–250.

Servaes, J., and R. Lie. (2008). Media globalization through localization. In J. Servaes (Ed.), *Communication for development and social change,* 58–67. Los Angeles: Sage

Servaes, J., Polk E., S. Shi, D. Reilly, and T. Yakupitijage. (2012). Towards a framework of sustainability indicators for "communication for development and social change" projects. *International Communication Gazette* 74 (2), 99–123.

Sunkel, O., and E. Fuenzalida. (1980). La transnacionalizacion del capitalismo y el desarrollo nacional. In O. Sunkel, E. Fuenzalida, F. Cardoso F., et al. (Eds.), *Transnacionalizacion y dependencia,* 45–63. Madrid: Cultura Hispania.

Therborn, G. (2013). *The killing fields of inequality.* Cambridge: Polity Press.

Thompson, J. (1995). *The media and modernity. A social theory of the media.* Cambridge: Polity Press.

Van Dijk, J. (2012). *The Network Society.* Third edition. London: Sage.

Van Dijk, J. (2013). Inequalities in the network society. In K. Orton Johnson and N. Prior (Eds.), *Digital Sociology. Critical Perspectives,* 105–124. London: Palgrave Macmillan.

Wilkinson R.G., and K. Picket. (2009) *The spirit level: Why more equal societies almost always do better.* London: Allen Lane.

Index

About the
Editors and Contributors

EDITORS

Jan Servaes, PhD, is UNESCO Chair in Communication for Sustainable Social Change; Chair Professor at the Huazhong University of Science and Technology, Wuhan, China; Chair Professor at the Department of Media and Communication, City University of Hong Kong; editor-in-chief of the Elsevier journal *Telematics and Informatics: An Interdisciplinary Journal on the Social Impacts of New Technologies*; editor of the Southbound Book Series Communication for Development and Social Change; editor of the Springer Book Series Communication, Culture and Change in Asia; and editor of the Lexington Book Series Communication, Globalization and Cultural Identity.

He has been president of the European Consortium for Communications Research and vice-president of the International Association of Media and Communication Research, in charge of Academic Publications and Research, from 2000 to 2004. He chaired the Scientific Committee for the World Congress on Communication for Development (Rome, October 25–27, 2006), organized by the World Bank, FAO, and the Communication Initiative.

Servaes has taught International Communication and Development Communication in Australia (Brisbane), Belgium (Brussels and Antwerp), the United States (Cornell), the Netherlands (Nijmegen), and Thailand (Thammasat, Bangkok) in addition to several teaching stints at about 100 universities in 43 countries.

He has undertaken research, development, and advisory work around the world and is known as the author of journal articles and books on such topics as international and development communication; ICT and media policies; intercultural communication and language; participation and social change; and human rights and conflict management. Some of his most recent book titles, include with Toks Oyedemi, *Social Inequalities, Media, and Communication: Theory and Roots* (2015); *Technological Determinism and Social Change* (2014); with Patchanee Malikhao, *Communication for Social Change* (in Chinese; 2013).

Toks Oyedemi, PhD, is interested in sociological questions around media and communication. His research examines communication, media, culture and society, digital culture, pattern of marginalization and exclusion in the communication and technology environment, communication for social change, and the intersection of social inequalities, citizenship and technology. He serves as editorial board member of the Elsevier journal *Telematics and Informatics: An Interdisciplinary Journal on the Social Impacts of New Technologies*; he also serves as a grant review panel member for the South African National Research Foundation. He was a fellow at the Center for Communication for Sustainable Social Change and at the National Center for Digital Government both at the University of Massachusetts. He was an academic member of NetTel@Africa: a transnational network of international academics and institutions for capacity building and knowledge exchange in the Telecom/ICT Sector in Africa. His research publications have appeared in international journals, such as *International Journal of Communication* and *Citizenship Studies*. He has contributed chapters to *Sustainability and Culture in Communication: Theory and Praxis* (2005) and *New Media: Technology and Policy in Developing Countries* (2005). He has taught at colleges and universities both in the United States and South Africa. He is currently at the University of Limpopo, South Africa.

CONTRIBUTORS

Stephanie Agresti, a 2015 alumna of the Department of Communication Studies at the College of New Jersey, is a winner of the $10,000 Judy Coreman Memorial Scholarship sponsored by Scholastic, the New York Women in Communications, Inc. She is currently account coordinator at UpSpring Public Relations in New York City, a firm specializing in design industries, architectural firms, and interior designers as well as hospitality, commercial, and residential real estate.

Roberta Bracciale PhD, is assistant professor at the Department of Political Science at University of Pisa, where she teaches Sociology of New Media. Her current research interests include the social integration of new media, with particular attention to the methodological perspective of media studies and the implications, theoretical and operational, related to e-inclusion.

Martin Caraher is professor of food and health policy in the Centre for Food Policy at City University London. He has worked on issues related to food poverty, cooking skills, local sustainable food supplies, the role of markets and co-ops in promoting health, farmers markets, food deserts and food access, retail concentration and globalisation. Martin has contributed to books on public health and health promotion, including a chapter on international public health in the *Oxford Handbook of Public Health*. He was a founding member of the London Food Board which advises the Mayor of London on food in London, and was the public health representative on the London 2012 Olympic Food Advisory Board. Consultancies include work for the UK Department of Health, the World Bank, and the World Health Organization. He was a member of the National Institute for Health and Clinical Excellence (NICE) advisory board on preventing CVD and is a member of two scientific committees: the Irish Government's safefood, and the International Obesity Taskforce. Current research involves collaborations with researchers in Australia, Portugal, and the United States. Martin was the Australian Healthways Fellow for 2008. In 2012 and 2013 he was the Thinker in Residence at Deakin University, Melbourne.

Mike Gasher, a former newspaper reporter and editor, is a professor in the Department of Journalism at Concordia University in Montreal, and director of the Concordia Centre for Broadcasting and Journalism Studies. He is the principal investigator of the Geography of News Research Project and co-author of the widely used textbook *Mass Communication in Canada* (Oxford University Press).

James Gibbons holds an MA in journalism studies from Concordia University. His research considers how the news media expresses exclusion through language. He presently works for Concordia University.

Tommaso Gravante, PhD, is a postdoctoral researcher in the Laboratory for Analysis of Organizations and Social Movements (LAOMS) at

CEIICH-UNAM, Mexico. His main research interests are: Self-organized Grassroots Movements, Emotions and Protest, Empowerment and Social Change, Micro-Politics, and Qualitative Methodologies.

Steven Harkins is an ESRC-funded PhD candidate at the Department of Journalism Studies at the University of Sheffield. His research examines news coverage of poverty and inequality. He is also part of the Joseph Rowntree Foundation's Expert Communications Group, and his research has been published in *Critical Discourse Studies, Critical Studies on Terrorism,* and the *British Medical Journal.* He has taught sociology at the University of Strathclyde and Journalism Studies at the University of Sheffield. He also contributes to *Spinwatch* and *London School of Economics Review of Books.*

Gyuri Kepes is a doctoral candidate at the Department of Communication, University of Massachusetts Amherst. Gyuri received his Master's degree from the University of Hartford, where his research focused on new technologies, development and pedagogy. His current research explores the intersection of critical pedagogy, media literacy and cultural studies. Gyuri has taught undergraduate courses in Writing, Mass Communication, Human Communication, Film and Television Production, and Public Speaking at several institutions of higher learning, including University of Massachussets–Amherst, University of Hartford, Westfield State University, Springfield Technical Community College, Holyoke Community College, and Asnuntuck Community College.

Archna Kumar, PhD, is an associate professor at the Department of Development Communication and Extension, Lady Irwin College, University of Delhi. In addition to gender and sustainable development, her research interests include community media and participatory communication. She has been consulting with UNICEF and other organizations in the use of participatory narrative based techniques for evaluation of C4D programs.

Lauren Longo is a senior at the Department of Communication Studies at the College of New Jersey, is president of the department chapter of Lambda Pi Eta, the U.S. national communication studies honor society. She and Stephanie Agresti are co-authors of several refereed papers presented at state, national, and international conferences on such topics as U.S. nationwide coverage of pediatric immunization, rape and rape culture on college campuses, and rape adjudication in the military, as well as cross-national coverage of Muslim immigration.

Jairo Lugo-Ocando, PhD is an associate professor in the School of Media and Communication at the University of Leeds. He is the author of several books and articles about news coverage of poverty. Before becoming an academic he worked as a correspondent and news editor for news media outlets in Latin America and the United States. He has taught in several universities in the UK and he has been a visiting Research Fellow at the Universidad Católica Andres Bello, Venezuela, and at the National University of Singapore. He has also been a visiting lecturer in the School of International and Public Affairs at Columbia University and is currently a visiting professor of the Doctoral Program in Media and Communication at the Universidad de Málaga in Spain.

Isabella Mingo is assistant professor of Social Statistics at the Department of Communication and Social Research at Sapienza University of Rome, Italy. She teaches "Data Analysis and Statistical Sources for Communication" at the Faculty of Political Sciences, Sociology and Communication at the University of Rome Sapienza. Her research focuses on the application of quantitative methods in the social and cultural domains, with particular attention to the Information Society and the life styles.

Aparna Moitra is a doctoral candidate at the Department of Development Communication and Extension, Lady Irwin College, University of Delhi, India. Her interests include Participatory Communication Initiatives, Community Media and ICTs for Social Change. Her doctoral research focuses on Mobile Telephony based Interactive Voice Response Systems in rural and marginalized communities and dimensions of empowerment of its users.

Greg Nielsen is professor of Sociology and research fellow at the Concordia Centre for Broadcasting and Journalism Studies in Montreal. He is author of *The Norms of Answerability: Social Theory between Habermas and Bakhtin* (2002); *Le Canada de Radio-Canada: Sociologie Critique et Dialogisme Culturel* (1994); co-author of *Mediated Society: A Critical Sociology of Media* (2011); co-editor of *Acts of Citizenship* (Zed Books, 2008) and *Revealing Democracy: Secularism and Religion in Liberal Democratic States* (2014). His current project includes a study of how mainstream journalism works to expand or reduce gaps between urban citizens and non-citizens who are regularly reported on but excluded from the ideal audiences implied by the journalistic address.

Louise North PhD, is senior research fellow in journalism at Deakin University, Australia. Her research focuses on the gendered production of news in the Australian media, and gender and journalism education. Her 2012 survey of female journalists in Australia in the largest ever undertaken. She is the author of *The Gendered Newsroom* (2009). She now combines her academic work with journalism and is the co-founder and editor of the hyperlocal online magazine, *Bluestone Magazine*.

Lucy Obozintsev, a senior at the College of New Jersey, is pursuing a bachelor's degree in communication studies with an interdisciplinary concentration in health communication and a minor in public health. She plans to attend graduate or professional school in a health-related area.

Fay Patel, PhD, has thirty years of teaching, research and educational development experience in higher education in an international context (Malaysia, Australia, Canada, New Zealand, the United States, and South Africa). She has co-authored and co-edited multiple publications, including journal papers and books on educational development, higher education learning design, intercultural communication, international development, technology innovation, and online learning. Selected recent publications include *Online Learning: An Educational Development Perspective*; co-edited book *Technology Innovation Leadership in Development: A "Middle East" (West Asia) Perspective*; and co-authored papers "Enabling Leadership in Teaching and Learning: Balancing Creativity and Compliance Agendas" in *Australian Higher Education, International Leadership Journal*; and "Cross-Institutional and Interdisciplinary Dialogue on Curriculum for Global Engagement" in *Journal of International Global Studies*.

John C. Pollock, PhD, is professor of Communication Studies at The College of New Jersey. He is the author of *Tilted Mirrors: Media Alignment with Political and Social Change – a Community Structure Approach* (2007) and edited *Media and Social Inequality: Innovations in Community Structure Research* (2013) as well as *Journalism and Human Rights: How Demographics Drive Media Coverage* (2015). He is a media sociologist pursuing interests in health communication, media and human rights, and media and social movements.

Alice Poma is a social scientist. At present she works as a postdoctoral fellow at UNAM FES Iztacala, Mexico. Her main research interest is the emotional dimension of protest. She studies the experience of people who take part in self-organized grassroots groups, employing qualitative research techniques.

Hannah Salamone is an alumna of the College of New Jersey. She received her BA in International Studies with a focus on European studies. She studied at a school in Italy that focused on social justice, where she worked specifically with asylum seekers. Her senior thesis analyzed the rising level of xenophobia in modern Italy.

Francisco Sierra Caballero is the general director at CIESPAL, senior researcher and professor of Communication Theory at the Department of Journalism at the University of Seville, Spain; and editor of the *Journal of Studies for Social Development of Communication*. He is also scientific director of the Latin Union of Political Economy of Information, Communication and Culture, and vice-president of the Latin American Confederation of Scientific Associations in Communication. He has written over twenty books and more than fifty scientific articles in academic journals, in addition to being a professor at prestigious universities and research centers in Europe and Latin America.

Kaan Taşbaşı, PhD, is an assistant professor of Communication at Yeditepe University's Department of Radio, Television and Cinema. He has conducted his PhD dissertation research at Lund University, with the financial support from TUBITAK. His research interests focus mainly on mass communication and critical theory. He is the author of several scientific articles published in international journals, and of chapters in national and international books.

Amanda Weightman has a Master's degree in Sociology from Concordia University, where she supported research for the Concordia Centre for Broadcasting and Journalism Studies and for the Canadian Regional Development Project. She currently lives in Calgary and is co-founder of Habitus Collective, a research and innovation consultancy that works to mobilize knowledge and develop creative strategies for meaningful social change. She supports a number of local grassroots initiatives and sits on the board of the Coalition for Equal Access to Education.

Rebecca Wells is a former BBC producer and a visiting lecturer at London's City University where she is studying for a PhD in food policy and journalism. A BBC producer specializing in food journalism for ten years, she now researches media coverage of food.

Lightning Source UK Ltd.
Milton Keynes UK
UKOW04n0140201217
314771UK00001B/141/P